D0895366

Duels and Duets

Why do men and women talk so differently? And how do these differences interfere with communication between the sexes? What judgments do women make about men, based solely on their speaking voices? In search of an answer to these and other questions, John L. Locke takes the reader on a fascinating journey, from human evolution through ancient history to the present, revealing why men speak as they do when attempting to impress or seduce women, and why women adopt a very different way of talking when bonding with each other, or discussing rivals.

When men talk to men, Locke argues, they frequently engage in a type of "dueling," locking verbal horns with their rivals in a way that enables them to compete for the things they need, mainly status and sex. By contrast, much of women's talk sounds more like a verbal "duet," a harmonious way of achieving their goals by sharing intimate thoughts and feelings in private. And because a third, "uni-sex" way of talking never evolved, men and women have to rely on the strategies at their disposal. As Locke explains, their contrasting styles also offer men and women an important benefit: the ability to collaborate with each other in everyday life.

John L. Locke is currently Professor of Linguistics at Lehman College, City University of New York. His articles have appeared in a broad range of journals, including the *Journal of the Royal Anthropological Institute*, *Evolution and Human Behavior*, *Behavioral and Brain Sciences*, and *Language Sciences*. He has published over 100 articles, chapters, and books. His books include *The de-voicing of society* (1998) and *Eavesdropping: an intimate history* (2010).

Duels and Duets

Why Men and Women
Talk So Differently

JOHN L. LOCKE

 CAMBRIDGE
UNIVERSITY PRESS

CAMBRIDGE UNIVERSITY PRESS
Cambridge, New York, Melbourne, Madrid, Cape Town,
Singapore, São Paulo, Delhi, Tokyo, Mexico City

Cambridge University Press
The Edinburgh Building, Cambridge CB2 8RU, UK

Published in the United States of America by
Cambridge University Press, New York

www.cambridge.org
Information on this title: www.cambridge.org/9780521887137

First published 2011

Printed in the United Kingdom at the University Press, Cambridge

A catalog record for this publication is available from the British Library

Library of Congress Cataloging-in-Publication Data

Locke, John L.
Duels and duets : why men and women talk so differently / John L. Locke.
    p.   cm.
Includes bibliographical references and index.
ISBN 978-0-521-88713-7 (Hardback)
1. Oral communication–Sex differences.   2. Conversation analysis.   I. Title.
P96.S48L63 2011
302.3′46–dc22   2011001070

ISBN 978-0-521-88713-7 Hardback

To dispute whether males or females are the higher, is like disputing the relative superiority of animals and plants. Each is higher in its own way, and the two are complementary.

Patrick Geddes and John Arthur Thompson

Contents

Acknowledgments

I wrote much of this book in the 2009–10 academic year, when I was on sabbatical leave from the Department of Speech-Language-Hearing Sciences at Lehman College, City University of New York. During that time I was privileged to hold a faculty position in the Department of Anthropology at Yale University. I am indebted to several scholars for discussions of issues that I take up here, including Richard Bribiescas and David Watts. On a more personal level, I must acknowledge a unique privilege. I am married to my muse. Thank you, Catherine.

John L. Locke
Old Lyme, Connecticut

Illustrations

Figure 2.1 *The Female Orators* (engraved from a painting by John Collett, 1768).   [51]

Figure 3.1 A "big man," or rhetoric thumper, settling an inter-clan dispute (from Reay 1959).   [66]

Figure 4.1 Testosterone of trial and non-trial lawyers (from Dabbs *et al.* 1998. Trial lawyers and testosterone: blue-collar talent in a white-collar world. *Journal of Applied Social Psychology,* **28**: 84–94).   [95]

Figure 5.1 Scene from *Le Caquet des Femmes* (woodcut, c. 1560, Bibliothèque Nationale de France, Cabinet des Estampes, Tf. 2, fol. 49, from Mainardi 2003).   [103]

Figure 6.1 Throat singing by Ainu women (from Malm 1963, p. 242).   [120]

1 Speech, sex, and gender

Men and women talk differently. We know this because we hear them conversing, and may have witnessed their failures to connect – or experienced these difficulties in our own relationships. Many of us have also read accounts in the popular press of "he said–she said" types of communication breakdowns.

By focusing on the ways men and women talk *to each other*, however, writers have overlooked an important issue: how members of the two sexes communicate when they are with "their own kind." This seems odd, since same-sex friendships are far more prevalent, and more natural, emerging spontaneously in the second or third year of life, intensifying in later stages of development, and continuing throughout adulthood. Opposite-sex friendships are relatively rare. Many people don't have *any*.

The fact is: if you want to witness speaking differences, look at what happens when men talk with men, and women with women. Now here are some *variations* – ones that are far more extensive, and far more compelling, than anything that has ever been described in the literature on mixed-sex conversations.

There is a second oddity nestled in the literature. Most writers see "culture" as the source, even the sole source, of men's and women's distinctive ways of speaking. Perhaps this makes some sort of sense, or is convenient or satisfying to believe. But there is not a shred of evidence that it is true.

I will attempt to demonstrate that the more dramatic differences that occur when men talk with men, and women with women, are not the "gendered" effects of modern culture but the "sexed" expression of ancient biological dispositions. These dispositions are as different as they are because ancestral men and women competed for the things they needed in two fundamentally different ways. This created separate evolutionary trajectories, endowing the two sexes, in modernity, with unequal bodies and brains, developmental paths, and patterns of behavior.

Men have characteristic ways of talking with other men, and women with women, and there are good reasons why these distinctive verbal styles or, better, *strategies* would have evolved. It is less clear that there was ever a need for a *third* speaking strategy, one that would be used exclusively in male–female relationships, or that such a "uni-sex" way of talking ever evolved.

I have now used a form of the word "different" several times. Some might wonder how it benefits us to think about the ways that one half of the world's population differs from the other half. Would it not be easier for men and women to live together if we downplayed, or even ignored, our differences?

As a scientist, my goal is to discover, describe, and explain what exists. It is surely not to look around for opportunities to express my personal views, or to gloss over inconvenient truths. But there are ways of putting these things in a larger – and possibly more harmonious – perspective. In the past there has been a tendency to write about the verbal styles that cause men and women to *clash* in their conversations. The paradox is that these same modes of speaking make it possible for male and female partners to *mesh* in their lives. I have come to believe that biologically supported sex differences in verbal behavior increase the benefits of collaboration in modern life, much as they once conspired, in antiquity, to broaden the foundations for human language.

~

Suppose that some ordinary people have been asked to speculate on why zebra finches sing. Reasoning that these birds must gain something by exercising their vocal talent, each person offers a theory of the possible benefits. Lacking evidence, the discussion quickly becomes a matter of personal opinion. Arguments ensue.

It is decided that the birds will have to be watched. In time, one of the new ad hoc empiricists notices that it is only the males that sing. Everyone's attention is now drawn to this sex difference. Eventually a further qualification is discovered – a seasonal one. It is that the males only sing in the spring. This raises a possible connection between singing and courtship. Finally, the more and the less tuneful males are compared, and a trend is noticed: the impresarios have more success with the ladies than the monotones.

Our amateur ornithologists are on the right track. Male melodies do attract females, and it is adaptive that they do. Research indicates that singing is enabled, and ornamented, by testosterone. This sex hormone acts directly on brain mechanisms that evolved specifically for singing. In the spring, testosterone levels rise, the song mechanisms expand, and singing increases.

These findings help explain the courtship and mating patterns of zebra finches. Females who cast their lot with a melodious male are likely to get a mate that has above-average levels of testosterone. This will facilitate reproduction, and it will continue to benefit the female long after she and her new mate take up housekeeping. One reason, among others, is that testosterone promotes self-defense.

This "androcentric" story is correct, as far as it goes. But it is incomplete. For there is something equally special about the role of females: they *like* the sound of male songs. If they did not, males would not sing as beautifully or as often as they do.

The females call the tunes. Literally.

If our amateur ornithologists had been forced to explain birdsong *without reference to sex differences*, they could only speculate on why "some birds" have complex and attractive songs and "other birds" do not. True, they still might discover the seasonal variations, but this would not be enough to understand the functions of birdsong. For science to work, everything must be on the table.

Now suppose that a second group of lay people is impaneled. They are asked to speculate on a different question: how *our own species* acquired the ability to produce complex vocalizations, including the multitude of sound sequences that are manipulated when a person speaks. In most languages, these sequences number in the tens of thousands.

This question intrigues the new panelists, because they sense that the emergence of this phonetic capacity may have paved the way for what is arguably the most important of all human traits: language. Unfortunately, the new theorists, unlike their predecessors, are told that they must solve the assigned problem *without reference to sex differences*, whether in other species or our own.

This injunction is no less limiting here than it was in the case of the finches. The abilities of modern humans reflect problems that were uniquely faced, and solved, by early members of the *Homo* line, who diverged from ancestors shared with the other primates millions of years ago. Since males and females were subjected to different selectional pressures, the brains and bodies of the two sexes evolved differently. To ignore these neural and cognitive differences would be to tie at least one hand behind the panel's theoretical back.

Since the brain controls behavior, the exclusion of sex differences could also cause some related – and possibly critical – differences to go unnoticed. The panel will surely miss two modes of vocal engagement that would have helped them to explain the speech of modern humans. In birds and mammals, including the other primates, sexually mature males are prone to contend with each other in highly public vocal displays that are aggressive or "agonistic" in nature. We may think of these engagements as "duels." In many primate species, sexually mature females have an equally strong disposition to affiliate with other females, in more private and intimate circumstances, by engaging them in subdued vocal interactions. I will refer to these interactions as "duets." Both words contain the Latin base *duo*, for two, but dueling represents a conflation of *duo* with *bellum*, war, creating *duellum*, a war between two. Duets, of course, refer to the harmonious behaviors of a duo.

When men compete with other men, and women with women, they display two distinct ways of speaking. These differences are revealed in their purest form when contests are waged over two

things that have always been critical to our species: sex, including
the things we do to get and keep mates; and dominance, or social
status.

~

What I have chosen to call duels and duets were first described in
raw form many centuries ago, and they have been documented in a
broad range of human societies around the world. As we will see, a
strictly vocal form of these strategies is enacted in other species. We
humans are thus an interesting blend. For each of us is possessed of
language – a codification of human knowledge that requires
extensive cognitive support, takes years to master, and is frequently
asserted as evidence of our species' rationality – but embed our
words in "primal" displays that are unlearned and biologically
driven, having originated long before the evolution of language.

At one time, of course, social scientists viewed allusions to
sex differences suspiciously, as efforts to reinforce inequalities
between women and men. I can only hope that this era has
passed, because a great deal of science requires investigation of
these particular biological variations. In fact, by exploring inter-
sexual differences we make it possible to see ways in which
modern men and women *complement each other* in the conduct
of everyday business, much as (according to my claim) ancestral
men and women collaborated in the evolution of language.

Of course, popular books on the everyday communicative differences between men and women have been rolling off the presses
for some years. In 1992, couples therapist John Gray claimed that
Men are from Mars, women are from Venus. When experiencing
stress, he suggested, men – the Martians – grow silent. They go
into their "caves." Women do just the opposite. They contact a
friend and talk out their problems until they feel better.

In a later book, *Eve's seed*, historian Robert McElvaine offered a
qualification. He said that men and women are not as different as
such separate planetary addresses would imply. "Men are from
New York," he amended, "women are from Philadelphia."[1] How

differently men and women *actually* talk, of course, is something that we will look at here.

Some years ago, researchers established that young men, in the speeches they gave in university classes, said "I" more often than women, produced more verbs of various kinds, and uttered more long or multi-syllabic words. In women's speech, there were more prepositional phrases, rhetorical questions, and fillers such as "um." Their utterances were also longer. Significantly, men's speech was *perfectly* discriminable from women's speech on the basis of these and other features.[2]

But let's not get sidetracked by the bits and pieces that make up speech. These things are interesting – my first book was only about speech sounds – but we would not want to make the mistake of archaeologists who become so interested in bits of bone and pottery that they forget to ask what such discoveries might be trying to say about human civilization.

If we turn our attention to the *speaking practices* of males and females, we come face to face with those larger issues.[3] In same-sex groups, according to summaries of this research, males are more likely than females to:

1. interrupt each other
2. issue commands, threats, or boasts
3. resist each other's demands
4. give information
5. heckle
6. tell jokes or suspenseful stories
7. try to top another's story
8. insult or denigrate each other.

By contrast, research indicates that females in same-sex groups are more likely than males to:

1. agree with other speakers
2. yield to other speakers
3. acknowledge points made by other speakers
4. be polite
5. cooperate or collaborate.

There is also a rule that applies to female groups: do what it takes to preserve group harmony. This rule underlies some of the female tendencies enumerated above, and influences women's conversational speech in additional ways. In the case of males, the corresponding rule would be: do what is necessary to be seen as *the most wonderful anything* – from strong and knowledgeable to brave and resourceful – whether that means building yourself up or tearing everyone else down.

The list above might seem to be fairly complete, but these items are merely what emerged when researchers scratched the surface. The reason? They had no theory as to *why* men and women might be disposed to speak differently, and therefore they could only pursue their intuitions or just wait for something to jump out at them. But we humans, no less than other animals, are physical creatures. Our bodies and brains evolved in environments that contained resources, dangers, and competitive pressures. Since our species lives in groups, each of us is wired to interact, and there are additional pressures here, ones associated with the need to cooperate with our competitors and compete with our friends. In this context, it is possible to ask if men and women were to use speech as strategies, ones that would help them achieve their goals *as men and women*, what would they do? Approaching the matter in this way enables scientists to generate principled questions, based on what we know about men and women, not merely to follow in the footsteps of other researchers.

But let us begin by examining their tracks. In *You just don't understand*, linguist Deborah Tannen wrote about men's tendency to use language as a vehicle for the transmission of information in factual, news-like bulletins. She called this "report talk." Women, on the other hand, devote more of their speech to an affiliative goal, "establishing connections and negotiating relationships." Tannen labeled this way of speaking "rapport talk."[4]

Tannen helped readers to appreciate some *linguistic* reasons why men and women, particularly married couples, might fail to communicate. But the trail ended there, almost as soon as it started. For there was no formal account of the *reasons* why men and women use language differently in the first place.

So we have questions. For example, if our ways of speaking do not *benefit* marital relations, why do we persist in these practices? Why don't couples naturally recognize and cast aside their counter-productive behaviors? If style differences are arbitrary and optional – not supported by anything deeply *biological* or particularly *useful* – why not jettison any that happen to work against us? Speakers can presumably discard anything that is arbitrary and optional.

Doing so might seem to be fairly easy. After all, speakers routinely move into and out of various "registers" or "voices" all day long, speaking formally to some people and casually to others. Most bilingual speakers naturally "code switch," that is, alternate between – or even combine – the languages that they know, without any particular effort. Surely, one might suppose, the rest of us can abandon styles of speaking when they no longer work for us. If we learned them, we can unlearn them.

But *did* we learn them? To be sure, we could not have acquired our native language without storing up many thousands of words and meanings. This material originated outside of us – initially in the speech of our parents – and it passed through a suite of perceptual and other cognitive systems before it came to rest somewhere in our minds. A portion of this experience may even have occurred consciously.

All of this relates to the stuff that we *talk with*. But the words we know and use – an abiding concern of linguists – have little or nothing to do with the dance of human interaction. This is enacted not only in speech but also in gestures, facial expressions, eye movements, body language, and tones of voice. Do we not care that those people are whispering? That something said to us with a straight face was actually a joke? That an insult was actually a misguided attempt to bond? If talking is the human way of *relating*, we must consider everything that goes on, whether the sights and sounds are reducible to printed words in a tran-script or not.

How we talk, that is, *how we use* the linguistic material that we know, is rather different from stringing words together. The ways we address and verbally interact with others are heavily influenced by internal systems that were already up and running when our ancestors left the trees. Today, aspects of this primacy of vocal communication over linguistic content are played out in human development. In the first six months of life, infants use their voices to greet, request, reject, and comment – things our prelinguistic ancestors certainly could have done – long before their newer and more abstract mental mechanisms kick in, the ones that enable them to understand and use words.[5]

All of which is to say that the differences between human males and females, like the avian sexes, have scientific value. We cannot achieve a complete scientific "story" about language (and many other complex behaviors) without them. Fortunately, the discoveries achieved in an impressive range of investigations have begun to come together, making it possible to tell a significant portion of that story. Important clues emerge from psychological and biological studies of human development and life history. Harmonious findings are also available in anthropological accounts of traditional societies, comparative research on primates, and studies of the human brain. Intriguingly, this material converges with trends in ancient history, and analyses of epic literature, to support a claim: men and women speak in fundamentally different ways largely because they are outfitted by Nature to do so.

Gender and sex

In our species, the most clear-cut differences between males and females are expressed physically. One look at the genitals of a newborn and we know that it's a boy or a girl. But if asked the *gender* of a neonate, the safest answer would be, "It's too soon to tell." The reason is that gender is largely a cultural construction, like *masculine* and *feminine*. This construction is sensitive to the individual's psychological make-up and the larger community's values and practices, and in special cases there is room for doubt about a person's gender.[6]

The distinction between sex and gender helps us to keep in mind important differences between biology and culture. These domains are where we go if our goal is to explore male and female ways of talking.[7] In fact, they are the only places that we *can* go, so our choice of one over the other is an important one. Which we choose – assuming that scientists will be more attracted to one or the other – is a matter of critical importance, for it determines what we will (and will not) discover, and this influences how we will (and will not) think about our human ways of relating to each other.

Unfortunately, the relative merits of culture and biology have been distorted by the personal responses of researchers. During the era when feminist linguists were attributing sex differences to gender, hence to culture, evolutionary psychologists Margo Daly and Martin Wilson were writing about "biophobia," a naked fear of biological explanation that was working its way through the social sciences. They noted that this fear initially expressed itself in the form of several myths about human behavior. Perhaps the most important was that some human tribes are completely fierce and others totally tranquil. If that were true (sadly it is not), we might think of violence as optional, and the human species as perfectible. That may be why the myth, as Daly and Wilson wrote, lives on in the academic and journalistic corridors of American life, and "*fills a need* for social scientists and commentators."[8]

I would never be confused with a "biophobe." Indeed, I naturally take a biological approach to human language, speech, and communication.[9] But I do not wish to imply that culture is a total weakling where the speaking habits of men and women are concerned. Over three centuries ago, Charles César de Rochefort, pastor of a French Protestant church, visited the West Indies. He reported later that the men "have a great many expressions peculiar to them, which the women understand but never pronounce themselves. On the other hand, the women have words and phrases which the men never use, or they would be laughed to scorn." In their conversations, Rochefort observed, "it often seems as if women had another language than the men."[10]

This example of gendered speech seems extreme until one reads a second account, by Cambridge anthropologist Sir James Frazer. In 1900, he described differences in the ways that men and women spoke in a variety of traditional societies around the world. Among the Caffre people of South Africa, for example, a woman was forbidden from uttering the Christian name of her husband and his brothers. Moreover, if the husband's name was, or merely sounded like, the name of something else, the woman had to find another word for that thing. She was also forbidden – and this one would have been difficult to enforce – from *mentally* articulating the names of her husband's father and male relatives. Finally, it was considered wrong for a wife to utter specific syllables if they appeared, in stressed form, in her husband's name. If she wished to say a word containing that syllable, she had a choice: she could substitute another syllable for the one that appeared in her husband's name – mutilating the correct form – or use another word altogether. These customs, wrote Frazer, produced "an almost distinct woman's language."[11]

∾

In the 1970s, women's speech became a topic of serious discussion in academic circles and it was occasionally the focus of heated debate. It started with linguist Robin Lakoff. In *Language and woman's place* and other writings, Lakoff described some ways that women's speech differed from men's based mainly on her informal observations (she had no actual data). For example, she pointed out that women are more likely than men to use color terms such as *mauve* and *lavender,* and "empty" adjectives such as *divine* and *adorable,* and that women more often end sentences with a tag question, such as "It's hot in here, *isn't it?*" Lakoff suggested that women are also inclined to use hedges ("It's *kind of* warm in here") and intensifiers ("I like him *so* much") and to converse in an emphatic way that she called "speaking in italics."

Lakoff suggested that the differences between men and women are "clues" to deeper things, but she was not thinking of biology. That the males and females who make unequal use of rare color words might have different visual processing systems, with unequal sensitivity to certain hues, did not occur to Lakoff, nor did she explain other variations by appealing to the differing social and emotional dispositions of the two sexes. Rather, Lakoff pointed to the possible effects of "attitudes." Unfortunately, she never attempted to demonstrate that the differences itemized in her book were *caused by* differing attitudes, nor did she identify the attitudes, or explain how one sex comes to possess more of certain attitudes than the other.

Casual references to "gendered" speech now occasion no particular notice, and it is possible to find references to the different patterns of male and female speech as "genderlects." Since words are learned, it could be appropriate to refer to men's and women's vocabularies as "gendered," at least if the processes of learning or usage were somehow associated with cultural constructions of sexuality.[12] Perhaps the same is true of genderlects, since "dialects" include word choices. But we should be clear on what is *not* captured by these terms: critically, the ways that we individuals deploy our linguistic skills when interacting with each other.

When Lakoff broached the subject of gendered speech, some linguists were bothered by what they took to be an implication in her writing – that women's language was *deficient* relative to men's. They asked why the focus was on women's speech, as different from men's, and not the other way around. But they did not doubt her observations.

How did Lakoff make her observations? Nothing was said about this, so I assume she simply collected aural evidence wherever she, as a listener or eavesdropper, was able to hear people talking. I do not mean to diminish this. Her over-hearings prompted linguists and others to think about some important questions. But what did she *not* discover? What one hears is

largely a function of what one listens for, and expectations typically arise from a theory that is held, consciously or unconsciously,
even if it is merely a "folk theory." *What was Lakoff's theory?*

The reason I ask about this relates to Charles Darwin's remark,
in 1860, that a previous generation of geologists had operated
without much of a theory, making them little different from any
other individuals that walk through a gravel pit, counting and
describing all the pebbles as they lie. "How odd it is," he wrote,
"that anyone should not see that all observation must be for or
against some view if it is to be of any service."[13]

Without a theory, linguists – like geologists – can only go
around listening for things, describing the verbal pebbles that
catch their attention. So where do we look for an appropriate
theory? We look in the only place that it is possible to find
a theory of *sex* differences: human biology. Components of this
theory will include information on who or what humans are, and
what human males and females are like before and after they
reach sexual maturity.

Once we know about these things, we can cast an eye on the
physical and social worlds that humans inhabit, and ask what
men and women, behaving adaptively, might conceivably want in
and from these worlds. This sets the scene for our questions about
how speaking assists the sexes, doing so in different ways.

This new orientation does not require us to throw out the
concept of men's and women's "roles." But the roles that make
the most sense are not the ones played by the *genders* in *social*
history, and transmitted across some number of generations to
the modern human mind. Rather, it is the differing roles played
by the *sexes* in *evolutionary* history, the effects of which were
transmitted genetically to the modern human brain, which
continue to influence our behavior today.

∾

What do men and women like to talk about? Linguist Jennifer
Coates has noted that in same-sex groups, men's stories often

focus on action and conflict. The teller frequently depicts himself as a masterful person, a man who stands up for himself, gets away with things, is not to be toyed with or taken for granted, and who emerges from every contest a winner – possibly even a hero. By contrast, women's stories feature people and family, and they typically include intimate details about others and themselves.

Beyond the topics of men and women's speech, there are differences in conversational structure. When in mixed-sex conversations, for example, male speakers "seem to feel free to take long turns at talk," Coates said, though the men "are encouraged in their story-telling by female co-participants."[14]

Why should men and women be like this? Coates' account encourages us to think about the reasons, but she, like Lakoff, does little to help us with the answer. Is it her responsibility as a linguist to do that? Other kinds of knowledge may be required. Perhaps that is why it is hard to find any serious references to *causality* in the gendered-speech literature.

Coates wrote about the narratives of men and women, but the two sexes also *converse* differently. Tannen attributes these differences to cultural factors. "Girls," she wrote, "*learn* conversational rituals that focus on the rapport dimension of relationships." Boys, on the other hand, "tend to *learn* rituals that focus on the status dimension." They "*learn* to use language to negotiate their status in the group by displaying their abilities and knowledge, and by challenging others and resisting challenges. Giving orders is one way of getting and keeping the high-status role. Another is taking center stage by telling stories or jokes." Childhood play-groups, Tannen wrote, "are where boys and girls *learn* their conversation styles."[15]

Tannen's ideas are framed as assertions of fact, but they are, if anything, hypotheses. Even if they were true, they would still raise a number of questions. For one thing, we would like to know why children form same-sex groups, and why their groups are different enough to continue, in perceptible ways, to affect their ways of talking decades later. We might also like to know what the connection is between speaking styles and status, and the reasons why boys and girls seek status in different ways.

I am intrigued by an additional comment by Tannen. "In every community known to linguists," she said, "the patterns that constitute linguistic style are relatively different for men and women." What makes this interesting is that universal patterns of behavior are normally taken to mean that *biological factors* may be at work. But her frequent references to "learning" suggest that Tannen holds this psychological process responsible for the differences in male and female speech. What kind of learning she has in mind is unspecified, but it is one that presumably involves assimilation – the process responsible for the subtle and often unconscious accommodations that occur when people are reared in different cultures and exposed to different behaviors. Boys and girls speak differently, Tannen wrote, because they *"grow up in different worlds."*[16]

Other like-minded scholars point to the disposition of boys to identify with their fathers, and of girls to identify with their mothers. They assume that children acquire their ways of speaking from the parent with whom they sexually identify. This sounds plausible. It may even appear to be "common sense." But is it correct? There is plenty of room for additional questions here. For example, one would like to know how long this has been going on. Has there been an unbroken chain from Adam and Eve to the present? What sustains it today?

My point is that anyone wanting to lay such findings at the door of learning and culture has a lot of hard scientific work ahead, just as biologists do. In science, it is not enough to raise a possibility and move on. Consider the fact that in some cultures, men prefer heavy women. In other cultures, men prefer thin women. If men's body preferences vary from one culture to the next it is tempting, I suppose, to attribute them to factors that are "cultural." But it turns out, on closer analysis, that men in the "heavy" cultures have fewer resources available to them than men in the "thin" cultures.[17]

It also turns out that this relationship between preferred female size and resource availability occurs *within* cultures.[18] Recently, two researchers asked several groups of young adults about their financial resources and their preferences regarding the body size of possible mates. Others were asked the same questions about preferred body size, either before or after dinner. It was found that men who had little money, or were hungry, preferred a heavier mate than men who had more money, or were full. These findings, the authors concluded, "provide evidence that temporary affective states can produce individual variation in mate preferences that mirrors an otherwise unexplained pattern of cultural norms."[19]

There is a larger conclusion possible here. Differences between human cultures are not necessarily "cultural," at least in a causal sense. But I am not arguing against culture. What would be the point? Individuals are obviously influenced by things that happen around them, in their social and physical environments. However, we need to be clear about something here: social learning, the cognitive ability that enables culture, is itself an evolved characteristic. Evolutionary environments have changed rapidly, making it necessary for individual humans to adapt. It is assumed that evolutionary ancestors who were able to do this were more likely to reproduce than their less adaptive peers, building the requisite abilities into the human genes. This explains an observation made years ago: some things are easier to learn than others because the relevant perceptual and storage systems were designed into the nervous system by preceding generations.[20]

It is easy – beguilingly easy – to assume that basic differences between males and females are the result of assimilation. Consider a basic and broadly relevant issue: the toy preferences of boys and girls. Psychologists have long known that boys prefer airplanes, tools, cars, dump trucks, and tractors to other kinds of toys. In general, girls eschew these things, but they do like dishes, sewing machines, cosmetics, baby buggies, and doll clothes.[21]

The reason for these preferences may seem obvious. Boys and girls enjoy different kinds of toys because they grow up in a society that shapes such preferences, though this, too, must be explained. One possibility is that once they find out the sex of their infant, parents go shopping, and bring home boy and girl toys for their male and female neonates. Infants spend time with these toys and ultimately express a preference for these more familiar objects.

Another possibility, also based on common sense, is that sons see their fathers mowing the lawn or hammering a nail, and daughters observe their mothers caring for siblings and serving dinner. Sensing that one of the parents is more like them than the other, the infants seek, preferentially, to absorb more of the "like them" behaviors. How infants do this needs to be explained, but on the surface it seems plausible.

So we have a story, or possibly two. Shall we relax and turn our attention to something else? Or should we attempt to find out if our stories are true? Or more cautiously, and scientifically, shall we see if it is possible to *disprove* them?

If the latter, we might begin by looking at the role of sex hormones. If imitation of the same-sex parent requires nothing more than *being* a boy or girl, infants with more or less of the primarily male hormone, testosterone, will not vary in their toy preferences. But research indicates that the play behavior of typically developing girls is traceable to the level of testosterone in their mother's blood during pregnancy. Girls who have higher levels of testosterone prenatally spend more time playing with male toys, and less time playing with female toys, than girls with lower levels.[22] This masculinizing effect continues into adulthood.[23] There is little here to support a cultural or "gendered" explanation.

A second test might be to look at children who are given no toys, or boys who grow up without a father. If modeling and imitation are responsible for masculine behaviors, surely boys who are raised by both parents will be more masculine than boys who are raised exclusively by their mother. But there is evidence that boys who grow up without a father in the home may be even more strongly masculine than other boys in their disposition to compete and aggress, and in their attitudes towards females.[24]

A third test of the parent-modeling explanation might be to look at infants who have *not yet* seen the relevant masculine and feminine behaviors. If toy preferences are due only to observing and learning, they will *never* appear *before* the infants have observed their parents modeling the relevant behaviors. In this context, a particular experiment is relevant, one carried out by Jennifer Connellan and her colleagues.[25] They measured the amount of time that day-old infants look at the face of a live female and an animated mechanical object. At this "age" there would have been no opportunity to learn which things to look at. Therefore, it is interesting that the male neonates, more than the females, preferred the sight of the mechanical objects; and that the female subjects, more than the males, spent more time looking at the human face.[26]

All these tests raise questions about the parent-modeling idea, but there was always something presumptuous about it in the first place. It would be one thing if this effect could be confirmed merely by showing that parents treat their sons and daughters differently. In fact, very few studies have found that they do.[27] But the modeling concept presumes that parental behaviors *cause* the sex differences that are observed in the children. Overlooked is the possibility that parents who treat their sons and daughters differently may be *responding* in a normally sympathetic way to their male and female offspring, who are the true source of the parents' behaviors.

If this seems strange, it may help to consider a fact about normally nurturant parents, one that was originally noted a half century ago: they watch their infants and attempt to provide them with the kinds of things and experiences that they seem to want.[28] If parents notice that their daughter doesn't like to play with boys, possibly because boys are too rough, they arrange for her to play with other girls.[29] If she shows an interest in cooking, they get her some miniature pots and pans, and on it goes with other toys and social experiences. These things seem entirely natural, so natural that it is easy to see how an unsuspecting psychologist could come along later, discover the parents' behavior, and misinterpret it as the *cause*, rather than the *consequence*, of their child's preferences.

If it's not looking good for a learning-based account now, a final bit of research is likely to make matters worse. If social learning is responsible for children's toy preferences, then we should not see any such effects in a species – yes, *species* – that has no exposure to toys and a limited capacity for social learning. Enter two psychophysiologists, Gerianne Alexander and Melissa Hines. They did an experiment with vervet monkeys, a species that, like the other primates, is not known for a love of human toys or any kind of culture.[30]

The monkeys were given six toys, one at a time. Two of the toys, a car and a ball, were considered "male toys" based on previous research with human children, and two of the toys, a doll and a pot, were considered "female toys." Two neutral toys, a book and a stuffed animal, were also included since they had previously been found to attract human males and females equally. When all the data were in, it was clear that the male monkeys had spent significantly more time handling the male toys and the female monkeys had expressed a strong preference for the female toys. The two sexes did not differ when it came to the neutral toys.

It would be hard to say that the monkeys had *learned these preferences*. After all, they had never seen a human or any other being using such objects. Even if they had, it would be daring, in monkeys, to speculate that mere exposure – without a protracted period of training – would be sufficient to produce the result that was obtained by Alexander and Hines.

I also have – if you will indulge me – a few existential-philosophical questions to add to the mix. Do male monkeys *know* that they're males? Do they know that something that looks like a truck *to us* is, in fact, *a truck* – has at least some of the properties of a vehicle that can be used for transportation or hauling, has an engine, makes a low rumbling noise, and can be made to run on imaginary roads – features that might, *in the minds of humans*, attract young males like them?

So *what does explain* the toy preferences of vervet monkeys? In a later article, one of the authors speculated that the trail might ultimately lead to characteristics of the primate visual system, reasoning that androgens affect development of the visual processing pathways and therefore endow males with somewhat different visual preferences than females. But for the moment the question remains unanswered.[31]

I have a brief anecdote to add. Several years ago, Lawrence Summers, then president of Harvard University, said that he had given trucks, and not dolls, to his two-and-a-half-year-old twin daughters. One day the girls were heard saying to each other, "Look, daddy truck is carrying the baby truck."[32]

~

In the 1970s and 80s, when neuroimaging studies were picking up sex differences in the human brain, popular books were still calling attention to gender differences in speech and feminist linguists were attacking each other. One *criticized* Deborah Tannen for *failing to politicize* her account of gendered speech when, if anything, a *compliment* for scientific objectivity would have been in order.[33] But we are now in the second decade of what is widely regarded as the "Century of Biology." If one were ever to seek a scientific account of sex differences, this would surely be the time to do it.

In recent years, a new field – evolutionary psychology – has demonstrated that a wide range of behavioral differences between the sexes is amenable to evolutionary explanations. These include mate-poaching tactics, infanticide and child abuse; sexual fantasies and the desire for sexual variety; specific fears, phobias, and anxieties; differential contributions to childcare; anger, aggression, jealousy; face preferences; and willingness to engage in casual sex.[34]

The neurosciences are also exposing sex differences in the structure and function of the human brain, including areas that are involved in language and communication. It is generally accepted that the evolutionary pressures responsible for the large neocortical area of the human brain, and some differences in men's and women's brains, were primarily social. This means nothing more complicated than, but every bit as complicated as, the ability to relate.

To form and maintain relationships, one needs a social brain. In the early 1990s, Robin Dunbar initiated a series of demonstrations that speak to this point. The first and most significant exhibit was a striking association between the size of primate groups and the size of the cognitively critical area of primate brain, the neocortex. Largely on the strength of this relationship, Dunbar framed the "social brain hypothesis," which holds that the challenges of living in social groups produced expansion and reorganization of the primate brain. This, he suggested, would have made it possible for primates to solve ecological problems socially, through the operation of brain mechanisms that enhanced social cohesion.[35]

Vocal differences

There are few indications that primates "construct" their sexual identity, so if male and female apes display different patterns of *vocalization* – the closest thing they do to *verbalization* – these differences are likely to be supported by biological factors. If they do, we may be forced to accept the possibility that some of the more important differences in men's and women's speech also originate in human biology.

Ten years ago, Cheryl Tomaszycki and her colleagues studied the vocalizations of rhesus macaque monkeys in the first eight months of life, when they were rejected by, or separated from, the mother. It was found that the male infants issued more noisy screams, and were generally louder than the females. Female infants, by contrast, made more coos and arched screams – calls that are relatively soft. The female macaques also produced more calls in general, more different types of vocalizations, and more calls that were long and complex.[36]

Did the infants learn these sex differences? It's a logical possibility, at least *if* their adult models displayed similar sex differences *and* macaque infants are able to learn such things. As for the "if," there is evidence for sex differences in adults to whom the infants were exposed. But there is little evidence of social learning in primate infants – and no evidence of vocal learning in primates at any age. Indeed, there is *negative evidence,* dating back to the early 1980s, when primatologists tried without success to locate anything in the vocalization of young gibbons that might have been learned from parents.[37] Some investigators concluded that the calls of young gibbons were under "strong genetic control,"[38] but none of these early studies was well controlled.

This changed in the late 1980s when Michael Owren and his colleagues arranged for several rhesus macaque and Japanese macaque infants, animals that as adults would normally have had slightly different vocal repertoires, to spend the first two years of life in the custody of foster parents – a primate couple of the opposite species. The infants were thus bathed in sounds that they would not normally make themselves, at least with the same quality or frequency, and this "bathing" occurred at an early and optimal stage of development, when exposure would be necessary if sound learning was to occur at all. Analysis of the audio recordings indicated that exposure to the foster parents' sounds had little or no effect on the youngsters' own vocalizations.[39]

What is the appropriate conclusion to draw here? It is *not* that parallels between the species – ones that especially relate to social communication – exist because the other primates, like humans, *learn* from exposure to the behaviors of others. Rather, it is that some of the more important patterns of human communication are *not learned*. As we go forward, I will attempt to demonstrate that the disposition of the human sexes to duel and duet originated long before the evolution of language had run its course. This disposition is now anticipated by genes, resourced by brains, and supported by obedient cultures.

2   Duels

At some point in the twelfth century, Ericus Disertus rose to prominence in medieval Denmark. He did so largely on the basis of his verbal wits. According to a contemporaneous history, *Gesta Danorum* "The Deeds of the Danes," Ericus was "superior in words" and "stronger in tongue" than other men. His followers came to think of him as "Eric the Eloquent."[1]

Eric's way with words was an attractive feature of his personality, but it was also useful. For Eric settled disputes, secured rights, and prevailed in a number of verbal skirmishes. Because he could fight with his tongue, Eric was able to avoid many of the militant engagements for which the age was known.

Eloquence also earned Eric a great deal of prestige and power. According to Saxo Grammaticus, the author of "Deeds," it was thought that Eric was "better spoken than all other people." His eloquence would eventually attract political opportunities. An attested "champion in argument," Eric became counselor to the King of Sweden and later ascended to the throne himself.

Flyting

There is a name for the contests that Eric the Eloquent won so easily. It's "flyting" (pronounced *flight* + *ing*). This English term is thought to have connections with Scottish *flyte*, to contend or argue – a descendant of Old English *flītan* – with links to Old High German *flīzan*, to argue. The essence of flyting was, as one scholar put it, "agonistically styled verbal disputation with martial overtones."[2]

Most flytings consist of insults and boasts, rendered in a stylized way, with the odd threat, curse, or vow thrown in for good measure.[3] Armed with a supply of these verbal tools and the ability to improvise, a medieval man could boost his stature while lowering the standing of competitors. From a societal perspective, it was, as one scholar noted, a zero sum game.[4]

In Old Norse, there were two kinds of flyting. One was the *senna*, a stylized verbal battle that began with a preliminary "squaring off" phase, followed by a succession of accusations and denials, threats and counter-threats, or challenges and replies.[5] At their core, *sennas* were thoroughly and obligatorily contentious, but they had a flexible structure that allowed the contestants to choose their own barbs.

The second type of flyting was the *mannjafnaðr*. In the thirteenth century, it was a way for Norwegian men to display their relative worth.[6] In fact, the name once referred to a legal procedure that was used by surviving relatives to "assess the cash value of slain men."[7] When one of these "man matching" contests was waged, the contestants took turns boasting and insulting each other, and the audience attempted to determine which was the better man.[8]

According to *Heimskringla*, written in c. 1225 by historian Snorri Sturluson, King Eystein hosted a dinner one evening for his younger brother Sigurd – also a king – and several of Sigurd's friends.[9] After they had finished eating, disaffected by the quality of the ale and bored with the conversation, Eystein suggested that they hold a verbal game to enliven the evening. The kind of game he had in mind was obviously a *mannjafnaðr*, since, as he said, "it is an old, established custom for men to compare themselves with others."

As it turned out, the man to whom Eystein wished to be compared was Sigurd. Provoked by Eystein – the brothers had had a long history of fraternal rivalry – Sigurd started the game himself by lobbing a barbed question at his brother, "Do you not remember that I could make you give way whenever I liked, even though you were older?"

KING EYSTEIN: I am not slower to remember that you could never master skills that required agility.

KING SIGURD: Do you remember how it was with the two of us regarding swimming? I could duck you whenever I wished.

KING EYSTEIN: I did not fall short of you in distance swimming, and I was no worse at swimming underwater. Moreover, I knew how to use skates of bone, so well that I knew of no one able to contend with me, and you are no better at that than an ox.

KING SIGURD: To me it seems a more princely and useful talent to be skillful with the bow. I don't imagine you would be able to use my bow, even if you struggled away with both feet inside it.

KING EYSTEIN: I do not have your strength with the bow, but there is less difference between us in accuracy, and I know how to ski much better than you, and that has always been called a worthy talent.

Several more of these true or semi-truthful boasts and insults were hurled before the match ended, according to Sturluson, leaving the brother-kings agitated but able to duel another day.

Beginning with the *Iliad* and continuing through to *Beowulf*, *Canterbury tales*, *The flyting of Dunbar and Kennedy*, and the *Battle of Maldon*, flyting played a dominant role in epic literature.[10] Clearly, verbal dueling was in, and for a good thousand years no country in Europe wanted to be left out.

In the *Iliad*, composed in about the eighth century BC, Achilles meets up with his opponent, Aineias, off the battlefield. Instead of drawing his sword, however, Achilles taunts his foe, insinuating that Aineias fights only because he wishes to be lord of the Trojans, or has been promised a piece of valuable land. In a previous encounter, he recalls, Aineias retreated as fast as his legs would carry him. Aineias responds that his opponent should not attempt to frighten him with words for "the tongue of man is a twisty thing."

According to a survey made by epic scholar Ward Parks, the twisty of tongue were uniformly male.[11] To pretend that women also engaged in flyting, he wrote, "would entail vast falsification of the ethological and human historical records." In saying this Parks evidently feared some sort of feminine backlash. For he went on to say: "To castigate men for behavioral proclivities that may owe in part to biology and evolution would surely be a lamentable form of sexism. Yet recognizing such realities does not mean playing the apologist for them." His own purpose, he said, was "neither to condemn nor to condone but rather to *understand* heroic contesting in a nonjudgmental way."[12]

So let *us* examine this sex difference when and where it emerges – whether in the historical records, in literary analyses, or in anthropological accounts – and let us also use it, in a "nonjudgmental way" to make sense of our species and the ways that we relate and communicate. As we will see, the impulses that give rise to verbal duels also reveal themselves in a great many other things that modern men do when they speak.

~

We begin with a simple question. Verbal battles consume energy. Why bother? Our Nordic and English ancestors must have enjoyed some impressive benefits – ones big enough to justify the risks – but what were these, and what made boasts and insults the perfect currency for this quirky-but-serious social game? Boasts and insults stand out from other kinds of utterances. Men who did these things were not attempting to inform, chat, or gossip. So what were they doing – *really* doing?

Rituals of sex and dominance

To answer this we must take a step back and look at the biological context in which the contests arose. The men who insulted each other so freely were engaged in a *ritual.* Just over forty years ago, English biologist Julian Huxley attempted to define ritualistic behaviors in a variety of animal species. He saw the process of ritualization "as the adaptive formalization ... of emotionally motivated behaviour" under pressures supplied by natural selection.[13] Huxley went on to identify key characteristics of ritualized behaviors, ones that may easily be seen as *benefits.*

Two of these benefits were general ones – to facilitate communication and elicit appropriate responses. The others were more specific: to reduce physical injury, and to facilitate sexual or social bonding. These latter benefits refer to things that we care about here: aggression – an important cause of injuries that rituals avoid – and access to mating opportunities.

How do rituals minimize injury? In the animal kingdom, it is not unusual for the threatening animal to make himself appear larger than he really is, causing foes to reassess his attackability and back off. In other cases, a ritual display may include some sort of moderating gesture. For example, one animal might approach another with his beak or other bodily "weapon" turned to one side. In other cases, an animal may make a submissive gesture that acts as a "releaser" or activator of mechanisms that were evolutionarily designed to inhibit aggression in the recipient.

Frequently, animals that engage in these rituals are negotiating dominance relations. When it becomes clear who does and does not have power, group living – which would otherwise be unrelentingly fractious – begins to settle down. Low-ranking animals rarely pick a fight with animals at the top of the hierarchy, and high-ranking animals can usually get what they want without fighting.[14] Since dominance hierarchies are biologically advantageous, the rituals that support them must also be seen as adaptive.

Inasmuch as females often prefer to mate with males of a high rank, dominance displays have sexual as well as social implications. But some of these displays, and direct combat itself, are explicitly waged over sex, and may even be incited by females who wish to avoid mating with anyone but the most virile male. During copulation, female elephant seals issue a call that attracts all the males within earshot. These highly excited males then proceed to fight for copulating rights themselves. The winner – the last and presumably fittest male standing – gets the green light. This is what Cathleen Cox and Burney Le Boeuf called the "female incitation" model of mating. Evidence of this mechanism extends beyond seals to include primates and other species.[15] Later, we will see examples of a similar mechanism in our own species.

Militant dueling: ritual but real

Rituals play an important role in the history of human communication, and I will have more to say about this later on. But rituals

have also played an interesting historical role. This was particularly clear in the case of militant dueling which, for a good four
hundred years, was held all over Europe and in other countries.
Many of these were *aristocratic duels*, which conformed to precise
rules, giving them an air of civility. The combatants were men.[16]

Although aristocratic duels were dangerous – even the presence
of rules did not prevent injury or death – they benefitted society in
several ways. The nineteenth century was a time of feuds. Like
duels, many feuds began with a slight or a slur, but lasted for
decades or longer – at least 11 percent of the Corsican feuds took
more than a century to run their course.[17] Duels offered an important advantage over feuds. They were self-terminating. They cleared
the air. "By giving the passions a limited mode of expression,"
wrote Donna Andrew, "dueling substituted a conventionalized,
well-demarcated conflict for a potentially endless state of war."[18]

Aristocrats chose to duel with pistols and swords, but ordinary
men used other weapons. In eighteenth-century London, many
duels were fought with fists, and these also followed rules of
conduct. In 1751, Charles Troop and George Bartholomew took
an alehouse argument into Marylebone Fields where they pro-
ceeded to engage in what one witness described as "fair boxing,"
but not without declaring "no animosity" and shaking hands
twice, a ritual they would repeat when the event was over.[19]

In the early nineteenth century, working-class Greeks fought
with knives. As in England, these fights usually began in wine
shops, where freshly loosened tongues led the altercants outside,
and ended with first blood, when other men intervened.[20] Some
of the victors turned themselves in to the authorities immediately
afterwards. In doing so they incurred a fine but it was a small
price to pay, for the victory became a matter of public record,
advertising the winners' reputations for toughness.[21]

These spontaneous fights were similar in structure and content
to the aristocratic duels of British soldiers, German students,
Italian liberals, the French bourgeois, and all classes of men in
the American South.[22] Most began with insults that targeted
indolence, drunkenness, sexual misdeeds, ineptitude, unreliability,

or dishonesty. Lying was one of the worst insults. To be accused of it was such a serious challenge, wrote Lodovick Bryskett in 1606, that a man "cannot disburden himselfe of that imputation, but by striking of him that hath so given it, or by challenging him the combat."[23]

Honor

It is interesting that militant duels were distinctly unlike other kinds of one-on-one contests in a particular way: the participants could accomplish their purpose *without winning*. The main thing was to exhibit the necessary courage *without dying*. This underscores their ritualistic nature.

But how could insults provoke such a confrontation in the first place? In many societies, they threatened the most important thing that men would ever have. It was honor, the *passe-partout* to practically everything that men cared about. Although honor is hard to define, it clearly involved rules that were used by men to control their own behavior and that of other men. But honor went deeper than specific rules. It was, according to law professor William Miller, "your very being."[24] Honorable people, he wrote, are those whose self-image and social standing are intimately dependent on the reactions they elicit from others."[25]

In England, duels were precipitated by some sort of dispute, usually an insult or charge of dishonorable conduct. The dueling began when both men were "ready," and ended when either of them was injured. Then, the fight officially over, the wounded party forgave his opponent.[26]

Merely by showing up, an insulted man could restore his honor and good name. Those who refused to fight incurred a bigger risk.[27] For honor was linked to masculinity. In the typical duel between two men, according to Ward Parks, the establishment of sexual identity was "a paramount preoccupation."[28] It follows from this that honor and masculinity would also be tied to another deeply male characteristic – autonomy – which we will explore later.

There is obviously something special about the honor →
insult → aggression sequence. It has occurred repeatedly throughout human history, so repeatedly and *reliably* that it has a hard-
wired look to it. What are the physiological conditions that cause
this honor-insult-aggression circuit to activate so predictably?

The epic flyters cannot help us here, but we need not look to
history for answers, nor must we extrapolate from apes. Thanks
to Richard Nisbett and Dov Cohen, there is experimental evidence
in modern humans. These psychologists recognized that the
American South had long displayed a stronger sense of male honor
than the North, and still does. Historically, the South has also had
the advantage in homicides. For Nisbett and Cohen, the question
was whether southern men are *unusually* protective of their own
interests, sensitive to insult, and ready to retaliate.[29] To find out,
they did an experiment with a number of young southern and
northern US men.

When reporting for duty at the lab, each subject was asked to
deposit some saliva in a vial, then complete a written survey and
place it on a table at the end of a narrow corridor. On the way back,
the subject was bumped into and insulted ("Asshole!") by a lab
assistant who pretended to be working in the corridor. This was
in full view of a young man and woman who were posing as
onlookers. After this "accident" the student was asked to deposit
a second saliva sample. Analyses of the saliva samples revealed
that the southern students displayed a significant increase in
cortisol, indicating a stress response, and a sharp rise in testosterone,
indicating a heightened readiness to aggress. Neither the northern
students nor a control group of un-insulted southern students
displayed a significant increase in either hormone. This bit of
physiological evidence exposes the action of biological mechanisms
that support the psychological, cultural, and historical evidence.

Males are naturally inclined to engage each other in various
kinds of contests, and we will inspect evidence that positions this
tendency in human biology. But the precise ways that men enact
the relevant dispositions is determined, to some extent, by external influences. In Colonial America, for example, boys "were

trained to defend their honor without a moment's hesitation," wrote David Fischer, "lashing out instantly against their challengers with savage violence."[30]

I was exposed to a little of this training in my own youth in Midwestern America. If one boy was insulted by another, an older bystander was frequently around to say: "Are you going to take that? He just called you a name! Aren't you going to be a man and stick up for yourself?"

When there is a role for teaching, there is room for cultural variation, and yet honor has one invariant feature: in every case, the individual is prepared to use force to protect his reputation. Historically, honor and violence traveled together, both showing up wherever there was strong economic competition coupled with a governing body that was too weak to prevent crimes and misdemeanors.[31] "The innate Desire of Honour and of what doth merit it," wrote John Cockburn in the early eighteenth century, "is a better Security of one's good Behavior than either publick Laws or private and personal Obligations."[32]

If honor was inherently linked to masculinity, of course, this meant that dueling was inextricably linked to dominance and sex. So there would have to be an audience and, naturally, the audience would have to include women.

The role of women

When men compete with each other, their reputations will usually be affected if other men are watching. But when men joust in public, women are likely to be involved too, whether they seem to do anything or not. For if males' "verbal plumage" is the result of sexual selection, components of this plumage may have evolved to exploit sensitivities in the female perceptual system, and these sensitivities may still be operating today.[33]

Men also dueled to protect the honor of their loved ones. Historically, a man's honor could be insulted in one easy step: raise a question about the fidelity or virtue of a woman in his life.

This automatically produced a "serious" or "gallant" duel, a contest usually fought over a wife, lover, or daughter, although the family name could also be at stake.[34] "For the man imbued with a chivalrous respect for the opposite sex," wrote Robert Baldick, "an injury or insult to a woman to whom he was related or attached was the gravest and most obvious reason for a duel."[35] In Amsterdam, according to a different historian, Pieter Spierenburg, "a number of knife fights originated in the defense of a woman against a man by another man."[36]

Chivalry has a good name. According to my dictionary, the chivalrous man takes personal risks in order to protect the honor of his lover. But were his motives always so selfless? Following a duel, the result would surely have reached the woman whose virtue had been so courageously defended, with results that are not hard to imagine.[37]

The possibility of such an outcome made it hard to put a stop to dueling, fussed German philosopher Alexander von Oettingen in 1889. Women have "a secret appreciation" for duelers, he wrote, and a feeling of "adoration" for their "chivalrous courage." Where it was said that a young man was opposed to dueling, von Oettingen continued, "it counts among many young ladies almost as a defect. They would rather converse and dance with a notorious duel enthusiast," he wrote. But he didn't actually blame the young women. They are, he said, "mostly unsuspecting of what pernicious influence they consciously or unconsciously exercise upon male youth."[38]

It makes good bio-logical sense that women would encourage men to display their masculine qualities, and if the desire to do so springs from innate dispositions associated with mating – which it does – it would be surprising if either party were consciously aware of the actual mechanisms at work. In view of the dispro-portionate effort that women contribute to reproduction and infant care, it makes sense that they would look for "honest signals" that men actually wanted *them*, not merely the oppor-tunity to have sex with them, and that these men would remain around, helpfully, after any babies were born. So if men had to incur some risk in order to protect their lady's honor, or even their own honor, all the better.

But there was an unacknowledged question here. How long could such risky behaviors be allowed to continue? How long could societies that prided themselves on their rationality and civility turn a blind eye to behaviors that were neither rational nor civil?

One sign of a growing disaffection for dueling was the growing use of pistols instead of swords. These weapons put a serious dent in the homicide statistics. Pistols, or the men who fired them, were not particularly accurate. In some cases, it was not even clear that they had *aimed them at anything.* In 1790, according to historical records, a pistol duel "ended after each party fired a single shot ... and one of those was in the air." This was play dueling, a ritual in which "neither party receive[s] any injury."[39] But this was not the only clue that serious dueling was becoming passé. According to one late eighteenth-century account, two men described as "Hibernian hairdressers" fought with tubers. Unbeknownst to the dueling hairdressers, the men serving as seconds had loaded their pistols with "half boiled potatoes."[40]

Finally, of course, campaigns were launched to put a stop to violent duels. Throughout Europe and the American South, anti-dueling leagues were established. Eventually, the use of weapons was outlawed altogether.[41]

∼

Individually, of course, men always knew that violence could be incited by words used crudely or in anger. In the mouths of ungifted speakers, words were an imperfect substitute for physical violence. Issued without skill or humor, words could threaten the victim's "face," and cause him to seek revenge. In 1297, Walter de Eure, a blacksmith in Oxford, England, stabbed a visitor, John Attehalle, following a "strife of words." It sounds like prototypical flyting, a humorless use of words that caused the very behavior for which it could have been – and in time, with modifications, would become – a substitute.

Mere recognition of this was not enough to stop it. No one could prevent public displays of anger, or penalize humorless speech. But it was possible to outlaw insults, and anti-slander legislation was eventually passed in many places. These new laws made it a crime to use untruthful words to damage a man's reputation and standing in the community, and they were put to work immediately. In late sixteenth-century England, defamation cases nearly tripled in a thirty-year period.[42]

Systemic controls were helpful, but men remained ready to take action on their own, and personal solutions were essential. Less harmful ways to channel aggressive dispositions were needed. One possibility was to develop a duel that preserved the concept of honor while offering continuing opportunities for male–male competition. If men were to continue contesting in public, this new duel would have to be fought with words, not pistols, and these words could neither be harsh nor humorless. Handled correctly, these more playful and artistic *verbal duels* would preserve the best of militant duels by producing winners and losers in the competition for sex and dominance, while holding the risk of violence to a minimum. As we will see, the verbal weapons in the new duels would say a great deal about the user's ability to manipulate what is perhaps our species' most valued trait in pursuit of our species' most valued resources.

New ways with words

In many cases of flyting the insults were a *truthful* recounting of some previous act of cowardice, ineptitude, or moral weakness. Nothing about this was amusing. Indeed, the accuser's intention was to injure his victim with authentic barbs – to cause him embarrassment or shame. There was no game here, no good-hearted jockeying for position. This was personal – there was a prior history, possibly a grudge or a bit of unfinished business – and there was certainly a desire to dominate or wound.

It is easy to see why insults are the preferred medium in verbal duels. Dueling has a call-response structure and insults usually elicit an in-kind response. But locking horns, in full view of peers, is a risky business. Taken seriously, insults can lead to fists or worse. This can be avoided with a clever use of humor, which usually takes the sting out of any offensive words that it accompanies.

According to psychologist Avner Ziv, some kinds of humor are a means of expressing aggression. If so, we might expect men to be unusually good at generating humor, or certain kinds of humor, and there is evidence that this is true.[43] They, more than women, enjoy jokes about people who are physically or mentally challenged, or who belong to an ethnic group that has been pre-selected for ridicule. In either case, the teller of the joke displays his superiority over some person or class of people.

Ritual insults

Men wishing to compete without risk have long made heavy use of ritual insults. These taunts are typically formulated or learned from someone else *prior* to the duel in which they are used. This gives them a displaced quality, making it difficult for victims to react *personally*. The more effective insults are also oblique. Many contain "information" about the rival that could not be known by the dueler. If the insult does relate to an intrinsic feature of the opponent, it is always factually absurd and, for that reason, both amusing and unbelievable.

For untruthful insults to work, of course, they must also be *obviously* untrue to the *audience*. If these observers think an insult is intended to injure, their silence or other reactions will surely embolden the victim to make an equally injurious response, and fists or weapons may not be that far behind.

Those who are able to fight with words, and to do so in a way that provokes nothing more violent, live to duel another day. Multiple skills and talents are required here. Saying something that is almost, but not quite true; or delivering a barb in a way that keeps it from being taken seriously – by this contestant, by this audience, in this situation – are skills that presuppose a range of social and cognitive abilities, ones that all of us would like our companions and teammates to have.

Cognitive ability may also be implied by the complex structure of insults. Shakespeare's plays contain more than four thousand epithets, including "prating peasant," "canker blossom," and "monstrous apparition," to repeat a few of the milder ones.[44] My colleague, Ljiljana Progovac, has compiled a shorter but sizeable list of two-word compounds that have been used as insults by men in several different cultures and languages, from America, where *kill-joy, pick-pocket,* and *scatter-brain* are used, to Serbia, where the men insult each other with *cepi-dlaka* 'split-hair' (hair-splitter), *guli-koža* 'peel-skin' (person who rips you off), and *vrti-guz* 'spin-butt' (restless person, fidget). Though many of the compounds are far more insulting and obscene than these, their use is understood to be playful.[45]

Some years ago, William Samarin studied the insults used by the Gbeyan people in the Central African Republic. He discovered that they had a "special genre of discourse" that enabled speakers to do something that, on the surface, poses exceptional risk: ridicule the listener's physical characteristics. This seems dangerous, and paradoxically so, since the Gbeyans feared any type of speech that could cause trouble between people.[46] Predictably, there was a special property that kept their insults from causing trouble, and a few examples are enough to see what this property was. "Your nostrils are cavernous," was one of the Gbeyan insults. In another, the victim's eyes are said to be "like the eyes of a frog that drowned." These insults are derived from the culture, not the mind of the insulter, and they are too preposterous to be taken very seriously.

The Gbeyans would also have been aware that their kind of insulting was a ritual. In many other places, there is another way to safely insult others, and that is to aim a jokey barb at some peripheral aspect of the individual's life rather than the person himself. This produces a glancing or harmless blow, as though the attacker's verbal beak were turned to one side.

Cavernous nostrils? You must be joking!

In many cultures, according to British anthropologist Alfred Radcliffe-Brown, people who joke with each other on a regular basis have a *joking relationship*. In these relationships, he wrote, one of two persons "is by custom permitted, and in some instances required, to tease or make fun of the other, who in turn is required to take no offence."[47] Radcliffe-Brown saw joking relationships as a "peculiar combination of friendliness and antagonism." In any other context, he pointed out, jokes are likely to express and arouse hostility, but they exert no such effects in a joking relationship.[48]

In many societies, men issue a humorous insult when they encounter a long-term male friend:

> How are you, you old son of a bitch?
> Well, look at what the cat dragged in.

In these "greetings" one man is attempting to elicit an in-kind response from his friend. The response, when it occurs, completes the ritual and affirms the friendship. The men are play-fighting with words, but how far can they go with this? Dogs seem to sense just how hard they can bite, perhaps from subtle reactions by the "bitee." How do men know that their lexical bites will not draw blood?

They could scan each other's facial reactions, and almost certainly do. But the fact is that duelers are aware, on some level, that what they are engaged in is indeed a ritual. They know that no part of it is intended to be hurtful. Anthropologist John Dollard once wrote about joking relationships between two male friends in which the jests flew about infidelity, though each seemed to be a faithful husband, and about impotence, though both men were married with children. "Both friends seem to have an unconscious perception and agreement on how far the joking may go," wrote Dollard. "It does not touch upon actual weaknesses."[49]

If there are limits on what can be said literally, or seriously, these can be relaxed with a smile, a wink, or some other movement. Sometimes, an inconsiderate or unfriendly remark is softened, or its literal meaning reversed, with a playful form of body contact. Toward the end of a visit, a father nudged his son-in-law with an elbow as he said, "Maybe we'll stay a few more days."[50]

There is a bit of theatre in the use of humorous insults. They are not hurled like spears; they are performed. Preparations begin when the actors learn their lines, typically canned insults that are acquired mainly through exposure to other members of the culture. These make up the "script." Next comes the performance itself, which requires timing and fluency. There is, to complete the analogy, an audience that is ready to respond.[51]

Successful duelers also have a sense of imagination, a sense of the *virtual*. Merely by performing a ritual, they seem to say: I am *portraying* a person who believes himself to be superior, or is attempting to pick a fight. In doing so, I express confidence in me, that I will be able to *play this role* convincingly – but not too convincingly – and confidence in my opponent that he will pick up the mitigating cues that I provide, and recognize the benign quality – the insincerity or playfulness – of my verbal charges.

In the years before organized sports, nightclubs, and television, verbal dueling provided ordinary people with a public event in which they, too, could play a role by cheering and laughing. Before the contestants on "Survivor" and other reality TV programs competed with each other for prizes, verbal dueling provided spectators with chances to applaud their favorite candidate and boo their rivals.

Dueling is also a form of public broadcasting, with social, cultural, and moral implications. For if a reference to some previous act qualifies as an insult, both to the audience and the recipient, then young listeners will know that it was *wrong* according to some standard. They will also discover – and directly observe – the chosen punishment: a dose of public humiliation for what may have been, until the moment, a private indiscretion. In this way, insulting shares properties with gossip, which offers some of the same benefits.

Song duels

When sampling behaviors across cultures, it is important to look for differences and similarities. When we see what varies we also discover core properties that remain the same. In some cultures, the words used in dueling are chanted or sung, occasionally accompanied by dancing and drumming. The anthropological literature contains several references to *song duels* by groups in various places around the world. It also contains references to *poetic duels* and *sung poetic duels*.[52] In the mountains of Sardinia, song duels routinely go on for four and five hours, not ending until the participating shepherds run out of material or motivation. A poet is able to win these contests, wrote Elizabeth Mathias, if he is able "to improvise freely, to entertain and amuse listeners, and to put down his opponent with his insults."[53]

Among the Greenland Eskimos, anthropologists have described what must surely be the epitome of rhythmic performances – *drum duels* – in which the participants issue good-humored taunts while beating a drum.[54] But the exotic form of these duels should not mislead us. Song duels work like their verbal siblings in a number of ways.[55] In both cases, the participants are men who use their wits to insult each other, humorously, before a responsive audience, the outcome of which affects their social standing. The contestant "who is most heartily applauded is 'winner'" in all these duels, wrote anthropologist E. Adamson Hoebel. "The sole advantage is in prestige."[56]

A linguist from Crete, Elli Doukanari, has described the sung poetic duels, or *chattista*, that occur on that island. These rhyming improvisations are held in public for the entertainment of mixed audiences. In the typical chattista, there are two male singers who set up a ritual conflict, which is ultimately resolved when one of the men produces a verse from memory that his opponent is unable to answer. In this way, the winner proves that he is smarter and, therefore, "the better man."[57]

Specially staged events like *chattista* dramatize the "appetite" of ordinary people for verbal competition. It is strong enough to fill soccer-sized stadiums. In Lebanon, where all-male teams perform "artistic verbal duels," contests are carried out before audiences of ten to twenty thousand people. They still talk about one in 1971 that drew over thirty thousand.[58] In the Basque country, poetic dueling contests are held in four-year qualification and elimination trials, in Olympian fashion – all witnessed live and on television, complete with running commentary and analysis.[59]

In Saudi Arabia, poetic dueling takes years of training and practice. "To be recognized as a good dueling poet," according to an account provided by Saad Abdullah Sowayan, "it is not enough to have a good voice and the ability to versify. One must also have a wide knowledge, deep understanding, quick mind, sharp wits, and the ability to twist words and turn phrases, say the same thing in different ways, and express ideas in veiled metaphors and figurative language. In the final analysis, poetic dueling is a match of wits and an exhibition of knowledge."[60]

These things matter because Saudi men need to be evaluated, much as their Scandinavian predecessors were appraised in the man-matching contests held nearly a millennium earlier. It is interesting, in this regard, that the etymology of *contest*, the Latin *contestari*, means 'to call upon to witness.' What is witnessed in verbal duels? What do the audiences learn?

Men who excel in verbal performances typically command more than some basal amount of colloquial and metaphorical language. They are also skilled in the physical act of speaking – being able to control their rate, loudness, fluency, and intonation, and they are good at reading their male opponents. Audiences infer from these things which men have the physical and cognitive abilities that *support* dueling. These enabling abilities were critically important to our pre-modern ancestors, for they needed to know, at a time when cooperation was essential to survival, who was sufficiently strong and smart to compete. There are also some deeper reproductive advantages associated with dueling behaviors, as we will see in Chapter 4.

In oral societies the audiences may also have been sizing up dueling men for possible positions of leadership, since leaders are usually selected, in large part, on the basis of their ability to speak. It would not be surprising if some of the better song, poetic, and drum duelers were also angling for political power. But on a personal level, men who enjoy the cut and thrust of public contests may also have, and thus put on display, what is indelicately called "cojones." Literally. Men with a tendency to aggress, swagger, or even to assert themselves, tend to have higher levels of testosterone, a product of the testes. As we will see, this translates into two elements that are indispensable to reproduction: libido and sperm.

Forensic debate

When one's own culture includes a particular feature, it is possible to miss it, or if noticed, to have no particular thoughts about its functionality. An example that is relevant here is forensic debates. In the early nineteenth century, debating societies cropped up in thousands of American communities.[61] These societies were solely made up of young men, who believed that participation in extemporaneous speaking, and the verbal skills that would be honed in the process, could lead to opportunities for professional advancement and civic leadership. It also gave them a chance to be evaluated, in a personal way, by large audiences of local citizens.

These evaluations could be comprehensive. The debates were physically demanding, since participants were on their feet – and under intense intellectual pressure – for as long as three hours; but they also placed a variety of other personal characteristics on review. When young men debated, community members assessed them "not just as brains engaged in calm, rational debate," wrote sociologist Nina Eliasoph, "but also as laughing bodies with tastes, passions, manners."[62] Viewed in this context, it is unsurprising that, as Angela Ray noted, the benefits of participation included socializing with each other and "preening themselves before potential sexual partners."[63]

In November of 1842, 20-year-old Isaac Mickle and his teammates prevailed in a very public verbal contest, a debate held
before a mixed audience in Camden, New Jersey. His team was
triumphant, he wrote in his diary that night, but Mickle himself
triumphed "because *ma chere amie* witnessed the tournament. To
conquer in her presence is doubly victorious."[64]

The following month Mickle participated in another debate,
one that he was careful to note had been held "before a crowded
house." There had been "some sparring," Mickle wrote, "all
however in good humor. Every inch of ground was *manfully
contested*, but we got the decision unanimously, so there could
be no appeal. This is indeed a compliment to us, and we feel it
properly. To get so unpopular a decision from prejudiced judges
and against able opponents, and that before *so many ladies*, is,
and ought to be, a source of pride."[65]

Clearly public debates were being treated like a dating service,
one that would enable enterprising young men to display traits
relevant to a decision that the women in the audience were hoping
to make. In this sense, a man's performance was, as Ray said of all
debates, "fraught with the perilous possibilities of triumph or
failure." As "visible bodies" the debaters ran "the risk of being
judged as personally inadequate for the role they inhabited." If
Mickle's *chere amie* had been wondering if her beau was willing to
take risks in order to surpass other men, the debates supplied
the answer. Mickle later became a lawyer, historian, musician,
playwright, translator, inventor, politician, newspaper editor, and
father of four – all before his untimely death at the age of 33.

A debate was far more useful if attended by women, and men
knew it. In the public speeches sponsored by Baltimore's union
halls in the late nineteenth and early twentieth century, the
presence of mothers, sisters, wives, and sweethearts was usually
acknowledged, wrote Roderick Ryon, with a fatuous reference "to
Baltimore's fame as a city of 'beautiful ladies.'"[66] Several debating
societies offered women free admission. Others extended honorary
memberships to women and attempted, by decorating the
meeting halls, to make them feel welcome. Later we will see that

modern women play a role that is less "showy" and demonstrative than that of men, but no less powerful.

In the effort to win their contests, the debaters would surely have chided their opponents on occasion. One can well imagine good-natured barbs such as "If my worthy opponent had gone to the trouble to read the US Constitution ..." But rules of engagement outlawed scorn, or anything that could be construed as seriously insulting. On the street, too, there are rules regarding what can and cannot be said, and how challenges can be issued. But insults – especially playful insults – are the name of the game.

"Sounding"

In the inner city areas of Los Angeles, Chicago, Philadelphia, and New York, black adolescents and young adults play a verbal game called "Sounding" (or "playing the dozens"). In this game, according to one account, "two opponents duel verbally, making derogatory remarks about each others' family members, usually the mother. Each player is appreciated and judged by the group, whose responsibility is also to urge the players on ... The winner of the game is determined by the audience, who judges both players' reactions to one another's comments. The cultural hero is the player who hurls the most linguistically derogatory comments and still maintains his composure."[67]

An educator offered that account, but thanks to H. "Rap" Brown, we also have a first-person description by a gifted performer. Sounding, he wrote, "is a mean game because what you try to do is totally destroy somebody else with words." Sometimes, he said, there would be "forty or fifty dudes standing around and the winner was determined by the way they responded to what was said."[68]

In a middle- to upper-class town in southwestern Ohio, studied in the late 1960s, white adolescent males regularly participated in Sounding matches.[69] A typical engagement, wrote the investigators, "starts from a chance remark innocently dropped which triggers a Sound as a comeback. This second Sound demands a rejoinder – and so on and on until one boy 'wins' the exchange. Victory," they went on, "is reckoned when either competitor is unable to supply a fitting retort or when the excellence of one boy's response evokes loud laughter and jeers from the necessary audience. In this way the audience serves as both catalyst and judge by goading the players on to making more daring Sounds and by tacitly recognizing a winner."[70]

Though much emphasis is placed on the words used in dueling, the contestants also display some characteristic bodily activity as well. According to one report, the typical adolescent dueler keeps his body stiff and chin turned upwards, evidently to look tough. There is also a reported gesture, which involves holding an arm parallel to the body with the hand pointing downwards during the issuance of the insult.[71]

The content of Midwestern American "Sounds," as reported by the adolescents themselves, included:

> Your mother smokes corn silks.
> Your mother goes down for the whole school.
> Your old lady gives Green Stamps.

In other places, including eastern communities, white adolescent males report dueling with their peers. Some of the milder of their stock insults:

> Your mother's like a birthday cake, everyone gets a piece.
> Your mother wears combat boots.
> Your mother is so low she could play handball on the curb.

As the examples suggest, references to "your mother" abound – in the US a TV program called "Yo Momma" first aired several years ago – and parental name-calling more generally occurs in other parts of the world, too.[72] In more or less typical cases, adolescents and young adults trade insulting phrases to the hooting and howling of peers and the entertainment of home viewers:

> Yo Mama's like a library – open to the public.
> Yo Mama's so stupid she stole a free sample.
> Yo Mama's so fat, when she backs up she beeps.

In real life, the insults are not purely maternal. In the Ohio study, the researchers' notes included "I went to your house but the garbage man already emptied it," and "You look like five hundred miles of bad road."

What happened to duelers who lacked a quick or clever retort? What happened to the losers? According to H. "Rap" Brown, "It was a bad scene for the dude that was getting humiliated ... The real aim of the Dozens was to get a dude so mad that he'd cry or get mad enough to fight."[73] The "dudes" who consistently lost duels had a name. In the poor black neighborhoods of New York and Philadelphia in the 1970s, they were called *lames*. These losers had normal linguistic ability but most were from another part of town and lacked the colloquial knowledge needed to participate in the local genres of verbal competition.[74] When black men fail with women, their "raps" are ridiculed as "tissue paper."[75] In other societies, according to New Zealand sociolinguist Koenraad Kuiper, those who cannot handle phrasal vocabulary – colloquialisms and other forms of stereotyped material – are considered "social lepers."[76]

The winners of duels are viewed very differently. Like Erik the Eloquent, they are known and admired as "men of words." These men usually have a good command of colloquial expressions and, in a number of black communities, are able to generate rhyme, and to deliver it with special rhythms that move with the rhymes.[77] This is functional, for rhyming draws attention to individuals. Just before his prize fights, young Cassius Clay (later Mohammed Ali) drew attention to himself with frequent boasts ("I am the greatest!") and rhyming predictions ("If he's hip, he'll take a dip, 'cos I'ma bust his lip").

Although duels abound in adolescence, and in the oral cultures that anthropologists love to study, they may erupt wherever competitive men congregate. Playful insulting occurs everywhere that men go. In the early 1970s, anthropologist Frank Manning spent some time in a black bar (or "social club") in Bermuda. One thing that stood out about the male patrons was their insulting, especially the artful and friendly way that they did it. Since there was always a responsive audience of men and women in the club, Manning thought these verbal exchanges could "be viewed as spectator games and public performances," opportunities for the participants "to display their personality and style for the benefit of an audience as well as their competitors."[78]

While Manning was observing the black duelers in Bermuda, E. E. LeMasters was busily at work in a white working-class tavern in southern Wisconsin. LeMasters, a sociology professor by day and patron of the "Oasis" by night, noticed a great deal of banter in his natural laboratory. In fact, some regular patrons light-heartedly attacked each other more or less continuously. In the Oasis, social success was dependent on men's "ability to 'dish it out' in the rapid-fire exchange called 'joshing,'" wrote LeMasters. "You have to have a quick retort, and preferably one that puts you 'one up' on your opponent. People who can't compete in the game lose status."[79]

Bars are one thing, but what about the workplace? Do men duel there? In the 1990s, two language specialists, Andrea Decapua and Diana Boxer, spent some time in a stockbrokerage in suburban Washington, DC. All of the stockbrokers were males in their late 20s or early 30s. Decapua and Boxer noticed that these men displayed a nearly constant stream of "intense bantering" or "jousting," a form of mock combat in which profanity was used in a way that was witty – at least to the stockbrokers themselves – and controlling. A contestant won if his opponent faltered or embarrassed himself. These bantering exchanges, the authors wrote, were "attempts by the brokers to display themselves as competent and powerful individuals," but the strategies – humorous bragging and put-downs – served as a release valve for office tensions as well as a means of social control. "In this brokerage house community," wrote Decapua and Boxer, "he who gets the laughs gets status."[80]

Core features of dueling

We have seen that men's disposition to lock verbal horns with other men goes back a good many centuries, and crosses a variety of regional, social, and educational boundaries. Verbal dueling serves some of the same purposes as the rituals that have been documented in other species, particularly domination. The calls and retorts take the shape of insults, which are served up with the expectation that the opponent will swat them back. Accusations, when they occur, are usually made humorously, even outrageously, and this keeps the banter from heating up.[81]

When we look at the various kinds of duels that have occurred in diverse cultures, what varies? This question is of great interest to cultural anthropologists, sociologists, and other social scientists. Here we are particularly interested in what is left over – in what stays the same. Competitive verbalization enjoys universal appeal. It occurs in a number of geographically dispersed cultures, from the frozen tundras of Greenland to the island of Malta, the mountains of Sardinia, the suburbs of Midwestern cities, the stockbrokerages of Washington, DC, and the streets of Los Angeles, Chicago, New York, and Philadelphia. The political and economic structure of these places varies widely. Predictably, there are, as we have seen, dueling "dialects." In some places men duel with spoken words, in other places verbal competition takes the form of sung duels, drum duels, poetic duels, and various combinations of these. The remarkable thing is the number of features that do not change. Most verbal duels, especially the highly stylized ceremonial types, have the following properties:

1. There is a ritualistic contest that is held in public space.
2. An audience is present.
3. The contest is won and lost based on the quality of the verbal performances.
4. The favored material is colloquial or "pre-packaged."
5. Each challenge must be met by an appropriate "in kind" response.
6. The material may rhyme or have other special linguistic characteristics.
7. Winning and losing affect reputation and status.

The spontaneous duels, ones that are enacted by juvenile and adult males, have the features listed above as well as these additional properties:

8. Boasts and insults are the primary content.
9. Most assertions and counter-charges are self-evidently false.
10. The content is issued humorously, or in a humorous spirit.
11. Words may be used as an alternative to, and may prevent, physical fighting.
12. Contests are lost, and may be ended, by anger or verbal ineptitude.

To this list may be added two natural and non-arbitrary features of the *participants* and the *audience*. The duelers are two males who are usually somewhat familiar with each other. The audiences are made up of women as well as men, and they are entertained, but potentially affected by the outcome.

Verbal duels are rituals, but we must be careful not to think of dueling only as a discrete ceremonial event with a clear onset and conclusion. The dueling disposition threads its way through the *ordinary speech* of men, with strands of it here in this challenge and there in that retort. Men duel when they distance themselves from others by *performing* in some way. The dueling disposition also emerges as an attempt to *dominate*, as revealed by excessive interruption, loudness, and refusal to yield the floor. The disposition to duel is never far from the surface.

Do women *never* duel?

If women were opposed to verbal duels, there are no indications of it in the historical records. It is unlikely that many were. As we have seen, the mere existence of chivalrous duels indicates that even where the weapons were swords and not words, and the outcome possibly bloody, some young women expressed appreciation for the heroism and sacrifice displayed by young men. Other types of militant duels were staged in order to preserve men's own reputation and honor, issues in which women had a stake. That is why these duels were staged so that women – not just men – would see them.

Men are overt competitors, and the more likely of the two sexes to display their biological wares. By contrast, women, as we will see, are more inclined to compete indirectly; and in sexual matters, to evaluate the displays of males rather than stage their own. What, then, of women's participation in anything as "duelly" as men's verbal contests? Perhaps we should begin by asking if women ever took up arms against each other.

There are a few cases where women dueled with swords, but this was rare. Women had virtue, but they clearly did not have honor in anything approaching the masculine sense. Did they ever duel with words? Do they do so today? It would be surprising if women *never* dueled with words, and yet it appears that they never do. There is no evidence that women have ever engaged in verbal dueling as performed by men, or that they do so now. This seems an extreme statement. How can I be so sure?

I have looked far and wide for cases of women's dueling, and when I find what looks like one, it invariably turns out to be a false positive. For example, until the 1950s, women in the Outer Hebrides sang poetic songs while pounding or "waulking" long swatches of woolen cloth. Some of these waulking songs pertained to the work itself, but most were historical or personal, and highly charged emotionally. In one case, two women from different islands, Barra and Uist, decided in a moment of apparent dueliness to see who was better at composing poetry. The women traded poetic insults until victory was achieved. The woman from Barra was thought to have won. As "the woman with the most *verbal* prowess," according to Jean Haskell Speer, she would have been "the most esteemed." But then, Speer went on to say, "a concession was made to the woman from Uist, for she was far better at *singing the tunes*. "Both are necessary," wrote Speer. "Like the communal activity of waulking, women of varying talents are required for the fully realized creative act."[82]

What about truly verbal duels, ones with no "musical accompaniment"? Whenever I have seen a reference to any sort of verbal confrontation I have chased it down to see what was entailed. A more or less typical account is the "conflict talk" of women in Gapun, New Guinea, investigated some twenty years ago by anthropologist Don Kulick. Conflict talk has been cited as an example of women going public in the settlement of disputes. Is this garden-variety dueling?

If we look at the details, we find, first, that conflict talk involved *angry complaints* by women about their husbands, relatives, and children, and anyone else that offended them in some way. These complaints were characterized by obscenity, sarcasm, threats, and insults, and voiced in loud, public displays called *kroses*. The typical *kros* occurred at day's end when villagers began drifting back to their homes and began the usual preparations for dinner. Then, Kulick wrote, it was "not uncommon to hear a high, indignant voice suddenly rising above the playful screams of children and the barking of the village dogs." According to his contemporaneous report:

> The voice will often begin in low, loud, dissatisfied mutters, but it rises quickly and peaks in harsh crescendos. It becomes rapid, piston-like, unrelenting – so fast that the words become slurred and distorted to the point where it sometimes takes the villagers a while to work out what is being said. As the voice grows in volume and rancor, villagers stop what they are doing, cock their ears, and listen.[83]

A *kros* is frequently set in motion by a belief that the "plaintiff" has been wronged or insulted, or compromised by a fellow villager. The culprit does not actually have to be present during the *kros*, which is actually a form of dramatic self-display.

Scolding

Women's conflict talk falls heavily on male eardrums, so heavily that the male-dominated legislatures of England made it illegal. The "scolding" statute went so far as to identify the probable breakers

Figure 2.1 *The Female Orators* (engraved from a painting by John Collett, 1768)

of the law *before they broke it*. A violator, an accused or convicted "scold," was "a troublesome and angry *woman*, who by *her* brawling and wrangling amongst *her* Neighbours, doth break the publick Peace, and beget, cherish and increase publick Discord."[84]

In the typical case of scolding, one woman raised her voice against another woman in a public setting, usually doing so in a strident and spectacular way. Figure 2.1 depicts some late eighteenth-century fishwives in a verbal quarrel run amok. Was this dueling? After all, the accusers did their brawling and wrangling verbally. Some of the more memorable insults, thanks to ear-witnesses who later testified in court, were "drunken fuddling fool," "drunken pocky-faced rogue," and "miserly knave and drunken miser."[85]

Do such creative insults qualify as verbal dueling? There are many reasons why they do not. For one thing, they are completely one-sided. Insults may act like "calls" but there is little evidence of any in-kind "responses." But before we rule out women's conflict talk we should look beyond the slurs and ask what was going on below the surface. Why were women so abusive of each other? What was the trigger? There had to be some gain, real or imagined, for in the tiny villages of England words echoed, reputations mattered, and victims could be expected to fight back.

In fact, the scolds were attempting to solve some highly specific problems, and it is in this context that their shrill or strident vocalization begins to make sense. In the vast majority of the fourteenth- and fifteenth-century scolding cases in England – over nine in ten – the charge was of a sexual nature. In over a third of these sexual allegations, "whore" was the charge. Women issued sexual insults at about seven times the rate of men, and the victim was almost invariably another woman – or *the other* woman.[86]

Were these women policing their villages? Certainly some would have been – the church implored parishioners to assume such responsibilities, along with the risks associated with confrontation – but the motive in many cases was more personal. Ear-witness reports suggest that in most cases a jealous wife was attempting to discourage a mate-poacher from further incursions into her marital territory.[87]

On a doorstep in Whitechapel in the winter of 1610, Alice Rochester insulted Jane Lilham in front of their neighbours. "Thow art a whore and an arrant whore and a common carted whore," screamed Alice. Was Alice acting in the role of moral guardian? Something rather more self-oriented emerges from the next phrase: "and thow art *my husbandes whore*," and it may not even have been her husband, *the man*, but her husband, *the provider*. For she continued: "my husband hath kept thee a great while at Newcastle and *all that he got he spent on thee*," while lying "oftener with him then he hath done with me."[88]

The whore charge statistics and ear-witness testimony expose the primary reason why ancestral women verbally aggressed in public. In the male-dominated economies of the day, the security of women like Alice Rochester was tied to the strength of their matrimonial bonds. Competition for marital alliances was intense, producing numerous threats to existing marriages. If wives had sex with another man, their husbands could easily get a judgment of adultery – equivalent to a divorce – and leave them without much in the way of support. But, as argued in an article aptly titled "The double standard," the wives could not do this. If they wanted to preserve their marriages, and the resources those contracts provided, wives would have to do something on their own to ward off poachers, and scolding is what they did.[89]

If sufficiently vocal, other women in the village who faced the same marital threats were likely to sympathize with the aggrieved woman. They would naturally spread the word, eventually reaching an individual the wife would not dream of confronting directly.

Her husband.

This is the flow chart husbands were afraid of. They were unconcerned that women would accuse each other of domestic failings – child neglect, bad cooking, or a failure to keep their homes tidy – though they did so indirectly. Rather, men's fear lay uniquely in charges – as potentially verifiable claims – that would send women scurrying to their social networks with gossip about *them*. How could men carry on clandestine relationships when the entire village knew what they were up to, and with whom they were up to it?

Research from several different academic disciplines sheds light on what was going on here. Psychological research indicates that young American married women issue "verbal possession signals" when fearing the loss of their mate to a competitor. These signals include warnings to sexual rivals that their mate is "taken." Anthropological research indicates that in Zambia, wives are in almost constant conflict with women who attempt to steal their marital resources. Female aggression, according to the report, "tends to be over a man himself ... a woman's husband or lover is always a potential target of other women ... wives and lovers will use any means available to protect their status."[90] Biological research indicates that when a wife feels jealous, it is not purely because another woman is threatening to take her *man*, though this may be a factor; it is because she is threatening to take the *resources* that the man provides.[91]

Were the scolding cases that occurred in early modern England isolated in time and space, or was defamation more widely spread and enduring? The historical evidence reveals that public insults

were also reported in France, Italy, Greece, South America, and
the American colonies – in some of these places over a period of
three and four centuries. But the anthropological evidence
extends far more broadly. In an analysis of verbal aggression in
over a hundred societies around the world, Victoria Burbank
found that twentieth-century women were the targets of female
aggression in approximately 90 percent of the societies; men were
targeted in just over half. Burbank's data indicate that in polygynous societies, the victim was one of the husband's other wives.
Otherwise, it was a sexual rival.[92]

The punishment

In a short essay published three years after the law was passed, the
common scold, "a Devil of the *feminine gender*," was caricatured
as "a serpent, perpetually hissing, and spitting of venom; a composition of ill-nature and clamour ... animated gunpowder,
a walking Mount Etna that is always belching forth flames of
sulphur ... a real purgatory."[93] The punishment was either a tour
through the village in a dunking (or "ducking") chair, followed
by submersion in a local pond or stream, or a few hours in a
scold's bridle, a "helmet" of thin iron bars that was placed over
the head with a "bit" that was laid flat on the tongue.

   That men reacted so violently against women's "disturbances
of the peace" means something in and of itself, and we will circle
back to this later. But our concern here is whether scolding is
verbal dueling. Clearly, scolding is a form of conflict talk, and all
such talk possesses certain properties. It is:

1. serious, not humorous or absurd
2. angry
3. focused on specific acts by others
4. usually inartful
5. vengeful
6. intentionally injurious
7. one-sided.

The verbal duels of men differ on each of these points. At the same time, women's acts of verbal disputation equally fail to qualify as dueling, since they are not:

8. performances
9. rituals
10. contests
11. attempts to dominate or show off.

This list gives us little reason to believe that women duel, nor have we come across any indications that they *want* to duel but for some identified reason do not actually do so. Can we assume from this that women do not see dueling as something they would like? Do they actively *avoid* dueling? Perhaps we can apply an even more stringent test. *What would happen if men tried to induce women to duel?*

Wanted: women duelers

One way to find out would be to look at women's experience in verbal disputation when it is institutionally supported and managed. How do women feel about, and perform in, verbal contests that are held indoors, regulated by rules and supervised by authorities, with no possibility of rudeness or *ad hominem* attack or discussion of personal issues? How do women feel about dueling when these safeguards are guaranteed? How do they feel about debate?

For some years, males have predominated in collegiate debate. In 1984, 85 percent of the participants in America's National Debate Tournament (NDT) were male.[94] In an effort to balance the sex ratio, attempts were made over the ensuing years to attract women. These efforts accomplished little. In 2001, the percentage of female debaters in the NDT had increased by 10 percent, but the distribution of *same-sex debate teams* was heavily skewed in favor of males: in percentage terms, the male dominance was 73 to 3. Accordingly, the investigators concluded that there had been no real increase in female participation.[95] In an analysis of women's involvement in a related tournament, similar results were obtained, women edging up no more than 7 percentage points in ten years' of vigorous recruiting.[96]

The women who did participate lost more often than the men did. But the reason is not that women cannot speak in public. When performing individually, as in poetry reading and oral interpretation, women's scores frequently equaled or exceeded those of men.[97] Debate was the area of specific difficulty.[98]

It is possible that women fall prey to a bias of some sort. Perhaps, one might suppose, there are some male judges who continue to think that young women should content themselves with poetry readings and oral interpretation and leave debate to the men. Some authorities did indeed wonder if women lost more contests because they were held to a higher standard. But analyses showed that both male and female judges scored males higher than females, and *male judges gave higher scores to female debaters than female judges did.*[99] "Although it may not be comfortable to think about," two analysts wrote, "it appears that female judges are the main contributors to the overall pattern of female speakers receiving lower points than males."[100]

Of course, young women could get caught in the "double bind" problem. "If a female is passive, she perpetuates the attitude that females are poor debaters," wrote a forensics specialist: "if she is aggressive, she is apt to be labeled as 'bitchy.'"[101] This expert may be right. I have several books on my shelf that discuss this particular response to vocally assertive women, all written by women. One is actually called *Bitching*.[102]

Were the female judges attempting to offset a bias, that is, attempting to counter a conscious or unconscious gender bias? Perhaps, but it's also possible that the male debaters actually did a better job than the females, and that the male judges were the ones that were attempting to control a sex bias. One specialist, unhappy with the reliability of scoring procedures, speculated that "other facts" were influencing the judges' decisions.[103]

What "other facts"? Nothing further was said about this. But from my perspective, these specialists approached the matter too technically, as though a few simple adjustments in the scoring or other procedures would enable women to do as well as men, increasing their enjoyment of participation. Perhaps debate procedures can be improved, and forensic societies can be made more welcoming, but there is something else to consider here.

It is the eight hundred pound gorilla in the room. Debaters are humans – women and men – who differ in their ways of dealing with competition. Little in the evolutionary history of women inclines them to engage in protracted verbal disputation in a large open space before an audience. Unusually egalitarian at heart, and free of any specific grievances, little would dispose women to sign up for an experience that involves openly adversarial behavior in a public arena – one in which their performance will be evaluated and scored. Indeed, as we will see, this is *exactly the opposite* of what is clearly a species-long preference of females to deal with rivals privately, indirectly, and cooperatively. Are women more hesitant than men to enter public space, and to perform in public? Do they shy away from the kinds of public contests that characterize dueling? Are women less likely to plunge into crowds, or take the stage?

There is a condition called "speech anxiety" (also "social anxiety"), a fear of speaking in public, especially before strangers. Fear of *speaking in public* is the primary symptom of social anxiety disorder; it arises primarily in adolescence. Females outnumber males in nearly every culture that has been evaluated. In a large investigation of residents of Canadian citizens, over 70 percent of the females admitted to speaking anxiety, fewer than 30 percent of males.[104]

Do women not like to joke, tease, denigrate, and insult?

If women do not want to debate, or to speak in public, perhaps there are some other duelly things that they do like. What about jokes?

To my knowledge, no one has suggested that women do not have a good sense of humor. The question is whether they like to tell canned jokes, or to create their own, and there is little evidence that they do. In 1900, there was so much doubt about women's humor that *The New York Times* asked readers to write in if they knew of a "real woman humorous writer."[105] Many did, but one respondent wrote, "I do think they are more apt to be witty and sarcastic than humorous. There are men to whom life seems all a joke, but I never knew a woman of that description." For the most part, women have seen little appeal in writing jokes or performing humor. Twentieth-century women constitute a minority in professional humor and comedy.[106]

In their personal lives, few women participate in jokey greeting rituals or maintain joking relationships, but as previously mentioned it is not unusual for some men, upon seeing an old friend, to give him a playful punch in the belly and say, "How are you, you old son of a bitch?" It is equally common for one man to comment on the growing paunch or baldness of another. How easy is it to imagine a woman who, upon seeing a lady friend on the street, feigns a playful punch in the midriff and says, "How are you, you old whore?" How often do women joke about a friend's bulging midriff, varicose veins, or sagging breasts *to her face*?

Anthropologist Mahadev Apte has written that women generally do not engage in ritual insults, practical jokes, and pranks, all of which reflect the competitive spirit and aggressive quality of men's humor. Nor do they participate in "frat house" or "Three Stooges" types of slapstick or in formal joking relationships with females.[107] Women are unlikely to "clown" around. All cultures that have professional clowns have male clowns, but none have women clowns only.[108]

When women do joke, their humor usually lacks the bite of men's humor. They rarely belittle or humiliate others in order to enhance their own status. In a study of "put down" humor, researchers played tapes of humorous routines in which males or females made fun of themselves or other people. It was found that males preferred jokes that denigrated others to self-effacing jokes. If males are dominant, the authors reasoned, the last thing they would be expected to enjoy is a man making fun of himself. Females, typically the more empathic of the sexes, were just the opposite. They preferred jokes that made fun of them, as the tellers, rather than someone else.[109]

$\sim$

More than five centuries of social history indicate that wherever women have raised their voices against rivals, they have consistently done so in anger, in a one-sided way. This is not to say that women are *unable* to do many of the things that verbal dueling involves. It does not say that they *cannot* debate, or debate as well as men. What it does say is that verbal disputation appears to be something that few women *seek* or expect to *enjoy.*

Men, by contrast, take great delight in verbal warfare, and many pride themselves on their way with words. There is lots of cultural and historical evidence that men love to *perform*, and to be compared to other men based on the quality of their performances, whether directly or indirectly. This disposition to perform is deeply rooted in male biology, surfacing when men assume the roles, imagined or real, of bards, heroes, Romeos, and clowns.

3   Bards, heroes, Romeos, and clowns

> All natural talk is a festival of ostentation ... It is from that reason
> that we venture to lay ourselves so open, that we dare to be so
> warmly eloquent, and that we swell in each other's eyes to such a
> vast proportion. For talkers, once launched, begin to overflow
> the limits of their ordinary selves, tower up to the height of
> their secret pretensions, and give themselves out for the heroes,
> brave, pious, musical and wise, that in their most shining
> moments they aspire to be ... And when the talk is over, each
> goes his way, still flushed with vanity and admiration, still trailing
> clouds of glory ...
>
> ROBERT LOUIS STEVENSON, "Talk and talkers"

In the preceding chapter we discovered that European kings
and noblemen waged ritualistic duels well over a thousand
years ago. We also saw that men around the world engaged in
verbal dueling throughout the twentieth century. In this range
of times and places, men of diverse backgrounds tried to dominate each other with ridicule and riposte, latterly tempered
with humor.

Some of the descriptions of verbal duels, as we have seen, were
specialized as song, drum, and poetic duels, and various combinations of these. These duels were ceremonial, and anthropologists
were drawn to them because such rituals figure into cultures
in important ways. But it would be naïve to think that when
ceremonial duels are over the male contestants abandon their
masculine ways, that they *quit being men*.

To be sure, *ritual* duels are episodic. Like other events that
occur in time, they have beginnings and endings. But the male
disposition to duel, once it comes on line in development, just
keeps going and going. It has no end, only moments of temporary satiation. Thus, the male reservoir of agonism is always filled

to some level, its contents leaching into a host of verbal interactions, regardless of whether they qualify, in the culture, as
dominance displays or not.

Educated men living in modern societies may think that they
never engage in anything like the ritual duels of the ancient Norse
and English – and never would – and they may believe that their
friends and co-workers do not participate in the kinds of song
and poetic duels held by traditional groups in far-away places.
But, as we have seen, modern men *do* engage in verbal duels, ones
that are powered by the same mechanisms that motivated the
contests of old, even if their own duels are fragmented, less
ritualistic, and performed less consciously.

The disposition of men to dominate and defeat other men, or
merely to distinguish themselves from them, is rarely far from the
surface. It emerges when they orate, tell stories, and court women.
It also bubbles up, less ceremoniously, in everyday conversation.
Thus, as distinctive as they are, verbal duels share important
properties with other types of speaking events in which men
spontaneously take it upon themselves to display or *perform*.

∼

After a flurry of thrusts and parries, spectators to the "man-
matching" contests in twelfth century Norway could tell which
of the two combatants was better at dishing it out and which was
better at taking it. That was what they wanted to know, and the
crowd-pleasing duelers did what they could to accommodate
them by broadcasting the relevant information.

Which of two men is the better *dueler* can only be gleaned from
direct, one-on-one contests. But who is the better *man*? What if a
performance involves no crossing of verbal swords, but is a
solitary display unto itself? What if listeners are exposed only to
the sound of one man speaking? What if two or more men
perform at different times and places, and are even unknown to
each other? Can spectators evaluate and "match" *these* performances, and rank-order *these* men?

My reason for asking will be obvious. There are many occasions in which men speak – not everything is a ritual duel – and since the human need for social comparison never stops, listeners have reasons to keep on keeping score. If personal information is needed, why not tune into whatever performances are going on at the moment? If the right people are present – the ones that need to be evaluated – why not go with whatever genre is likely to work best under the circumstances? The absence of an opponent should pose no problem. Witnesses have memories. They are perfectly able to compare an isolated bout of speaking by one man to an earlier or later performance by some other man, or to an internal standard. Were this not the case, storytellers and humorists could not develop a reputation for their own way with words, as they clearly do, nor could orators. If individual performances could not be compared, forensic societies would be unable to sponsor and judge individual speaking events, and there would be no toastmaster's clubs and storytelling festivals.

Of course, there's a catch here. A solo performance will accomplish little if it is not memorable – *favorably memorable.* To make it so, men do things that, if successful, will cause them to appear eloquent, riveting, seductive, or amusing, which they are in their roles as bards, heroes, Romeos, and clowns.

Slow-motion duels

Many men, like circus hawkers, love to *draw a crowd*; and to be up on their feet in front of it, laughing, boasting, swaggering, showing off, clowning around, and doing what they can to make themselves the center of attention. If it is important for men to compete with other men for status, and for access to mating opportunities, it is axiomatic that men must also be freely open to, if not eager for, a public presence.

In some ways, two individual performances that are separated in time are like a *slow-motion duel*. What would normally have occurred at a single point in time, that is, *synchronically*, takes place across time, or *diachronically*. But of course the time scale is not the only difference. Individual contributions lack the call–response format that lies at the heart of ritual duels, they provide little information about a speaker's stomach for verbal warfare, or his ability to deal in ridicule or insult, and they offer few clues as to a man's chances of succeeding in direct confrontation.

But audiences do not go away empty-handed. Solo performances provide personal information that would be hard to extract from duels. Planning and rehearsal are frequently possible, enabling speakers to develop and express their ideas more fully than is possible in a rapid alternation format. Without fear of interruption, speakers can pause for dramatic effect; and they can use the time to work out what they want to say next, editing out anything that might fall flat. In self-paced discourse, a quality of self-expression unachievable in fast-paced duels becomes possible. The more thoughtful selection of vocabulary that is possible in extended and unhurried monologues gives listeners clues to a speaker's familial and social background. From the use of metaphor, colloquial language, and novel turns of phrase, members of the audience learn about his learning capacity, and ability to think creatively.

We have seen some of the things that audiences learn from men's dyadic interactions. What new possibilities – what additional judgments – do their monadic performances allow? To turn the question around, what would be lost if solo performances were outlawed? How would the members of both sexes find out the things they needed to know about men? How would they select their allies, mates, and leaders?

One possibility would be to follow individuals surreptitiously, waiting for them to solve some number of moderately difficult – hence discriminative – real-life problems. This is impractical, and risky. Alternatively, one could interrogate people who know the individual. But if intimately familiar with him, they might well be personal – and loyal – friends, or former friends with axes to grind.

Fortunately, men understand the benefits of self-display, so they can usually be counted on to stage personal performances with some regularity. This is one reason why male conversation, as Robert Louis Stevenson said, is a "festival of ostentation." In their not-so-wild dreams, men hope to appear wise, adventurous, and masterful, even heroic. But such lofty impressions presuppose something more basic. To be evaluated as anything, they first need to be noticed, and that means they must receive more attention than other men.

Attention and eloquence

In other primate species, the most watched individual is typically the one that holds the highest rank. Jane Goodall once described the antics of a low-ranking chimpanzee that she called Mike. By loudly clanging together two kerosene cans that he found near Goodall's camp, Mike was able to spook several higher-ranking males, elevating his own rank in the process.

In our own species there is evidence of a strong causal relationship between verbal ability, the attention it commands, and the status or power created by these unusual levels of attention. "Th[e] ability of a person to use active and copious verbal performance to achieve recognition within his group," wrote ethnologist Roger Abrahams, "is observable throughout Afro-American communities in the New World. It has given rise to an observable social type which I have elsewhere called 'the man-of-words.'"[1] In each performance, he said, the man of words "must incessantly call attention to himself as an unexcelled speaker or singer."[2]

But of course he does more than this. Lots of people can attract attention, at least momentarily. They can be loud or bellicose or shrill. But if a sole performer is to succeed, his audience will have to *continue* paying attention, and form a lasting impression. To be a man of words, the speaker must use material that is sufficiently artful to be remembered until later times, when competitors seize their turn.[3]

There is one rhetorical property that creates lasting and favorable impressions. It is eloquence – the capacity, as we might define it here, to achieve riveting levels of attention with ornate language that is delivered in a personally forceful way. If a man seems eloquent, he must have some pretty powerful cognitive and neural machinery at his beck and call, and listeners need not worry about deception. Eloquence cannot be faked. If a man seems eloquent, he is.

"Rhetoric thumpers"

Some of the tribes described by anthropologists are led by "Big Men," who represent local interests in various matters, including disputes. In the Kuma tribe of New Guinea, these Big Men are also called "rhetoric thumpers" (see Figure 3.1). "The rhetoric thumper," according to Marie Reay:

> is a skilful orator, fluent in idiom and eloquent in delivery. He struts vigorously backwards and forwards about eight paces as he orates. He swings his hatchet as he walks, and often holds a carved spear upright in his other hand. He speaks in clearly measured periods: the shorter statements extended by repeating *a-a-a-a-a*, the longer ones spoken more rapidly, so that each corresponds in time to a set of paces in one direction. What is said as he goes is often balanced exactly by what is said as he comes back; the subject perhaps is varied in twin sentences of identical construction ('Our clan has decreased *a-a-a-a-a*; Our pigs have decreased *a-a-a-a-a*').

There are, Reay said in closing, "subtle uses of alliteration, rhyme and consonance, and . . . a kind of sprung rhythm after an initially regular metrical form."[4]

On one level, rhetoric thumpers are obviously unique. One would have to search far and wide for an account of other tribal leaders that speak in precisely the same way. But on another level, Reay's description is typical. For it is generally the case that tribal

Figure 3.1 A "big man," or rhetoric thumper, settling an inter-clan dispute (from Reay 1959)

orators are gifted in speech. They use an exceptionally broad range of words, and their phrases are "ornamented" by material from outside the more limited repertoires of their listeners. To wit:

In New Guinea, Bronislaw Malinowski noted that linguistic "power" was achieved through the use of "archaisms, mythical names and strange compounds, formed according to unusual linguistic rules."[5] Kenneth Read described the speech of village leaders as "florid and theatrical." Men who possess oratorical skills, he wrote, "stand out at every gathering."[6]

In Samoa, according to Lowell Holmes, leaders "demonstrate their skill at weaving verbal garlands of flowery words and phrases."[7]

Among the Maori people of New Zealand, wrote Anne Salmond, "oratory is the prime qualification for entry into the power game."[8]

According to Ferdinand Santos-Granero, the Amuesha people of Central Peru "describe a true leader as ... 'the one who is powerful due to his or her words.'"[9]

When speaking in public, the Suya Indians of Central Brazil employ a special rhythm and style of delivery, according to Anthony Seeger. "The phonetic and rhythmic features of speech are altered, generally by exaggerating rhythms and stressing unstressed syllables."[10]

These examples – and there are many more – reveal strong links between oratorical skill, attention, and leadership or power. One would expect to find the same association in modern societies, and there is evidence that individuals who speak in long sentences or hold the floor for long periods of time tend to be perceived by their conversational partners as more powerful than those who produce shorter utterances.[11] In fact, a speaker's talkativeness – quite apart from topics, vocabulary, rhythm, and colloquial expressions – may be sufficient for listeners to determine his status, since there is evidence that volubility, attention, and dominance are all related.[12]

Bards and storytellers

In a number of small societies around the world, there is a resident or "official" storyteller who is expected to represent the group not to outsiders, as a leader would do, but to itself, reminding members of who they are, where they come from, and what they believe.

It makes sense that there should be a formal arrangement of this kind. From an anthropological perspective, one of the more important functions of language is storytelling. Stories enable the transfer of information within and across generations. This contributes to culture – a group's traditions, technology, history, and morality – so it is important that the individuals responsible for this transference be ones who can attract, and hold the attention of, a large number of group members.[13]

A storyteller that has been studied somewhat intensively is the griot of Western Africa. Griots are wandering poets and musicians who perform in public, especially in tribal initiations, courtships, marriages, installations, and funerals. Griots sing traditional songs but also speak out on current events and politics, and instruct people in their history and traditions. Their speech is sprinkled with proverbs, sayings, and metaphors. Thomas Hale referred to griots as *bards*. They are "guardians and shapers of perspectives on the past," he wrote, "respected for the power of their speech and their ability with music and words."[14]

Most griots are men. There are no published epics that were narrated by women.[15] But it is not just the *official* storytellers that are men. Readings of Martin Gusinde's fieldwork in Tierra del Fuego with the Yamana Indians, originally published in German in 1937, suggest that storytelling formed an integral part of Yamana life. It was men, not women, who told stories during the long evenings around the campfire.[16]

There are two studies of storytelling that say something about the way men tell stories, both, coincidentally, based on fieldwork done in the Canadian Maritimes. The first study was carried out by James Faris nearly forty years ago. Faris concentrated on a tiny fishing village in Newfoundland called Cat Harbour. He noted that the stories told by men – most of the stories in Cat Harbour – were filled with adventure. Most were eye-witness accounts of the things that men had actually seen and done while out fishing.

The fishermen treated these personal experiences as a precious resource. When asked about their day at sea, the men frequently gave a vague answer. "It was really something," they would say, without necessarily defining what the "something" had actually been. Then, when the time was right, or the villagers asked, the men began to dribble out facts, and when attention flagged, more facts, and on it went until they had wrung themselves dry.[17]

The second study was done off the southwest coast of Nova Scotia, in an island store that could only be reached by rowing. Each night in the summer, somewhere between twenty-five and forty men gathered in the store to play cards and talk. Women went to the store, too, but usually shopped and left. Young people, if present, mainly listened. It was "the premier speech situation of the community," wrote the anthropologist Richard

Bauman, "an occasion in which the display, maintenance, and development of personal identity was of paramount importance, through the exploitation of a conversational resources in personal terms. The chief vehicles of this personal expression were yarns and arguments."[18] A yarn was a narrative about the teller's personal experience. Although accepted as true, it was understood that storytellers often embellished their yarns in order to attract or maintain the attention of their listeners. But the benefits of storytelling, personal as they were, did not end with the teller. The evenings at the store constituted "a forum in which wisdom could be shared," wrote Bauman. They enabled listeners to react safely, properly, and productively when similar situations were encountered in their own lives.[19]

Romeos

Clearly, men see words as valuable allies in their search for prestige, status, and dominance, and in their effort to distance themselves from other males. Men also put their faith in words when engaged in sexual display, and when they speak directly to women in courtship.

It is appropriate here to recognize that where mate selection is concerned, males are typically the displayers and females the choosers.[20] Women do need to be choosy, and in some cases, skeptical. Some of the men that drift through their lives are natural "dads," reliable, likely to be faithful if they commit, and helpful with any children that come along. Others are "cads," rebellious, potentially unfaithful, and neglectful of offspring.[21] Though cads are more exciting, tempting women to make a decision that may not be good for them, there are borderline cases that are difficult to spot, and men do not walk around wearing sandwich boards that announce their mate-worthiness. Even if they did, their claims could not be believed. But the stakes are high. If women cast their lot with a cad, there may be huge price to pay later on.

Thus, women are faced with an important decision, and it must be made under the pressure of time. If a woman takes too long to make up her mind, the male might move on. If she acts too soon, she could make the wrong choice. A solution of sorts is coyness – a pretense of shyness or modesty that is intended to keep the man interested but stops short of a flashing green light. It has been proposed that coyness was an evolutionary adaptation in socially monogamous species, a female strategy against philandering males, which gave them the time they needed to evaluate a male without discouraging him before the process had been completed.[22]

This sets the stage for a bit of pageantry. Sensing that women are waiting to appraise their mate-potential, men must cast about for some tests that they are likely to pass – tests demonstrating that they have the ability to bring home the bacon, and the resolve to remain helpfully in place if the domestic going gets rough. Aware that cads, like good duelers, can also be wonderful actors, women must pay close attention to every available clue and attempt the most discerning analysis possible. How do men talk when they're trying to impress or seduce a woman?

Rap

Since the topic here is male *performances*, we should certainly look at rap. I refer not to rap music, of course, but a way of speaking that some men have created and used specifically to court women. Rap is a traditional African-American verbal ritual that is issued humorously, is not to be interpreted literally, and has one and only one social function – to induce a woman to have sex.[23] The man's purpose, according to Virgil Anderson, is to "get over" women's resistance. "To get over," he wrote, "the young man must devise a 'game,' whose success is gauged by its acceptance by his peers and especially by women. Relying heavily on gaining the girl's confidence, the game consists of the boy's full presentation of self, including his dress, grooming, looks, dancing ability, and conversation, or 'rap.'"[24]

The most important thing is to get the attention of the intended "target." To do this, the rapper may change his pitch, volume, and rhythm, emphasize a syllable that is normally unstressed, and vocalize in a rasp, growl, falsetto, or whine. "The rapper uses active verb forms in his effort to "throw a rap" or "run it down," wrote E. B. Dandy. "His rap is filled with slang, colorful exaggerations, and incredible comparisons."[25]

Social anthropologist Ulf Hannerz, who studied Afro-American rap in Washington, DC, wrote that "A good line can attract the attention of a woman who passes by in the street and open the way to a new conquest, while at the same time it may impress other men with one's way with women."[26] An African-American teenager in Los Angeles told Edith Folb that rap was a good way to compete for sex. "Hey baby, you one fine lookin' woman," the teen supplied as an example. "Let's you and me get better acquainted." A teenage girl from the same neighborhood said, "I likes to hear a brother who knows how to talk. Don' hafta blow heavy, can sweet talk you too. Don' hafta make whole buncha sense, long as sounds pretty."[27]

Clearly, rap has special properties that make it stand out from other ways of speaking. There are other features of speech and voice that men manipulate, and that women like, and we will take a look at these things in the next chapter. But first we have two remaining male performances to consider, including humor and heroism.

Comics and clowns

In their performances, men try to get others to like or admire them. One strategy is humor. It has been estimated that 85 percent of the famous twentieth-century comedians have been men.[28] This male dominance extends across the globe from Australia and Belgium to France, Great Britain, Israel, Italy, and Yugoslavia.[29] But humor is not just amusing. No matter how mild one's jokes, wrote Alice Sheppard, the performance of a stand-up comic "is an act of aggression."[30]

Let's take a look at the kind of joking that occurs in everyday life. Have you noticed that when a man tells a joke, his male listeners begin to smile and nod well in advance of the punch line, sometimes at the *beginning* of the joke? They know their friend is performing, that he is "on," and wishes to make them laugh. The joke-teller says "Stop me if you've heard this one," but even if the listeners have indeed heard the joke, they are unlikely to stop their friend. That would be to miss what is going on. The joke-teller is not telling his friends *about* a joke, though when he gets to the end they will know it. Rather, he is *telling* the joke. This may or may not be done well, even if a transcript proves that all the relevant details were recited in exactly the right order. Telling a joke requires timing, pausing, and appropriate affect. Jokes are *performed*.

In joking relationships, there is an additional conspiracy. The listener will usually laugh or make some other sign of appreciation even if the joke is old or unamusing. Failure to do so could hurt the joke-teller's feelings. The listener may also laugh even if he does not "get" the joke – to not get a joke can be to fail a folk IQ test, which is, in some cases, what a joke is.

There are many reasons to suppose that women would not see the attraction of canned jokes. Even if they "got" the jokes, the *telling of jokes* has certain duel-like properties that may not interest women. Joke tellers and receivers are, for the moment, in a relationship that involves dominance. The teller has the upper hand – he alone has the floor, and knows what is coming. The receiver of the joke does not. One reason why men tell more jokes than women, wrote Jeffrey Mio and Arthur Graesser, is that in jokes the teller "is the one *controlling the flow* of the communication process, especially with an audience present."[31]

What about clowns? To "clown around" might seem a pointless waste of time, but clowns perform an invaluable function in some societies. In his book, *Wayward servants*, Colin Turnbull pointed out that small bands of African pygmies cannot afford hostility, which threatens social harmony, and ultimately the ability to cooperate in hunting and other important activities. Hostility threatens the food supply. It also threatens the group itself. If hostility is allowed to build, the band may dissolve into two smaller groups. Pygmies prevent this with clowns. Every band of pygmies has its own designated clown. "His function," Turnbull wrote, "is to act as a buff between disputants, deflecting the more serious disputes away from their original sources, absolving other individuals of blame by accepting it himself."[32] Their primary tools are ridicule and mime.

Every modern culture that has clowns has male clowns, but no culture has only female clowns. "In general, women individually do not clown for humorous effect," wrote Mahadev Apte, "especially in social situations that are public."[33]

Heroes

Folk wisdom, wrote Nicholas Emler, tells us that men "build ships, discover continents, fight wars."[34] In their own minds, even the most mousy and insignificant men are heroes, and these heroes are featured in the stories they tell.

In the first chapter, we saw that in same-sex groups, men's stories frequently focus on action and conflict. The typical storyteller presents himself as a masterful person, one who stands up for the things he believes in, is able to get away with things, and is not to be underestimated or taken for granted. He is a winner. Studies carried out independently in the USA by Barbara Johnstone and in the UK by Jennifer Coates indicate that contests form the core of men's stories. The most popular themes include fights with other men (including organized sports); Hemingway types of battles with charging rhinos and elusive marlin; struggles against nature; and cases where a man takes on "the system."[35]

Storytelling has been investigated in Greek men and women. Alexandra Georgakopoulou found that the men in her study told more stories, and longer stories, than the women. Moreover, over 90 percent of the characters in the men's stories were men (as they were even in nearly 80 percent of the women's stories). Typically,

the storyteller was the protagonist. He was involved in – and by
the end of the story had heroically resolved – contest and conflict.
It may come as no surprise that when a man and woman
witnessed the same event, it was the man, almost invariably, that
told the story, frequently doing so "as a result of *the woman's
insistence that he tell it*."[36]

Oral historians have learned about this male storytelling
dominance the hard way. "It is notoriously difficult even to tape-
record women remembering in the presence of their husbands,"
wrote James Fentress and Chris Wickham in their book *Social
memory*; "most men interrupt, devalue their wives' memories, take
over the interview, tell their own stories instead, or even, most
bizarrely, themselves recount their wives' life stories."[37]

Serial monologues

There is a tendency for men to continue telling stories even when
the speech event in which they are participating happens to be a
conversation. When several men are present, there may be *serial
monologues*, one long string of independent or semi-independent
stories.

Like quilts in which the sections are all made by different
people, working together, men's stories are a blend of individualism and collectivism. Bauman pointed out that collaboration is
not unknown in men's stories, but it occurs within episodes of
storytelling. For, the men stay on topic, and build on each others'
remarks as the storytelling progresses, working toward a conclusion that greatly exceeds individual contributions. Men's storytelling, Bauman concluded, involves a form of accretion. At any
given moment, a single speaker is telling his story, but if one
looks at longer stretches of time, there are multiple speakers
telling many stories.[38]

If a man falters while doing his monologue, his "act" as it were,
it is unlikely that another man will step in to help him. If he mis-
states something, his fellow storyteller-listeners are unlikely to

correct him. Doing so would not be appreciated. Each man knows what he wants to say – it may even be his own original experience, and no one else has any authority in the telling of it. But when there is an impromptu storytelling fest, the individual stories tend to summate – a series of calls and responses after all.

～

What happens if men treat a genteel conversation as an opportunity to perform? The social historian Alberto Manguel wrote that at one time he regularly attended the social gatherings of Roland Barthes, Severo Sarduy, and François Wahl around a table at the Café de Flore in Paris. These interactions were never communal, he wrote, for "nothing mingled and became one. Their talks had the feel of oral essays, of recitations and quotable repartee." But as brilliant as the talk was, and as memorable, it was not a true conversation. What it was, he said, borrowing a term from a scholar of gendered speech, was "intersecting monologues."[39]

While the men at the Café de Flore were having a congenial conversation over a drink, it is clear from Manguel's account that their talk had some of the properties of a spirited duel. Were they dueling *about* something, or was their talking merely carried out in a *dueling format*? It has long been known that if three or four men are introduced, they immediately begin to test each other, and to arrange themselves hierarchically. Perhaps the men in the café were doing that. But why, and why was verbal dueling their strategy?

4 Why do men duel?

Our cast of characters now includes a motley crew of flyters, rappers, orators, sounders, debaters, insulters, Romeos, jokers, comedians, and clowns. What is going on here? What special connection exists between men and all these sex- and dominance-oriented verbal performances?

In the previous chapters, there were hints that dueling is inspired by something embedded in the biological make-up of human males. But we cannot content ourselves with hints. No, if we are to understand why men duel, we must seriously look for factors that cause and shape this way of acting. If the disposition to duel is a biological trait, it should be possible to see that this is so – not by looking outside men, at the things going on around them, but by examining factors that operate within them.

Normally, to find out what a biological trait includes, one begins by looking for variations in its expression across a range of different environments or, in the case of human language, dissimilar societies. The trait will consist of those features that are relatively invariant. In the case of duels, the qualifier "relatively" is unusually important. This is because the available accounts are due to a number of different fieldworkers, some trained in anthropology, others in ethnography or linguistics. Even within these disciplines there are no uniform rules of description, and of course individual investigators are just that – individuals – with their own personal goals and perspectives. Thus, the features that are noticed, and the descriptive language that is used, vary from one account to the next, and would do so even if the trait were expressed in exactly the same way everywhere.

Under such circumstances, it is difficult to know how much uniformity *to expect* in accounts of behaviors that are biologically supported. Still, when we examined reports on diverse cultures around the world, we repeatedly found evidence that pairs of men do raise their voices against each other in rituals that function in highly specific ways. To be sure, these duels are sung in some places and spoken in others, with durations that vary from a few seconds of spontaneous jousting to several hours of ceremony. But all of these contests, whether held in tiny villages, rural encampments, or modern urban societies, have certain core features. For all involve verbal ritual, and all are held in a public space, typically before an audience, with the quality of the performance affecting the outcome and, therefore, the performers' reputation and status.

In the social sciences, descriptions of behaviors are usually based on their appearance to modern observers, but we have also looked back in time – over periods that are measured not in years or decades, but centuries. Thanks to historians and authors of epic literature, thirteenth-century duels vividly came to life. These writers were unaware that they were producing "data" that would be used at some future time to construct or embellish a theory of human language and interaction. Like Darwin's geologists, they were theoretically innocent. Yet their accounts have blended in with modern anthropological and linguistic research with remarkable ease, bolstering the conclusion that dueling is deeply entrenched in the male repertoire.

∼

How do we begin to answer our Why questions? Aristotle was both a philosopher and a biologist, so he was uniquely positioned to suggest formal ways to think about Nature. Famously, he suggested that one cannot truly understand natural phenomena without knowing their cause. There is one academic discipline that took up Aristotle's suggestions in a serious way. From its inception, the field of ethology has been pre-eminently concerned with the causes of behavior. In 1963, Niko Tinbergen defined ethology as the *biology of behavior*, and offered a theoretical framework to be used specifically for the study of causation. To understand what causes a behavior, he said, it is necessary to consider four things: how the capacity for the behavior evolved in the species, how it develops in the young, what the behavior actually does for the individuals who emit it, and the mechanisms in the brain or body that produce the behavior.[1] This accepted framework will help us when we ask why men duel. But they are not the only duelly ones.

Dueling in other species

Several of the epic scholars pointed to an interesting fact about dueling: it also occurs in other animals.[2] Which animals they had in mind is unclear, but there is no shortage of contentious species, including insects. It is important that we take note of the circumstances in which they duel, and the benefits they derive, for these alert us to ways that dueling may work in our own species.

Some years ago, a zoologist reported on the physical dueling of horned aphids in the leaves of bamboo trees in western India. The contests of these tiny insects are usually fought over access to a feeding site. By dueling, they stand to save a great deal of time, for a typical duel lasts about three minutes, but it takes over five hours to develop a new site.[3]

Fish duel too. In a rather ingenious experiment, biologists put two male fighting fish (cichlids) in chambers that were separated by a partition. For three days, these solitary "actors" were viewed, without their knowledge, by other male cichlids that were situated on the other side of a one-way window. Then, the partition was removed. Predictably, the actors instantly began a fight for dominance. What they experienced is unknown, but the audience must have found it exciting. Their testosterone levels shot up, and remained high for some time afterwards.[4] In other work by the same team, it was found that fish who witness a battle later swim out of their way to avoid the winner.[5]

Aphids and fish duel silently but a number of species do so vocally. In wild canaries, for example, males "oversing" their competitors by issuing similar calls in an overlapping fashion.

These bouts of oversinging are male-on-male contests for dominance. As with rituals generally, the outcome requires no interpretation. The victor knows to a certainty that he has won, and that this result will favorably affect his social status. But he is not alone in knowing these things, for there is always an audience in the wild.[6] Studies indicate that when one male is sufficiently competitive and adept to oversing another, male eavesdroppers, like the fighting fish spectators, will avoid him in the future.[7]

The duels of canaries are fought to establish dominance over other males, but they rival a Harlequin novel for their sexual implications. Experiments indicate that female canaries, unlike their male counterparts, *prefer* victorious males.[8] Following a duel, they approach the winner, and sexually display to him.[9] This makes good sense from a biological standpoint. By winning, the victor does females' evaluative work for them, showing that he has the ability to fight for the things that they would like him, and them, to have.[10] It is unsurprising, therefore, that in one species that has been studied, nightingales, the more aggressive males have greater reproductive success.[11] Predictably, losing can have the opposite effect. In chickadees, females are known to "divorce" mates after seeing them lose a song contest, then hook up with a different male.[12]

Later, we will discover, remarkably, that human dueling shares some of the properties and benefits of dueling displayed by birds and other animals. But of course we are not just interested in parallels between our species and others. We want to know where our own duelly behaviors came from. So it makes sense to ask: when adult male primates compete for sex and dominance, what do they do and why do they do it?

Evolution of dueling

Chimpanzees resembled our ancestors at a time, six million years ago, before our ancestors struck out in a different direction. Thus, chimps can tell us something about the duelly behaviors of pre-modern males, as they occurred nonverbally.

Early in their lives, male chimps come out swinging, and this produces no end of physical injuries – frequently fatal ones. In *Demonic males*, Richard Wrangham and Dale Peterson write at length about the injuries and homicides that are committed by orangutan, gorilla, and chimpanzee males. What is there about these "demons" that causes them to fight so often, and so much more often than females?

The story begins with disparities in reproduction. Female primates contribute a great many physical resources to their infants before birth, including fertilization, placentation, and gestation. In the case of chimpanzees, lactation and infant care continues for a good five years after birth. All this is extremely taxing, and from a reproductive standpoint, limiting. Since lactation suppresses ovulation, and the child-bearing years are limited, most females can only get pregnant five or six times in their life.

These reproductive burdens of females contrast starkly with those of males, who commit none of their bodily resources to infants prenatally – beyond the calories burned by sex – and may invest little or nothing in their offspring after they are born. As long as males are able to achieve sexual access to females, there is nothing to prevent them from fathering hundreds of infants in their lifetime.

From a biological standpoint, the generous reproductive role played by females makes them highly attractive to males, but there is something that boosts the competition even further. It's polygamy. In many primate species, the males are polygamous, mating with many different females. This changes the effective ratio of sexually motivated males to available females from something like one-to-one to three- or four- or even ten-to-one.

Victorious males get the sex they want, but when they win a series of individual contests they also develop a dominance that causes others to defer to them. Thereafter they can achieve preferential access to sexually receptive females without fighting each and every future battle from scratch.[13] In recent years, genetic analyses have begun to confirm what fieldworkers noticed many years earlier: high-ranking males sire more infants than other males.[14]

Traits that gave males a competitive advantage were usually selected and thereby found their way into the genes of succeeding generations. One such characteristic was size. Today, males who are unusually large tend to get what they want. In evolution, this benefit produced massive differences between the sexes. Today, the size discrepancy ranges downwards from gorillas, where males are well over 100 percent larger than females, to chimpanzees, where the male advantage is closer to 26 percent.[15]

Ritual aggression

Primate males are off the charts when it comes to homicide, but there would be even more fatal injuries were it not for ritualized forms of aggression. Since larger males tend to win their battles, it makes sense for males to show off their size if they are large, and to do what they can to make themselves *seem large* if they are not.

When animals attempt to *seem anything* they are engaged in a social display. Years ago, Martin Moynihan suggested that "hostile displays" evolved as a way of achieving certain advantages *without having to fight for them*.[16] He wrote that one of the more common hostile displays involves threats, which intimidate an opponent or force him to retreat or flee.

How do primates intimidate each other? What do they do to seem larger than they truly are? In 1962, biological anthropologist Frank Livingstone noted that it is not uncommon, in agonistic situations, for gorillas to rear up on their hind legs and thump their chests; and also to stand just before attacking another animal. Later, several biologists suggested that this use of standing as a threat display was so successful in establishing order, and preventing violence, that it reduced injuries to individuals and therefore improved reproductive success.[17]

If standing on hind legs can make males *look large*, roaring can make them *sound large*. For the fact is that adult males have lower-pitched voices than juveniles, and primate species that are physically large also have a characteristically lower pitch than small-stature species.[18] Within a species, large animals also have a greater space between the resonance bands (or formants) of their voice than do small animals.[19] There are bluffing opportunities here. Males can literally "call" off looming battles with rivals.

In many species, adult males roar for dominance. By itself, a loud roar can mean that an animal is vigorous, and may have the physical power to back up his vocal "assertion." Male orangutans of high rank and unusual stamina are known for their "loud calls," which can be heard up to a half mile away. These are also called "long calls" because they sometimes last as long as three minutes. The physical mechanism that is responsible for these long-and-loud calls is uniquely male. When male orangutans reach or pass the threshold of sexual maturity, at around 5 to 7 years of age, they develop cheek pouches, or flanges, which greatly broaden the face.[20] Testosterone encourages the growth of these flanges. Flanged males also have air sacs (or throat sacs). These sacs are thought to amplify vocalization and expand respiratory capacity.[21]

What do long calls do for males? One possibility is that they help with advertising and self-promotion, that is, bring their location and personal characteristics to the attention of females.[22] Where there is a tendency for unflanged males to approach females directly, flanged males frequently issue long calls and then "sit and wait" for females to come to them.[23] How well they actually work is unclear,[24] but male calls contain clues to rank, age, and physical condition, and this is the sort of information that females (and other males) need.[25]

In chimpanzees and the other apes, vocal duels do some of the work of physical fights. In an experiment carried out in the early 1980s, the same chimpanzees were observed in crowded and uncrowded conditions. Crowding usually increases aggression, but in the experiment it caused less than the expected increase in fights, presumably because the animals made more liberal use of vocal displays. Some lasted as long as ten minutes.[26]

At some point in human evolution, of course, the capacity to speak emerged, and when it did, new ways to advertise one's reproductive fitness became available. This, among other factors, may have contributed to the demise of throat sacs.[27] What was lost on the road to humanity, wrote one voice scientist, was "the joy of sacs."[28]

Neandertal murdered: man wanted

Perhaps the earliest known homicide occurred about fifty thousand years ago when a Neandertal man in his early forties, living in the Zagros Mountains of Northeastern Iraq, was stabbed in the chest. The killer was almost certainly a right-handed man. The knife entered the chest between the 8th and 9th ribs, penetrated the left pulmonary pleura, and possibly the lung. The victim died several weeks or months later, the knife still in his ribs.[29]

The handedness of the killer can be guessed from the location of the wound. I infer his sex from a blend of chimp and human murder statistics. It is exceedingly rare for women to kill anyone, and even rarer for them to kill a man. Women may refuse to speak, cook, or have sex, as Victoria Burbank's work indicates, and they may throw things.[30] But if a man is stabbed in the chest, the police should risk accusations of "gender profiling" and go looking for a man.

In an analysis of data from nearly twenty different countries and a dozen American states, and extending back to the thirteenth century, Margo Daly and Martin Wilson found that upwards of 95 percent of same-sex homicides involved men killing men. Interestingly, the figures for medieval England were on a par with Uganda and St. Louis eight centuries later.

In reality, the sex bias is even more lopsided than this. If cases of infanticide are removed from the data, and one looks only at *peer violence*, the incidence of male–male homicides is about 98 percent. "The difference between the sexes is immense, and it is universal," wrote Daly and Wilson. "There is no known human society in which the level of lethal violence among women even begins to approach that of men."[31]

In humans, as with the other primates, women contribute a disproportionate amount of time and energy to reproduction, and this adds to men's willingness to fight for mating opportunities.[32] Historically, a great deal of men's fighting can also be traced to the shortage of sexual opportunities. As with the other primates, some amount of this shortage can be traced to polygamy and some to a distinctly human practice – polygyny, in which men have more than one wife. In practice, these are not mutually exclusive. In Mesopotamia, around 1700 BC, it was not unusual for a man to have one "main" wife and a few secondary ones, and to have sex, additionally, with thousands of slaves, a pattern repeated on a similar scale in Egypt, India, Peru, China, Mesoamerica, and Rome.[33]

From a reproductive standpoint, polygyny pays huge dividends. In a survey of Xavante Indians in Brazil, carried out in the 1960s, 40 percent of the married men were polygynous. Approximately 70 percent of the surviving offspring came from these polygynous unions. The chief and the heads of clans were the most covetous. They had four or five wives and two or three times the number of offspring as other men. The chief had twenty-three children.[34]

Of course, we need not limit ourselves to places as historic as Mesopotamia or to tribes as exotic as the Xavante Indians. In Utah, polygyny became a central feature of the Mormon religion in the mid-nineteenth century. Brigham Young started the ball rolling with fifty-five wives, though he got a poor "yield," with just fifty-seven children. Polygyny is still practiced by fundamentalist church members in the southwest United States.[35] Before he was jailed for statutory rape in 2007, Warren Jeffs, a church official, is thought to have married more than eighty women.

All this marital and sexual gluttony contributes to male competition, of course. "If you have men marrying twenty, thirty, up to eighty or more women," observed a former member of the church, "then it comes down to biology and simple math that there will be a lot of other men who aren't going to get wives."[36] Before they draw that conclusion for themselves, of course, hopeful men will do all they can to become the kind of mate, or to acquire the resources, that they think women want. That means, among other things, seeking higher social ground.

Little wonder, then, that Daly and Wilson found that most American homicides are "the rare, fatal consequences of a ubiquitous competitive struggle among men for *status and respect*."[37] Many of these struggles, like the flytings of old, begin with a "trivial altercation" comprising an insult, accusation, or other verbal act that threaten status and "face." Some murders have followed the escalation of a showing-off contest between two or more men who tried to best each other before an audience of mutual acquaintances.[38] Remarkably, the prototypical murders in places like Detroit contain elements of both the chivalrous duels of previous centuries and the humorless accusations and threats of the *sennas* that, as we saw in Chapter 2, were so common in Scandinavia a thousand years ago.

∼

When ancestral men recognized the need for less injurious forms of competition, the most obvious solution was to perfect their ape-like bluffs. They could begin by experimenting with more playful or humorous ways of contending. That they did so may be one reason why males and females have become closer in size since our species broke off from the last ancestor shared with chimpanzees. Men are just 12 to 16 percent larger than women.[39] Some amount of this "shrinkage" may reflect a transition from physical to more social and psychological forms of domination.[40]

Reproductive benefits of verbal dueling

Thirty years ago, Peter Marsh, a British psychologist, spent some time in England's football stadiums observing angry young men – fans of the opposing teams – as they squared off with each other in the stands. From their verbal taunts and swagger, it looked like these hooligans were about to come to blows at any minute, but they rarely fought physically. Instead, they bluffed and postured, behaviors for which Marsh coined the term "aggro." Aggro, he said, is "a way of expressing aggression in a relatively non-injurious manner." "In its purest form," Marsh wrote, "aggro is the art of subduing one's rival simply by conning him into thinking that his cause is lost from the outset."

His cause. Conning *him*. It hardly needs to be stated, but aggro is "an all-male affair," wrote Marsh. Women, he pointed out, "are irrelevant – they form no part of the ceremony and, more importantly, they are not legitimate objects of attack. There is no conflict here except with other males."[41] In saying these things, of course, Marsh was obviously thinking of the disputants themselves. Women usually, have an interest in the outcome of male competitions, as we have seen.

Men who are dominant, or wish to appear so, do not curl up in a ball or cower. They, like the other primates, literally stand up for themselves. Even without doing so, postural openness can make observers think an individual is taller than he really is, and this can also add to the impression of dominance. Aware of this on some level, when young men talk to women they make unusually expansive gestures.[42]

Strutting and gesturing tell onlookers something about the motivation and emotionality of the agonists, but fully fledged verbal dueling tells them much more. Indeed, the flow of information is so rich, and so functional, that to duel *without an audience* would be to hold a political debate before an empty house. In cities, especially in crowded areas, there are always people on the street, so duels can break out spontaneously at almost any time. Passers-by stop and watch – and may even be drawn into it, cheering, jeering, and commenting like a Greek chorus – doing so for deeper reasons that even they do not suspect.

What the audience does know is that it's exciting when two men square off in public. But they also learn things that they need to know about the contestants and, in the comparison, about themselves. Dueling is a perfect medium for "man matching," for it is a public broadcast of an agonistic contest that showcases the verbal and behavioral skills of two young men. Onlookers find out which has more of the assertiveness, humor, and quick wittedness that verbal duels require, but they get answers to some deeper questions in the process.

∼

What *do* women want? It sounds like the lament of a romantically frustrated man. But women are not hesitant to say what they want. From "want ads" that they place in newspapers and magazines, it is clear that intelligence is at or near the top of the list, for women specifically identify this characteristic among their "wants."[43]

These wants can also be traced to romance novels. When women readers are asked what qualities they like in a hero, intelligence leads the list, followed by tenderness, a sense of humor, strength, and protectiveness.[44] They also say that heroes should never be cruel or weak. Novelists know these things, of course, and the heroes they create are never murderous, muddled, or puny.[45]

Want ads and romance novels are not usually seen as "data," but they coalesce with more formal types of research. When asked in psychological surveys what they want in a mate, women in nearly forty countries have indicated that they place a high value on intelligence.[46]

The voice by itself

In the bird world, as we have seen, males sing and females call the tune. Their perceptual preferences also influence male coloration and other physical characteristics and behaviors. So when men duel, do they go out of their way to display their intelligence, or to hide their ignorance? Do they attempt to demonstrate their strength and dominance?

It turns out that some of the properties of the male speaking voice are there not because men put them there, but because they possess anatomical features that are automatically displayed every time a man opens his mouth to speak. One of these things relates both to dominance and sex. It is vocal pitch. On average, men with low-pitched voices, and lower resonances, have more testosterone than other men, and males with high levels of testosterone are unusually virile – they have higher sperm counts and are more sexually active.[47]

Men with low voices also have more sexual partners than other men.[48] In one hunter-gatherer society, men with low-pitched voices fathered more children than men with higher voices.[49] Among opera singers, baritones report more affairs than tenors.[50] In study after study, women reveal a preference for men with low-pitched voices, whom they consider more dominant and attractive than other men.[51] Predictably, this preference is stronger when levels of their own sex hormone, estrogen, are higher than usual.[52]

Although it is impossible to guess the size of any particular man from the pitch of his voice, women who listen to audio recordings believe that men with low-pitched voices are taller and more barrel-chested than other men – and height is also something that women want in men. In romance novels, the hero is rarely if ever a little guy.[53]

The characteristic voice of men is largely influenced by physical factors that, as we have seen, are important to women and men, and are hard to discover any other way. But one rarely hears a man's voice without also hearing a sample of his speech. What is in the spontaneous speech of men that audiences to a duel or other verbal performance stand to learn?

A way with words

"Some people have a way with words," joked comedian Steve Martin, "others not have way." What about men who "not have way"? Are they less intelligent than others? Do they experience unusual difficulties when it comes to dating and mating?[54]

In various traditional societies around the world, there is an association between the ability to speak well and the speaker's presumed intellectual capacity. In the anthropologists' own words, we see that among the Igbo of southeastern Nigeria oratorical ability "is directly equated with intelligence and success"; that the

Barundi people of central Africa associate verbal ability with "successful cleverness"; that in Sierra Leone "it is noticeable how strongly the Limba connect intelligence and speaking."[55]

Historically, women have consistently sought men who could *take care of them*, that is, provide the things that they and their children require. In modern societies, this translates, indelicately, into the ability to make money (note: rhetoric thumpers have more pigs). Some level of intelligence is required here so we may assume that young women are drawn to intelligent men, with better than average opportunities to become successful, and research bears this out.

But it is not just about money. There are some surprising additional benefits associated with male intelligence. For one thing, intelligent men live significantly longer than less intelligent men.[56] For another, the intelligence of men predicts the quality of their semen. In a study of over five hundred US army veterans, intelligence was correlated with the number, concentration, and motility of their sperm.[57]

What might a man do to convince women that he is mentally (and seminally) dressed for success? One thing he could do is display an impressive knowledge of words. This would imply that he was used to being with worldly people – whatever precisely that might mean – and that his word-learning systems were working at a high level of efficiency. Possibly this lexically sophisticated man might be able to do other things that are enabled by the same neural and cognitive systems.

That people who know many words are likely to be more intelligent than people who know few words is almost definitional. For over a century, intelligence tests have included measures of verbal ability. In the early 1900s, French psychologist Alfred Binet made language a major part of the intelligence tests that he had been commissioned to develop. These tests instantly swept into the US and other countries, and they are still in use.[58]

For these reasons alone there is a relationship in modern societies between intelligence, as measured, and linguistic knowledge. But how do listeners know the extent of a man's vocabulary? When men duel, tell a story, or converse, they use only a tiny fraction of the words that they know. In a singles bar the problem is even worse. A phrase or two may be all that a man can say before the woman moves on. How can he effectively court if all his linguistic knowledge must be shoehorned into a single "chat-up line"?[59]

But all is not lost. People who know many words also know more *rare words*.[60] If a man who utters a rare word – something that could be done in a single phrase – he is likely to appear intelligent. If a man says that some event was "boring" he will do nothing to boost his perceived intelligence; if he says that it was "insipid" or "jejune," he will.

Recent research indicates that women do indeed want a man who has a way with words. In one study, young men were asked to define novel two-word constructions when tested by an attractive young woman, in a competitive situation with other men, and under control conditions. It was found that the men produced far more creative definitions when they were tested by an attractive young woman, or in the competitive situation with other men, than they produced in the control condition.[61] In the other study, it was found that young men used more low-frequency words in a written exercise following an imaginary assignation with a younger female, an effect not observed following encounters with older females. There was no effect in females who had an imaginary liaison with males.[62]

Warm, sensitive, and... amusing

Every woman wants a man who is warm, sensitive, and caring. Or so we have thought. But not the 37-year-old English woman who placed this ad:

> Attractive graduate, 37, wonders if there are any articulate, caring, funny men left. I haven't been able to find any.[63]

In an analysis of nearly four thousand personal ads in eight American newspapers, Robert Provine found that females requested humor more than twice as often as they offered it, and men offered humor about a third more often than they sought it.[64] A sense of humor is something that we recognize as an independent trait, but it is not unrelated to other items on women's wish lists. In fact it is also related to intelligence. Several years ago, two psychologists gave young adults a humor-generation task and found that the humorous stories and pictures created by individuals with higher IQs were rated as more humorous than the stories and pictures of individuals with lower IQs.[65] By itself, this suggests that women may prefer men with a good sense of humor. Do they?

Yes. Psychologist Eric Bressler and his associates asked a number of students to indicate their level of interest in dating individuals based on photographs and accompanying statements that had been pre-classified as humorous or not humorous. The principal finding was that women thought humor increased the desirability of a dating partner, but men did not. "Men say they value a partner with a good sense of humor," wrote Bressler and his colleagues, "yet do not rate funny women as more desirable."[66]

Other studies report similar findings.[67] When asked, both men and women *claim* that they value a sense of humor in a romantic partner, but on further probing an interesting detail comes out. What men *mean* is that they want a woman who will appreciate *their* sense of humor. They do not want to be amused by the woman. In a study of Israeli married couples, it was found that husbands' marital satisfaction was significantly related to wives' appreciation of their humor.[68]

Some kinds of male humor work better with other men than they do with women. Jokes that denigrate others are typically more amusing to men than to women, probably because men are less empathic. In a study of "put down" humor, men and women listened to recordings of humorous routines in which males or females were making fun of themselves and others. It was found that men preferred other-denigrating to self-denigrating jokes. Women displayed just the opposite pattern. The authors reasoned that if males have a high regard for dominance, the last thing in the world they could be expected to enjoy is the sound of a man making fun of himself.[69]

Dueling mechanisms: the endocrine system

As much as women appreciate creativity and other forms of intelligence, there may be cues within the male speaking voice that independently influence fitness evaluations. In one study, listeners were able to appraise intelligence purely from recordings of the men reading newspaper headlines.[70] In a second study, women who were asked to evaluate men, based only on recordings of their speech, displayed a preference for men who happened to be physically stronger, based on tests of upper-body strength.[71] Thus the two studies, taken together, suggest that there may be something about the *speech* of men with high reproductive fitness. Are there subtle cues, perhaps in the timing or force or precision of men's articulation, or in other aspects of their vocal behavior, that women find appealing? If so, these may be traceable to aspects of male anatomy and physiology and the neural systems that control the movements of speech.

Being larger than women, men also have larger respiratory systems and chests, and longer necks, and they also have more massive vocal folds. These anatomical differences enable men to sound large and powerful, possibly even menacing. They also have something that inclines them to use their voices in aggressive ways: testosterone.

Much has been written about testosterone in relation to competition and aggression in men and other sexually mature primates.[72] Predictably, dominance and status are also linked to testosterone.[73] But there has been less interest in what testosterone-laden men are like when they are not actively competing, dominating, or aggressing. Several studies by James Dabbs and his associates indicate that young adults with high testosterone levels tend to be more forward or business-like than others. They seem to display a "get-it-done" manner. When entering a room, they do so more boldly than subjects with lower levels of testosterone, who tend to look around tentatively or nervously before proceeding more deeply into the room.[74] Subjects with high testosterone levels, the Dabbs team said, appeared "engaging, sociable, friendly, even charming." The picture they present is one of "uncontrolled and unselfconscious friendliness."[75]

Testosterone is also related to two features that show up in proficient duelers: acting and extraversion. As we have seen, many boys and young men are natural performers – they love to show off before an audience – and male violence, as we saw, often occurs as a result of "escalated showing-off contests." When duelers act as if they are superior to their opponents, they are doing just that – acting. It is therefore interesting that professional actors have significantly higher levels of testosterone than members of several other professions. Significantly, they have about the same amounts as professional football players.[76]

∿

What about verbal duelers? Do they have sex more often than other men? Do they have more children? There are hints that they may. But there is one profession, largely controlled by men, who are consummate duelers. In fact, they get paid to duel, and some things have been learned about these gentlemen that bear on their reproductive fitness.

Trial lawyers

This brings us to trial lawyers. Trial lawyers are highly voluble, not just in the courtroom, but in their personal lives as well. In her dissertation research, Bettyruth Walter had no difficulty getting trial lawyers to talk about their work. In fact, she found that once she got them started, there was little she could do to get them to stop talking. In one of her late afternoon interviews, "a lawyer talked for two and a half hours with no sign of concluding, and since he had strayed far from the topic, the interviewer terminated the discourse, or tried to, by physically leaving the office. This lawyer," Walter wrote, "followed and continued speaking up to the door of the elevator."[77]

Trial lawyers, who also attracted the attention of James Dabbs and his colleagues, are "good at presenting concrete details in a straight-talking and compelling way that dramatically captures the attention of a jury in trial court."[78] Many are highly skilled performers. When one trial lawyer was told that he was so convincing in the courtroom that he should have been an actor, he retorted, "What do you mean 'should have been.'"

He was not alone. In an article in *Plaintiff Magazine*, a seasoned trial lawyer looked back over his career in the court-room. In the title he posed a question that he had wrestled with for some years, whether members of his profession were "actors or boxers"? For most of his career, the lawyer wrote, he had likened a courtroom trial to a fight, a one on one, head to head boxing match. But he eventually began to see that a trial lawyer "is also an actor who is on stage during the entire trial."[79]

I recently asked a trial lawyer about this flair for theatre. He told me about a case in which he was taking a deposition from a client in the presence of four other defense lawyers. "One of the lawyers objected to my line of questioning," the lawyer said. "I responded in a firm tone, that it was not his client, he was not taking the deposition and the rules did not allow for his objec-tion. He backed down. Remarkable, considering I made the whole thing up regarding the rules."[80]

In view of the argumentative and dramatic aspects of trial law, it is interesting that trial lawyers have *30 percent more testosterone than other kinds of lawyers* (see Figure 4.1 comparing testosterone levels in trial and non-trial lawyers).[81] One wonders if they would be verbally combative in the courtroom whether it helped their client or not.

Trial law, like forensic debate – which has long been considered an academic preparation for the law – is a field that has attracted far more men than women.[82] According to my calculations, 93 percent of the US's top-rated trial lawyers in 2010 were men.[83]

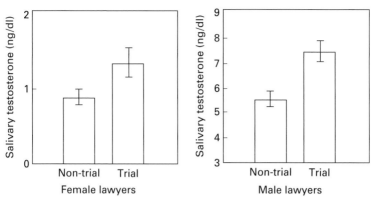

Figure 4.1 Testosterone of trial and non-trial lawyers (from Dabbs *et al.* 1998)

It is clear that few women have sought or succeeded in a career that requires them to lock verbal horns in a public arena.

～

"Born, not made." Occasionally that statement is made in relation to leaders, heroes, entrepreneurs, and violent criminals. One wonders what trial lawyers were like as little boys. Were they assertive? Did they like to argue, perform, and show off? How do duelers come by this way of dealing with others? Are duelers born or made?

Little duelers

The question we might like to ask is when sex differences emerge in the development of dueling, but of course there is little chance that either of the sexes could plunge into fully fledged verbal jousting without some period of preparation. This means that we have to look for components or immature forms, behaviors that have some if not all of the characteristics of dueling as it occurs in adults. So here we ask about the emergence of agonistic behaviors, some of which precede the acquisition of language and the ability to speak.

Physical aggression is, by definition, active, so it is interesting that males get off to an early start when it comes to physical activity. As fetuses, males already have more testosterone than females, and are also more physically active in the birth canal. They remain so after birth.[84] Within the first two years of postnatal life, males are already physically pushing others more than females do, and may continue to do so as they get older.[85] At 18 months, boys kick their siblings more often than girls do. At 2 and 3 years of age, males continue to out-kick females, and assume an advantage in two other acts of aggression, biting and hitting.[86]

How sensitive are these postnatal sex differences to cultural expectations? Do male infants see their father wrestling in the grass with the man next door, and surmise that this sort of behavior is expected of them? Do they, more than their sisters, see their father pushing and kicking their mother?

It is unlikely. In the mid-1950s, Beatrice Whiting and Carolyn Edwards did a study of children and juveniles in six different cultures, including Kenya, Okinawa, India, the Philippines, Mexico, and the US. The main finding was that in all these places males surpassed females in their tendency to engage in rough and tumble play, to physically aggress, and to respond to an act of aggression with an act of counter-aggression.[87] The rise of this male edge in physical aggression demonstrably continues until early adolescence, with no indication that the discrepancy between the sexes ever stops at some later time in adulthood.[88]

It takes nearly twenty years to build a fully fledged practitioner of human language. A great deal of linguistic content accumulates in infancy and childhood, but the ability to use language in a truly effective way must await developments that occur in juvenility and adolescence. Dueling is complex, so we should not expect it to break out overnight, but to develop gradually, over a number of years. That said, it is certainly the case, as I commented earlier, that even in the first year of life infants naturally express themselves emotionally in ways that are completely intelligible. They naturally use their voices to greet, affirm, object, and comment. Even before they have the words to duel, and the vocal control to respond quickly and alternately to the vocalizations of others, infants are surely able to act in an oppositional way!

In his fieldwork with the Chamula Indians, Gary Gossen heard attempts by 2- or 3-year-old boys to verbally duel with their older brothers.[89] In a rare report, verbal performances of 3- to 5-year-old African American boys were captured on audiotape and transcribed. In one case, a spontaneous rap, a boy expressed his feelings toward one of the female research assistants on whom he had developed a crush. In the other case, three boys engaged in "the dozens."[90] It began over a trivial matter. Very quickly, one of the boys made reference to the mother of one of the others.

> Your mother don't have no mother.
> Your mother don't have no mo-tor and your mother. . .
> Your daddy don't have no car.
> Your mother have a car but she don't have no keys.

"It is clear," wrote the author of the report, "that the children understand that a primary requirement of this speech event is to engage in some discussion concerning one or more members of another participant's family. . . They also know the importance of trying to 'play off' each other's lines."[91] These boys were indeed playing, but a decade later they would be expected by their culture to use their verbal abilities adaptively to attract females, to avoid violence, and to compete for status with other men.

Riddling and joking

Knowing about the male penchant for clowning around, it is not surprising that research generally indicates that boys initiate humor more often than girls do. In childhood, boys laugh, joke, and act silly far more often than girls, and there is more hostility to their humor.[92] In the transition to juvenility, boys treat jokes as an opportunity to out-perform others, and they attempt to dominate in joking relationships.

Around the world, boys show an interest in riddles in late childhood. By "riddle" I refer to knock-knock and moron jokes as well as riddles themselves. All of these have a competitive or agonistic flavor, and they conform to a call–response format. In other words, the riddler issues a call and the other person responds:

RIDDLE:
Call: What has eyes but cannot see?
Response: I don't know, what?
Call: Potatoes.

KNOCK-KNOCK JOKE:
Call: Knock-Knock
Response: Who's there?
Call: Delores.
Response: Delores who?
Solution: Delores my shepherd, I shall not want.

MORON JOKE:
Call: How do you make a moron laugh on Saturday?
Response: I don't know, how?
Solution: Tell him a joke on Wednesday.

In every case, the caller is the dominant one, by definition, since he knows something that the other person does not.[93] The subordinate individual, or "victim," responds by guessing, typically with unfavorable results, or by admitting ignorance or defeat. The poser of the riddles, and only the poser, is allowed to evaluate the acceptability of any answers.[94]

Riddles are a means of achieving dominance. Since riddles are memorized, boys need not be creative to get the upper hand on their peers. In other words, riddles enable the young to bluff their way to success in a new verbal league, long before they know the rules of language and social interaction.

Teasing, insulting, and bragging

There are two ways to improve one's relative standing. One can attempt to elevate it directly, and boasting is obviously a way of doing that. Alternatively, one can attempt to lower the status of others.[95] In the US, children get off to an early start in the status-changing business: 8- and 9-year-old boys do significantly more bragging and insulting than girls,[96] and in late childhood and juvenility, boys are far more likely to tease girls than vice versa.[97]

Insulting makes heavy use of colloquial material. A great many insults are "off the rack," that is, were heard at some earlier time and committed to memory. As with riddling and joking, this aspect of insulting means that children can jump into the game before their linguistic and cultural learning are complete. "In societies where verbal insults are a major means of aggressive behavior and social ridicule," wrote Mahadev Apte, "children learn the formal aspects of insults *without understanding why they are insults.*"[98] This adds to the ritualistic nature of verbal dueling in the young.

In Turkey, there is a traditional form of ritual insult exchange that takes place in rhyme. Here, too, success depends on the young person's skill in remembering and selecting appropriate retorts to provocative insults. In a typical duel, described by Alan Dundes and his colleagues:

> It is the first boy who is the aggressor. He begins with an initial boast or insult. The second boy must come up with an appropriate rhymed retort or an acceptable portion thereof. The first boy can only "win" if the second boy fails to respond with a rhyming retort. So long as the second boy succeeds, the first boy must go on proposing other retorts, each time posing a different word which the second boy must counter with a proper rhyming word. The first boy is, however, obliged to use only traditional retort sequences. He cannot make up new retorts.[99]

If one is the victim of such an insult, "he is expected to come back with the most appropriate traditional retort," wrote Dundes and his team. "It is thus to an individual's advantage to memorize as many of such traditional retorts as possible inasmuch as such memorization thereby arms him against any sudden attack."[100]

Only boys participate in these rhyming duels, doing so, typically, between the ages of 8 and 14 years.[101] Homosexuality is an obvious and frequent topic – boys attack each other's masculinity and courage, and the sexual practices of their relatives.[102] Given the topics and the age of the participants, the duels of Turkish juveniles and adolescents – one step away from the responsibilities of adulthood – seem to serve as "rites of passage."

It is no coincidence that when the Turkish duels are getting off the ground, there is a dramatic increase in male testosterone levels. This contributes to sex differences in all forms of verbal dueling, from riddling to teasing, insulting, bragging, and joking. Testosterone may also underlie the verbal distancing, disparaging, and disputation that most males will have mastered by the time they reach adulthood.

≈

In exploring the biology of dueling, I looked for evidence wherever it could be found. Some was available, some not, mainly because the necessary studies had not yet been done. But dueling seems to meet the standard tests of a biological trait fairly well. The attraction of men to dueling is not something that could be predicted based on our knowledge of how culture works. Indeed, if we attempt to approach dueling from a cultural standpoint, a question raised earlier will plague us unrelentingly: how, if unsupported by biology, did men become "duelly" in the first place?

Why women do not duel

Women do not show much of an inclination to duel, as we have seen. They rarely lock verbal horns with other women, and certainly do not do so for any inherent love of disputation. They rarely hurl insults at the people they know, and they do not go around looking for points of difference between them and their friends. As we will see in succeeding chapters, there are reasons, stemming from the evolutionary history of our species, why this would not serve them well.

There may also be something in women's physiology that causes them to contend less openly and vigorously than men. They have very little testosterone. In men, as we know, this hormone is related to status and aggression. Relationships do not prove causality, of course, but in cases where testosterone has been administered to normal young women, there have been corresponding increases in aggressive tendencies.[103]

Women are no less sensitive than men to the pressures of group living. Many of their problems are caused by social competition, too. When thwarted, however, women do not necessarily go to the responsible party and stage a mock battle for all to see. More naturally, they seek out the company of other women, and repair to a private space. There, outside the awareness of others, they exchange thoughts and feelings about people and personal problems. They pool information. They duet.

5   Duets

> Both she and her daughter then leaned towards Martha, smiling
> with warm friendship, and proceeded to tell her how happy they
> were that Douggie was married at last, how wonderful, how suitable,
> how ... As one woman arrived at the end of a breathless phrase,
> searching for the superlatives that could not express what she felt,
> the other took it up; it was a duet of self-immolation ...
>
> DORIS LESSING, *A proper marriage*

In *Le Caquet des Femmes* (The Chatter of Women, see Figure 5.1),
an ancient woodcut, one sees a working village that is somewhere,
and everywhere, in mid sixteenth-century France. Because a few
of the exterior walls were chiseled away, it is also possible to see
inside some of the buildings.

As one's eyes play over the scene, a number of different interactions spring to life. All are obviously vocal, most of the talk
occurring in the context of various tasks that have brought
the village women together. The well, bakery, and laundry are
beehives of activity, as they have been in countless villages around
Europe, South America, and other places. Some of the women at
the well are actually getting water or waiting their turn; the rest
are merely congregating at this most public of meeting places. In
the bathhouse, two groups of naked women converse in an
animated way, their speech punctuated by manual gestures. Elsewhere in the village, one sees intimate talk co-existing indiffer-
ently with a surprising number of ongoing verbal and physical
assaults.

There is one room in *Le Caquet* that carries unusual meaning for
us here. It's a bedroom in the building that stands behind the
central action. In the foreground, four conversations occur at once.
A midwife stands at the side of the bed, conversing with the mother

Figure 5.1 Scene from *Le Caquet des Femmes* (woodcut, c. 1560) (Bibliothèque Nationale, Cabinet des Estampes, Tf. 2, fol. 49)

of the baby in her care. Two pairs of women elsewhere in the bedroom speak privately, and at the foot of the bed is a semicircle of six other women, also conversing. In the background, one can make out an additional cluster of five or six women engaged in some activity, and they are evidently talking as well.

This scene may not be particularly vivid, being part of an ancient woodcut, but it is readily recognizable as a particular cultural ritual, elsewhere labeled *Le Caquet de l'Acouchée* (Chatter at the Lying-in). The activities therein took place in French (and English) homes at the time of natal events. Why was such a personal event so widely attended? What explains the presence of all the women visitors?

A part of the deeper biological answer relates to the extreme difficulty of human birth, as we will see later. Due to structural problems that are particularly acute in our species, a specialist is often needed to ease the passage of the fetus though the birth canal. This explains the midwife, who told the mother when to push and when to rest; whether to remain in bed, kneel on the floor, or sit on a special midwife's stool; and what to eat and drink before the delivery. But who were all the others, and what were they talking about?

God-sibs

In England and France, historically, an approaching birth was often the occasion for a collective female ritual. Usually six or more guests – friends, relatives, and neighbors – were invited to the home, the guest list having been drawn up in advance. Sometimes there were twice that many – attendance was an honor, and a mother could be embarrassed if a close friend or relative was left off the guest list. This social function explains the number of invitees – far more than were needed to accomplish natal tasks. But what, if anything, did all these women do?

When the guests arrived, the first thing they did was convert the bedroom into a "lying-in chamber" by sealing all windows, doors, and apertures, including keyholes, and by hanging curtains. Then they lit candles, creating an additional sense of ceremony, and mixed up some "caudle," a hot spiced and sweetened wine that the mother consumed during the labor period, and after the birth, to keep up her strength and spirits.[1] The midwife and invited guests witnessed the birth and baptism, and it was in this capacity – as witnesses – that they played the role of "God's siblings."

But when the baby was born and swaddled, the women did not leave. They stayed behind to do more of what they had been doing all along. They "god-sibbed." According to social historian David Cressy, this "gossiping," as it came to be known, "transformed a biological event into a communal affair, bonding women among women and incorporating family and neighbours, baby and kin."[2] One late seventeenth-century writer quipped that preventing gossip at a lying-in would be equivalent, in difficulty, to "damming up the arches of London Bridge."[3]

Cressy was correct about the transformation of a concretely biological event into something else. But the communal affair was also an expression of female biology. Just because interactions with friends and relatives constitute a form of "psychological support" does not situate this benefit in some extra-biological realm. As we will see, there is evidence in other primates, too, that social grooming – arguably the closest equivalent of intimate talk – raises the level of endogenous opiates and lowers heart rate in the receiver. Animals cannot achieve this calming effect by stroking their own fur.[4] The "communal" component of the lying-in offered real and measurable health benefits to the mother, the infant, and the relationship between the two.

Duetting: a first glimpse

Attendance at the lying-in also stood to benefit the God-sibs themselves. After all, they had come together in a private, candle-lit chamber in a spirit of warmth and celebration, and may have had a sip of caudle themselves. They had attended a lying-in expecting to bask in the glow of a new birth. They knew they would also be disclosing intimate thoughts and feelings about their lives and relationships, as well as the lives of others, for this is what sixteenth- and seventeenth-century English women did on such occasions.

The conversations of the God-sibs, as well as the animated talk of the bathers, and surely the whispers of the women in close embrace, are all examples of the class of verbal interactions that I have chosen to call "duets." Duets involve the mutual exchange of intimate human material – mainly thoughts and feelings – an exchange that occurs in a context of closeness and trust. Duets typically break out spontaneously, in private spaces, or in a relatively private way. As I use the term, "duet" refers to the mode of verbal exchange, which is frequently secretive or confessional, or to the material, which relates to the lives of the participants and, frequently, mutual acquaintances.

In a typical duet, the women feel something. Merely by watching two women duet, one may be able to identify the emotion that is experienced by both women, since the two are likely to have similar facial expressions, postures, and head movements. Duetting women often sit very close to each other – close enough to hear each other's whispers – and it is not unusual for duetters to hold or touch each other.

Who duets? The participants are at least two close women friends, but there may be more, and any other women that are present may join in – at least if they are bound together by emotions and shared experience.

Although linguists usually focus on language – it's in their job description – it would be a mistake to think of duets as the transmission of *messages* on an alternating basis, or any other basis. Duets are inherently interactive, almost as interactive as dancing. What they do involve, at their deepest level, is two beings working together to locate, hence to share and express, some sort of personal enjoyment or meaning.

When men duel, the presence of women is encouraging – almost obligatory. When women duet, the presence of men can be inhibiting.[5] In many cases, two women will duet *only* if there is no one else around – and certainly if no men are. It could be foolish or even dangerous to discuss certain things if uninvited listeners were able to tune in, and it might invite contempt or ridicule if men were present. This explains a certain type of "signal," one that British biologists John Krebs and Richard Dawkins called the "conspiratorial whisper."[6] Much of the material exchanged in whispers qualifies as privileged – for the listener's ears only.

Evidence for duets may be found in art, literature, and social history, and in modern studies of language. Jennifer Coates has written that in their stories, women frequently incorporate intimate details from their lives, and that women are "intent to meld or mesh their statements."[7] She referred to a great deal of women's talk "as a kind of jam session."

> Women friends arrive at each other's houses and, after a brief warm-up over a glass of wine or a cup of tea, start playing. Solo passages alternate with all-in-together ensemble passages. We improvise on each other's themes, share painful and funny experiences, laugh at ourselves and with each other. The construction of a collaborative floor symbolizes what friendship means to us: as we create utterances together, as we say parallel things on the same theme at the same time, we are demonstrating in a concrete way the value we place on sharing and on collaboration. Our individual voices merge and blend in a joint performance. Laughter occurs frequently not just because people say funny or shocking things, but because we take huge pleasure in the talk we create and in our skill at "melding in together."[8]

The goal of these jam sessions, she wrote, "is the maintenance of good social relations." The exchange of information "is not a priority."[9] If it were a priority, women's melding and meshing sessions would be less natural, less frequent, and less conspicuous.

There is no shortage of seventeenth- and eighteenth-century European paintings that depict women sitting in close proximity to each other, frequently (but not always) caught in each other's gaze, sharing a facial expression, and in many cases touching or grasping each other. In many paintings, the women are speaking in a secretive way. In other paintings, the women are highly animated, physically and emotionally. No man is immediately present in any of these scenes.

Duetting might seem to be "gendered," an arbitrary way of speaking that has no physical properties that link it to characteristics possessed, uniquely, by the sex of those who use it; nor does duetting exist purely because unknown events in ancient history set this way of talking in motion and now enable modern women to associate themselves with a cultural concept, that of "feminine." Duetting is neither of these things. It is, because of its physical properties, concretely related to characteristics of human females, and it receives little or no sustenance from its capacity to conjoin women and any cultural concepts. Duetting is "sexed."

Although I occasionally refer to men and women's ways of speaking as their "styles," duetting is not a variant of standard speech that can be classified as *stylistic*. Duetting was never "selected" from a list of more or less equally attractive alternatives, like short hems or narrow neckties, which "work" equally well as long as they satisfy a transient need for novelty, or a desire to appear socially aware. Rather, the disposition of modern women to duet exists because it lingers in heritable form, having solved problems that were faced by numerous waves of ancestral women, and thereby entered the genome in the way that naturally selected behaviors do. It is now as deeply entrenched in the biology of modern women as dueling is in modern men.

As an adaptive trait, duetting confers benefits on its practitioners. The most obvious and superficial class of benefits is psychological. People in close relationships are usually able to discuss personal problems, and to receive expressions of empathy along with suggested solutions. In bouts of mutual grooming, trusted friends remind each other that they are "not alone" and can readily get help in time of need. Individuals who mesh with others are more likely to experience a feeling of well being than individuals who would like to achieve connection but, for various reasons, cannot. I will say a great deal more about the less obvious and superficial – and possibly even more important – benefits of duetting in the next chapter.

≈

The God-sibs in *Le Caquet* were "jamming," like the women in Jennifer Coates' account, or "self-immolating," as the women in Doris Lessing's book. They would have been discussing, in a lively spirit, the things that evolution put on their plate, from marital and family relations to housekeeping and childcare.[10] They would have been describing the people in their lives, offering a free personal evaluation of any questionable or inappropriate behaviors, or pooling information about the activities of an absent friend or neighbor.

But was every bout of God-sibbing so domestically dutiful? Did the participants *never* talk about the other end of the reproductive continuum? Surely it would be surprising if women that were momentarily insulated from the outside world – close friends that were gathered together for such an intimate thing as child birth – *never talked about sex.*

According to Marina Warner, they did talk about sex – and none too subtly. The chatter in the lying-in chamber, she said, was often so sexually detailed that men, who were specifically excluded from the birthing rituals, were tempted to eavesdrop from behind the bed curtains. Warner has reported that these eavesdroppers later passed on to their pals "tales of erotic adventures, remedies for unwanted pregnancies, and various hot tips for lovers."[11]

Women's noise

Two hundred years after the chiseling of *Le Caquet*, an English artist made a copy. It bears the caption, *Tittle-Tattle; Or, the several Branches of Gossip. Tittle-Tattle?* One would have to search far and long for a less euphonious name, and the same goes for *chatter* and *chitchat.* Were the English attempting to ensure, phonetically, that women's speech would never become respectable? In fact, there is abundant evidence that gossip was heard on both sides of the English Channel as *unwanted sound.* When I was a graduate student, taking a course in psychoacoustics, that's how "noise" was defined.

If there was something worse than the sound of words, of course, it would be their semantic associations. Gossip has been considered a "vacuous, aimless activity," according to Nicholas Emler, one that "contributes little or nothing of value to human affairs." The noun, *gossip,* is frequently preceded by unsavory adjectives such as *idle* or *malicious.*[12]

But it gets even worse. Diego Gambetta looked for the etymology of the primary Italian word for gossip, *pettegolezzo.* He was surprised to find that this word "comes from *peto,* to fart. In some northern Italian dialects," he found, "a common expression, 'contar tutti i peti', 'to tell every fart', refers to the habit of reporting and speculating about trivial events."[13]

Words like *chatter* and *pettegolezzo* are not just relics of earlier times. They are still in use today. No better sounding and meaning words have come along to replace them. This can make it difficult to *think about*, and certainly to *study*, this kind of speech fairly and objectively. One might suppose that it is beneath the dignity of social scientists to seriously study gossip, or to develop very much respect for the people who do it.

I think of myself as a moderately dignified scientist and I have a suggestion. Let us look at what ancient women were attempting to accomplish by speaking, and examine what modern women actually do. Let us see if we can discover why they whisper, and why men wish they wouldn't.

Whispering

As we have seen, men detested the "loud calls" of the human female, the shrill and unwelcome sound of women on the attack. But, paradoxically, *whispering bothered them more*.

How does one stop a behavior that is inaudible to everyone except the principals? The only solution seemed to be public education, something that men also controlled. Gossip was disdained in a diverse collection of ditties, lectures, poems, and books, including William Gearing's *Bridle for the tongue*, published in 1663, and Henry Hooton's book by the same title, published in 1709.[14] A verse at the base of the *Tittle-Tattle* woodcut localizes gossip to the places that we have seen – the lying-in, bakery, well, and bath-house (or spa) along with the river's edge, market, alehouse, and church – and ends with a plea:

> Then Gossips all a Warning take,
> Pray cease your Tongue to rattle;
> Go knit, and Sew, and Brew, and Bake;
> And leave off TITTLE TATTLE.

It's hard to see how men could have expressed more convincingly their fear of what whispering women might say. What was it about hissing sounds that tripped off such negative reactions? Which male nerves were hit by the feared wave of sibilance? For one thing, men were afraid that this subdued waveform would be an unusually powerful way to transmit intimate information *about them*, including their sexual peccadilloes. In *Anatomy of a Woman's Tongue*, published in 1638, Robert Harper wrote:

> A Man that had a nimble-tongue Wife,
> With whom he liv'd a discontented Life;
> For she would tell all that her Husband did,
> And from her Gossips nothing should be hid.
> If he sometimes did come Home drunk to Bed,
> About the Town it should be published.
> If he a Woman do salute or kiss,
> Why all the Town forsooth must know of this.[15]

Men who were physically or psychologically abusive had other problems. A review by Bernard Capp indicates that fifteenth-century women complained about a variety of spousal misbehaviors, from violence and infidelity to meanness and intoxication. "Even worse from a bad husband's point of view," Capp wrote, "was their readiness to shame him, shelter his wife, or pressure the parish officers to intervene."[16]

Even perfectly innocent men had things to fear. They knew, as men always have, that a few facts about their private life were likely to enjoy some level of circulation, and that there was no way to find out how far these facts had actually progressed.[17] Moreover, they knew that women "enjoyed bawdy talk among themselves," wrote Capp, "sometimes even in mixed company."[18] The danger was that embarrassing details about their sexual anatomy and performance would be disclosed. In *The Fifteen Plagues of a Maiden-Head*, published in 1707, a spinster complains that while she must toil, those that are married are invited:

> To labours, christenings, where the jollitry
> Of women lies in telling, as some say,
> When 'twas they did at hoity-toity play,
> Whose husband's yard is longest, whilst another
> Can't in the least her great misfortune smother,
> So tells, her husband's bauble is so short,
> That when he hunts, he never shows her sport.[19]

In some cases, lacking "male supervision and distracted from godly prayer, gossipings could be construed as potential sources of disorder," wrote David Cressy. When women met in private, they "were temporarily unsupervised and ungoverned," according to Capp. "Men predictably wondered what they discussed, imagining older women teaching the tricks of deceit and subversion, and wives complaining or, still worse, deriding their husbands' behaviour and sexual performance."[20]

There was no law against whispering, of course, and no way to catch anyone discussing the intimate lives of others in such a subdued register. If anti-gossip campaigns failed to do the job, how could the reputations of *respected men* be protected? In desperation, governments did exactly what governments have always done when gossip was feared. They shut down the venue.

That's what King Charles II did. Fearing insurrection, he ordered the closing of English coffee houses in 1675, saying that "false, malicious and scandalous reports" were being devised there "and spread abroad."[21] In Sweden, the king was less direct. In a period of political unrest, he suddenly "discovered" that coffee was unhealthy. What choice did he have but to close the places where this harmful beverage was served?[22]

Moved by the threat of anti-male gossip, according to David Cressy, some town governments in sixteenth-century England did something similar. They attempted to regulate birthing celebrations.[23] In 1568, councilors in Leicester voted to control "the superfluous charge and excess" of natal events. In Kirkby Kendal, a village in northwest England, legislation was passed to limit (*to twelve!*) the number of women permitted at lying-in ceremonies. Church officials also sought to control these gatherings.[24]

If sixteenth- and seventeenth-century Englishmen were afraid that women might say things that would curtail their personal freedoms or threaten their standing in the community, there is no evidence that women had any similar fears of men's speech, or that they made any attempts to get them to change men's communicative habits. Is this because women had less to lose, or less influence in English communities; or did English men not gossip? Did men not huddle together with trusted others and discuss personal things?

Do men never duet?

In the second chapter, I referred to the "intersecting monologues" of three men friends with whom the writer Alberto Manguel used to gather in a Parisian café. Nothing that was said, he wrote, ever "mingled and became one."

Those men may have been typical, but Manguel also spent evenings talking with three other men, and they behaved rather differently from the first. "For hours on end," he wrote, "the three would discuss an infinite number of subjects with intelligence, lightly carried erudition and wit. Listening to the three friends talking was like listening to a *chamber orchestra playing an improvised concerto.* One voice would suggest a theme, the others would pick it up and play on it, then abandon it in order to simultaneously attack several others, the whole peppered with quotations, anecdotes, tidbits of esoteric information and jokes."

In some ways, this sounds like one of Jennifer Coates' jam session-duets, with several notable exceptions. There was evidently no discussion of personal feelings, no talk of relationships, and no self-disclosure. One of the men made a list of the subjects that he and his friends had discussed. It included "the autobiographical books of George Moore, Victor Hugo, Housman's poems, Toulet's contrerimes, and the formulation of ethical principles."[25]

Well, of course, intellectuals like ideas. Why would they be discussing their doubts or fears, or the foibles of friends, when thought was on the table? But these men were just that – men. Listen to this man:

> I wish my life and decisions to depend on myself, not on external forces of whatever kind. I wish to be the instrument of my own, not of other men's acts of will. I wish to be a subject, not an

object; to be moved by reasons, by conscious purposes, which
are my own, not by causes which affect me, as it were, from
outside. I wish to be somebody, not nobody; a doer – deciding,
not being decided for, self-directed and not acted upon by
external nature or by other men as if I were a thing, or an animal,
a slave incapable of playing a human role, that is, of conceiving
goals and policies of my own and realizing them.[26]

Those are the words of Isaiah Berlin, a distinguished philosopher. He could not have been more intellectual, or more
autonomous.

There are reasons why all men, not just intellectuals, are less
inclined than women to disclose privileged information about
their feelings. Autonomy is placed at risk if friends know things
that could be passed on to others, perhaps to strangers who owe
them no loyalty. For this reason alone, men are cautious about
self-disclosure, and therefore about full participation in emotionally intimate relationships with other men.

The desire to be – and to be seen as – free of external control is
not just a property of *some men*. Recently it was reported that
when testosterone is administered to naturally trusting women,
they become less trusting. The authors suggested that this
occurred because testosterone increases competition, and it
would be adaptive for competitors to feel wary around rivals.[27]
We might extrapolate from this that men's naturally higher levels
of testosterone keep them in competitive mode, therefore perpetually on guard against vulnerability. How, under such circumstances, could they give other men – their natural rivals – the
information needed to weaken or control them, or to bring
them down?

As heroes, men may also be less interested than women in co-
authorship, less inclined to credit others with thoughts that they
would rather represent as their own. The story that men would
like to tell, for better or for worse, is their story, their personal
statement; their possibly unique contribution. There are indications of this in a range of literary genres, from autobiographies to
tales of adventure.

If men disdain self-disclosure, do they also avoid telling what they know about others? Studies carried out on people of different educational levels, from different cultures, and across eight decades in the twentieth century all indicate that men gossip *less* than women.[28] But they do gossip. When men discuss their mutual acquaintances, how is this different from what women do?

In a study of the gossip of Kung hunter-gatherers in Botswana, anthropologist Polly Wiessner found that the men in one village were primarily concerned with misdeeds that involved politics and land, followed by trouble-making and anti-social behavior. They were far less disapproving of behaviors that bothered the women: jealousy over possessions, failure to share, inappropriate sexual behavior, and failure to meet kinship obligations.[29]

American men also treat gossip as a means of punishing the objectionable behavior of other men, especially if it occurs in business or some sort of joint venture. Twenty years ago, Robert Ellickson, a law professor, reported that cattle ranchers in Northern California used gossip in an attempt to prevent various kinds of misbehavior, including failure to pay debts. "The lash of negative gossip," Ellickson wrote, "helps prompt its target to square accounts because a person's opportunities typically depend to a significant degree on reputation."[30] In a study of gossip by a collegiate rowing team, Kevin Kniffin and David Wilson found that young men used gossip to deride the behavior of a "slacker" who lacked the motivation to practice.[31]

These studies make it clear that men use speech to identify the misdeeds of other men, and to discuss what to do about them. In their gossip, they enforce group norms and punish offenders. True, they also harmonize with men friends on some level, but there are few indications that they set aside time to meet in private to discuss their innermost thoughts and feelings, and most men would never dream of phoning a friend in order to do those things.[32] Even when men grow to like each other, it may be difficult for them to "admit" this.

For some, according to sociologist Robert Bell, an expression of affection takes the form, "you're not such a prick after all."[33]

~

Women talk about the things they care about, and the things they care most about are the people in their lives. In casual dialogue, wrote Susan Harding, "women's speech is wrapped around people and their personal lives. The first thing a woman wants to know when she meets someone is about her family. In her daily life in the home and village, a woman is likewise more interested in how someone feels than in what someone thinks, in who a person is and what a person does in the private, rather than the public, sphere."[34]

In doing these things that bear the name "gossip," women are discussing business just as surely as men are when they talk about their work. People and relationships are the business of women. But topics and words do not make a duet any more than lyrics make a song. Some form of human music is essential, some harmonious uses of the voice. If we wish to understand verbal duets, we must pay special attention to the feelings that animate their interactions, and draw women closer together. We must come to see women's conversations as a form of complicity.

6 Complicity

> Women are ... bound together by their immanent complicity.
> And what they look for first of all among themselves is the
> affirmation of the universe they have in common ... They
> compare experiences: pregnancies, birth, their own and their
> children's illnesses, and household cares become the essential
> events of the human story.
>
> SIMONE DE BEAUVOIR, *The second sex*

Duetting is a way of relating while talking. When words are
used, there is a tendency for linguists to get involved, but
duetting is less about language than it is about action – human
inter-action that is expressed in movement of the body, face, and
voice. Timing is important. Eye movements matter. Duetting
reflects women's reactions to external events, but it responds to
internal forces – emotions and memories and ongoing life
events. Though much of this operates beneath the surface, it
is, paradoxically, only the immediate experience of something
that lies deeper still. For duetting expresses evolved dispositions
for one woman to coordinate, perhaps even to coalesce, with
another.

≈

In a tiny Inuit village in Northern Quebec, a woman arrives at the
house of a friend on a cold night in January. After removing her
parka, she and her host go into the kitchen, where other women
are gathered around a stove in cheerful conversation.

The visitor is expected. It was agreed earlier that she would stop
by for a *katajjaq*, a "throat game" that they often play on such
nights. When the two women take their place, the others draw their
chairs in a semi-circle, anticipating a lively performance.

The two contestants are old friends. As they approach each other, they smile and reach out, grasping each other by the arms. One woman starts the game, drawing a breath in anticipation of the sounds she will make. Her partner waits, as she must. The challenge, for her, will be to mimic perfectly the sounds and cadence of her friend without a split-second of hesitation. This will not be easy, for her friend will compose the sounds as she goes. When a string of sounds has been repeated, it is back to the first woman, who must be ready with a new and different set of sounds, and she, too, must begin without hesitation.

Sometimes, remarkably, the women sing in a whisper, under-scoring the difference between throat games and the necessarily public "man-matching" contests of twelfth-century Norwegian men. To be sure, there is a contest here – word of the winner's skill makes its way through the village – but what is being performed is something that is inherently intimate, an intimate use of the female voice.

How long the women will be able to play the first round before they stumble, or let even the smallest moment of silence pass between them, will literally be told by time. This may happen after a few seconds, or the women may go on for several minutes. But, inevitably, one will run out of air or material, or the other will make a mistake or fall out of synchrony. When this happens everyone in the kitchen will laugh, the contestants as well as their appreciative audience, and the first round will be over.

One would have to search high and low to find a purer form of *structural duetting*. One of the enthnomusicologists who studied throat games, Nichole Beaudry, commented that even after one discovers how the games are played, it is hard to tell which sounds are produced by which player. Although each woman is seeking to win, "the pair of women must give the feeling of a *perfect cohesion*," wrote Jean-Jacques Nattiez; "people from the audience should not be able to discover who is doing what."[1]

Throat games have been repeatedly documented among Inuit and other indigenes in the eastern Arctic region of Canada, including Northern Quebec.[2] By one estimate, these games have been around for at least four to five thousand years.[3] Among the Inuits, occasions for throat games include the celebration of a successful hunt or the arrival of visitors from another camp or village. Women also turn to throat games when entertaining themselves or their children.

These games are rituals. One ethnographer described them as "a friendly type of duel or competition," and yet the goal is to sing a perfect duet.[4] In that sense, throat games may be regarded as *duet duels*, since the two women compete to see who is *better at cooperating*.[5] As if to emphasize this possibility, there is a word in the Inuktitut language, *illuq*, that means *both partner and opponent*.[6]

All throat games, whether ceremonial or recreational, are played only by women. Young boys may play, but men do not – when boys are old enough to go hunting with their fathers, they quit.

～

In another remote place, a Russian island off the northwest coast of Japan, two Ainu women sit facing each other (see Figure 6.1). They are ready to play *rekukkara*, a different kind of throat game. The women's faces nearly touch. One woman cups her hands around the lips of the other, forming a tunnel to her own mouth. When the first singer begins her tune, the second singer achieves a "percussive accompaniment" in her throat. She does so, remarkably, on the air exhaled by the first.[7]

It is hard to imagine what these women, or any others, could do to make a joint exercise more intimate; hard to see what they could do to create a greater degree of fusion of their individual voices and identities into one.

When the women begin to sing, the sounds of exhalation and inhalation are alternated in a panting style. The impression to the listener is a complete fusion of lower ("throat") sounds and higher sounds. If one of the two women decides to alter her sound-making pattern, the other woman has to follow the

Figure 6.1 Throat singing by Ainu women (from Malm 1963, p. 242)

change, and the new pattern is repeated until the women decide to try something else. The goal is to perform as long as possible without making a mistake. If one of the women runs out of breath or gets out of synchrony with her partner, she loses. These performances rarely last more than thirty seconds.

Inuit and Ainu women have engaged in such vocal engagements for centuries, but what does that signify here? To me, the message is clear. There is something within women that senses or places a value on vocal coordination. If in some cultures women take delight in achieving a feeling of vocal unity – even when they are *not talking* – and this feeling of "one-ness" is achieved in a physically intimate way, it is possible that all women possess the enabling mechanisms. Is there any reason to think that vocal coordination should stop where these singing games end? Why not use the voice to share everyday emotional experience? Why not help each other talk?

Complicit conversations

Thirty years ago, Jane Falk wrote about these kinds of harmonious experiences in her doctoral dissertation at Princeton. To appreciate the significance of her contribution, it helps to pause for a moment and review the way people have traditionally thought about human conversation. According to the standard view, every conversation has a speaker and at least one listener, and these individuals have distinct roles. The speaker donates information and the listener takes it in. During her turn, the speaker pauses occasionally and looks at the listener to make sure she is being understood, and the listener occasionally signals her reception or approval with a nod, murmur, or some other gesture. Everything is very orderly.

So there was bound to be some surprise when Falk, in her dissertation and a short note published the following year, pointed out that "the speaker" can be *two people*. These speakers negotiate and execute their topics *jointly*. All that is required for this, she wrote, is mutual knowledge, shared authority, and a feeling of camaraderie. Mutual knowledge equips the speakers to collaborate, shared authority allows them to do so, and camaraderie motivates the participants to play at the same game.[8]

The "same game" is an appropriate metaphor. When old friends meet, their talk resembles a team sport. No single player does all the work or gets all the credit. At times it is unclear who has the ball. The game may be guided by shared understandings as to how team sports are supposed to work, but if a "cultural" rule seems to be in effect, this does not mean that the rule – if it is a rule – was woven out of whole cloth, with no threads from human biology.

The deeper dynamics of duets begin to surface when we ask a simple and obvious question: who engages in them? Remarkably, Falk said nothing about this, or about the possibility of a sex bias, nor did she comment about the relationship of the individuals who speak duets. But she did supply a telling piece of information.

Duetting, she suggested, should be unattractive to speakers who are "sensitive to the sensation or appearance of intimacy."[9]

∾

Jennifer Coates, the linguist who likened women's talk to "jam sessions," has catalogued a number of women's structural duets.[10] One type involves repetition of single words, as in Duet 1, below, which involves a pair of speakers.

Duet 1

J: because they've only got to win two seats
R: two ... yes, I know

Note here that just as R is saying "two," she hears J say that they only had to win two "seats," so she does not need to add that word, as she would if she were the sole speaker.

Duet 2

Duet 2 was created by five women. As we tune in to the conversation, Speaker C is saying "I mean, in order to accept that idea you're...

C: having to   completely change your view of your husband
E: mhm/   completely review your view of your husband /
B: yes/
A: yes   yes, that's right
D: yeah   mhm

E: and to have him become a person who can do the undoable
D: mhm   yes

C: and how easy is it to do that?
E: that's right   mhm

This is a group effort if ever there was one – a *quintet*. The thought set in motion by C is instantly embraced and supplemented by E with rapid agreement from B (yes), then A (yes, yes that's right), and D (mhm, yes), and E again (that's right) and a return to C, with a final contribution from E (mhm), all in a matter of seconds.[11]

Duet 3

A: I was sitting in my living room and without meaning to I was looking out into the garden and I was looking straight into Levers house, and I saw him get undressed in his living room. There's no reason why you shouldn't get undressed in your living room if you want.

B: Yeah!

A: And I thought, "My God...

B: Yeah!

A: if I can see him..."

B: He can see you!

A: and I don't always just get undressed in the living room. You know I mean OK I'm sure he's not...

B: peeping

A: peeping or anything

B: but he

A: but it just

B: you accidentally saw him

A: that's right

B: Oh I don't blame you. I think it needs screening trees round it.[12]

When women friends harmonize with each other they share the floor, overlapping in time, but transcripts indicate that they overlap at the level of linguistic content, too. When the second speaker chimes in, she is likely to use many of the same words as the first speaker – In Duets 2 and 3 "view" and "peeping" are repeated – and may employ a similar prosody, or intonation pattern. Were that not the case, it is unclear that duetting would appear harmonious.

Obviously, transcripts cannot do justice to duets. A page filled with written symbols tells us nothing about the fleeting movements of faces, voices, hands, and bodies, nor does it give us any information about the temporal relationship between these "nonverbal" activities and the words that are said. We are left with a partial but distorted picture of duets, our attention diverted from the emotional flow that forms their central core.

Talkers traffic in the behaviors for which we have no symbols. They nod, smile, murmur, and move together. They take on the

face and body language of their fellow talkers. They dance.
Women are clearly more active in these ways than men, since
they are generally more empathic and emotive.[13] If you doubt
this, do a little (more) eavesdropping and cast a furtive glance at
two women friends who are talking over a glass of wine. What
you will see is matching facial expressions. When one woman
discusses something that frightened or pleased or worried her,
similar emotions usually appear on the face of her friend.

Interruption?

In the third duet above, Speakers A and B – let us call them Adele
and Beth – appear to continually interrupt each other. At the outset,
Adele is recalling an event from her own experience. Suddenly Beth,
though she has no independent knowledge of the event, suddenly
chimes in, without waiting for Adele to stop speaking.

There is a simple question right here. What did Beth do? If we
ask conventionally trained conversation experts, many will
answer that she *interrupted* her friend Adele. Some may point
out that the women *clashed*. On the surface, this may seem
obvious and uncontroversial. Normally, it is understood that
listeners wait, or should wait, for a speaker to yield the floor
before taking their own turn. But as we see in the transcript,
Adele was not actually interrupted, since she continued speaking
when Beth jumped in. She and Beth then seemed to collaborate
on the next few phrases. Adele seemed *willing* for Beth to share
the floor with her, and might even have *wanted* Beth to do so.
Perhaps, like the lead singer in an Inuit song contest, Adele was
hoping that her partner would be able to keep the game going
just a little longer.

In the conversation of Adele and Beth, do we still feel that
interruptions occurred, that the two women clashed? Is there
such a thing as a *welcome interruption*?

It would seem that there is. Marianthi Makri-Tsilipakou counted
up all the cases in Greek conversations where one participant

intruded into the "turn space" of the other in order to signal agreement or disagreement. She found that women interrupted to *agree* almost twice as often as men did, and interrupted to *disagree* half as often as men did.[14] Reacting to these findings, Makri-Tsilipakou called women "support or agreement prone."[15] Others have referred to women's smiling and nodding as "silent applause."[16]

Perhaps Adele and Beth were not truly two *independent* women in the first place, or were happy to abandon that status in order to enjoy a moment of *duality*. Some years ago, Jeanne Watson and Robert Potter wrote about a process that they simply called "sharing." In sharing, two or more speakers surrender their individual boundaries and form a single larger system. When a speaker shares, they wrote, she "invites the listener to participate vicariously in the world of the speaker as if it were [her] own."[17]

≈

In the next chapter, we will see that duetting, in parallel with men's dueling, is a biologically adaptive strategy for acquiring basic resources that women need for a successful life. By reposing their trust in the power of allies and coalitions, women put their confidence in the strength of friendships. Friendships offer the possibility of assistance in time of need, but these relationships must already "be there" for this benefit to be called in. What do women do to create standing alliances? If there are bonds between women friends, what are they made of? What's the glue?

Intimacy

As we saw earlier, Jane Falk believed that duets would be unappealing to people who are "sensitive to the sensation or appearance of intimacy." Any guesses about the sex of these people?

Let us take a look at intimacy, and ask how duets promote (and reflect) intimate relationships. Much as attachment holds mothers and infants together, a critical process if helpless infants are to survive and pass on their mother's genes along with their own, I will suggest that one of the chief functions of intimacy in our species is to facilitate the survival of women who think, feel, and act cooperatively.

The word intimacy comes from *intimus*, Latin for 'inner' or 'inmost.' The English word, *intimacy*, refers to an understanding of the deepest nature of another. In general, intimate friends of the same sex share information about themselves that is privileged in the sense that it is not shared with just anyone, and is confidential, that is, could prove injurious if it were to be spread to others. Partners in intimate relationships, that is, close friends, tend to think alike, occasionally anticipating each other's views and behaviors. Frequently, they experience a sense of unity, of indissoluble "we-ness."

Women's relationships with other women, which are largely enacted in conversation, are typically more emotionally intimate than men's are.[18] In social interactions, women tend to stand and sit closer to each other than men do. This, among other things, enables them to whisper and thus to foil eavesdroppers.[19] When sitting fairly close together, women make far better eye contact than men do at the same distance.[20] They also speak more softly. When forced to sit farther apart, women relax their usual levels of eye contact, and they speak less intimately. [21]

Men behave in precisely the opposite way. The rule seems to be this: if men are to look into each other's eyes and to share intimacies, they must have the protection afforded by some amount of intervening space.

Look around and you will see that women also touch each other more than men do. In some countries, they hold hands, something that (heterosexual) men in most cultures would never do. Years ago, two researchers carried out a naturalistic study of touching behavior. In many cases, members of the opposite sex did the touching. But when the focus was on same-sex touching, women did about *four times more touching than men*.[22]

These physical and social conditions undoubtedly produce emotional satisfaction by themselves, but they also favor the transmission of a certain kind of information, one that binds women together in remarkable – and highly useful – ways.

Self-disclosure

The glue is self-disclosure, a critical ingredient in the development and maintenance of intimate relationships.[23] According to Jean-Philippe Laurenceau and his colleagues, the "feeling of closeness" that we call intimacy "develops from personal disclosures ... of personally relevant information, thoughts, and feelings to another."[24] That feeling of closeness is linked to trust.

Gaining trust is a delicate process. It requires that participants begin, on a trial basis, to see if they are able to keep each other's secrets. An important tactic is to release a measured amount of personal information that is just interesting enough to others, potentially, that the listener may be tempted to pass it on. The check against this is a return flow of equally sensitive information. This completes the implicit "I won't tell if you don't tell" circuit. The reason for the caution, of course, is that self-disclosure makes one vulnerable to social injury. By making both parties equally vulnerable, reciprocal disclosure makes both parties equally secure.[25] But the "material" is not just naked facts. In their work, Laurenceau and his team found that the disclosure of emotion was more important to the experience of intimacy than the disclosure of facts by themselves.[26]

There is no shortage of research to indicate that women communicate more intimately than men.[27] They discuss personal problems, doubts and fears, family problems, and intimate relationships. Women discuss these things more often, and in far greater depth than men do.[28] Research indicates that women are more likely than men to have close intimate same-sex friends, and to spend time just talking with a same-sex friend. Men are more likely than women to have a number of good but less intimate same-sex friends.[29] This intimacy gulf is partly explained by the strategic advantage that intimacy affords women in their relationships with other women, and the threat that confidences, if violated, pose to men.

As much as holding and touching keep people together, at least momentarily, an act of self-disclosure can work like a "spot weld" that ensures the continuing attachment of two people. Aware of this on some level, women self-disclose their way into stable and enduring relationships.

The evidence on this is clear. Women are far more likely to tell other women things that men would never tell their male friends.[30] Studies of women's first-person narratives indicate that fully a third contain "sensitive" information about a range of personal topics, from doubts and fears to intimate relationships and family problems. This is more than triple the rate of self-disclosure by men.[31]

Studies by sociologist Robert Bell revealed a sizeable difference in the number of friends with whom women and men are able to disclose personal information. Typical of the women was this 42-year-old divorcée, who said:

> I love my women friends for their warmth and compassion. I can share anything about my life with them and they never pass judgment or condemn. They are very open and share much of their inner thoughts with me. These friends have helped me tremendously in my own personal growth and through great changes in my life. They are fun to be with and have a great sense of humor. I would tell those women anything. There are no limitations on disclosure that I am aware of. The special quality of these female friendships is the openness. I have never been able to talk and share my feelings and experiences in the same way with any man.[32]

By contrast, this 38-year-old male, an advertising executive, told Bell:

> I have three close friends I have known since we were boys and they live here in the city. There are some things I wouldn't tell them. For example, I wouldn't tell them much about my work because we have always been highly competitive. I certainly

wouldn't tell them about my feelings of any uncertainties with life or various things I do. And I wouldn't talk about any problems I have with my wife or in fact anything about my marriage and sex life. But other than that I would tell them anything.

Then, suddenly realizing how ridiculous this must have sounded, the man added: "That doesn't leave a hell of a lot, does it?"[33]

Autonomous men fear loss of control, the threat posed by unauthorized disclosure of their personal secrets.[34] "The disclosure of areas of privacy reveals the underlying causes and motives of the individual's behavior," wrote psychologist Peter Kelvin, which "potentially gives those to whom they are disclosed power over him; and in doing so, disclosures make him vulnerable to exploitation."[35]

Men and women feel differently about *physical risk*. Men are more likely than women to drive fast, climb mountains, explore caves, dive off cliffs, and jump out of airplanes. But the same men will not sit next to a close friend and make softly buzzing noises with their mouths, at least if the friend could extract from these sounds something that could be used to injure him.

Other-disclosure

When women friends disclose things about mutual acquaintances, they usually express their emotional reactions to the information that is exchanged. There is nothing inherently wrong with this, but it is usually done in secrecy. Thus we see women leaning in, whispering, and moving their lips in silence. We see them nod, and give knowing looks. These are the subtle and familiar signs of collusion. In their choice of material, the participants expect expressed reactions that are similar to their own private ones, perhaps set up their stories, and choose their partners, to ensure this. In doing these things, the women are duetting.

In their book *I know just what you mean*, writers Ellen Goodman and Patricia O'Brien recall the comments of two young

mothers, Mendy and Jane, who had quit their jobs in order to
spend more time with their babies:

> They talked, how they talked. They talked about the decision to
> quit work ... They talked in the park, at Gymboree, at the mall, at
> the aquarium, while pushing strollers, changing diapers. When
> they couldn't be together, they talked for hours on the telephone.
> They began calling themselves members of the Society of the
> Cordless Phone.

> They talked while making beds, doing dishes, tucking their
> cordless phones under their chins while they scrubbed the kids in
> the bathtub. "Gradually we opened up and talked about more
> than kids and work and whether we'd get any sleep that night,"
> said Jane. "We would have long, intense conversations, and
> then my husband would come home and I wouldn't have
> much to say." She added with a laugh, "Why can I talk forever
> to Mendy and not to him?"[36]

As we have seen, men talk about mutual acquaintances, but they
usually do so for other reasons. When they talk about other men,
there is little indication that they reveal much that is personal or
emotional. When they bring up romantic relationships, which is
rare, they seem less interested in exploring their nature than in
asking how they might get out of one that has gone bad. Men
rarely discuss much of anything in a tender way, or use gossip as a
means of indirect aggression.

I have found a number of paintings of women that refer to
gossiping in the title. In these paintings, the women are portrayed
as *conspirators* who operate in relative silence and secrecy. The
women stand or sit close together – almost as close as the Inuit
women and Ainu women in their throat games – their faces
almost touching. In *The Gossips*, a French painting from the late
nineteenth or early twentieth century, one sees three wealthy
young women having a glass of wine in a public place, one
leaning agreeably toward the others while she talks. In *The
Friendly Gossips*, an Austrian painting from the same period,
three women are sewing. Two sit very close to each other, one

leaning in and laughing as they talk. In other paintings, the women touch or embrace.

The tendency of women to speak in personal and emotional ways about the people in their lives, to trusted others, is expressed in every culture that has been studied. This is something that benefits women in ways that it does not benefit men. When asked, women say that they value opportunities to engage with other women in precisely this way. In the next chapter, we will see some of the deeper reasons why they do.

7 Why do women duet?

There is a hidden bias in the sex data, one that has never been discussed, perhaps because it has not been recognized. I am not referring to the "biological bias" that was created when ancient events put the sexes on different evolutionary paths, altering the way future generations of men and women would talk, for that is a central issue of the book. Nor am I referring to the "gender bias" of researchers who may have secretly hoped to show that one sex is superior to the other. A century ago, Helen Thompson Woolley thought that no area of science could equal gender studies when it came to "flagrant personal bias, logic martyred in the cause of supporting a prejudice, unfounded assertions, and even sentimental rot and drivel."[1]

The bias that I have in mind relates to neither of these things, though it may lie somewhere in between human evolution and the practice of science. For it involves the subtle ways our ancestors continue from the grave, as it were, to influence the investigation of women and men's speech today.

In the second chapter, I described the verbal duels of men in some detail. This was possible for two reasons. The first is that duels are rituals that were *designed to be conspicuous*, and still are, for their continuing purpose is to display masculine traits that are valued both by women and by men. The second reason why it was possible to achieve a detailed account of duels is that rituals of all kinds, including verbal ones, have been a high priority of social anthropology.

For these reasons, it has been *natural* for fieldworkers to describe the verbal features that men manipulate when they duel, and it was also *fairly easy* for them to do so. As a consequence, we now have an impressive list of duelly media that extends from riddling and joking to teasing, insulting, and boasting.

Under the radar

A major portion of this previously unrecognized bias is perceptual. Imagine what would happen if two men held a duel but there was no one on hand to observe them. To ask a form of Bishop Berkeley's question about the tree that falls when no one is around to hear it, could an unattended duel produce triumph or shame? Would it be possible for one contestant to outshine his rival?

Duels tap into a pre-existing need of both sexes to know certain things about men. The search for these features – the evaluative component of verbal duels – is a mental process. It is carried out silently, under the radar, as it were. This makes it hard for anthropologists or any one else to witness or describe it.

My point here is not solely that women play this evaluative role – clearly they do – but that the cognition supporting that role itself *escapes the notice* of those who limit their studies to observable behavior. We *see* that peacocks have colorful feathers, and we *notice* that peahens are more responsive to brighter than duller males. Aware that long and colorful tail feathers make it difficult to forage or escape predators, we *reason* that sexual (and not natural) selection may be the preferred explanation for male coloration. Accordingly, we *infer* that peahens have good color vision, but to *know* this someone will have to do some experiments.

Fortunately, as we have seen, research is now being done on women's evaluation of men's speaking voices. To date, this work indicates that the "vocal plumage" to which females are drawn happens to be a reliable guide to males' reproductive potential – specifically their virility, assertiveness, and social dominance – and women are unusually drawn to these things when it could benefit them reproductively. But these findings have yet to be assimilated, and theories of human communication make no provision for this indirect and silent activity of women.

If women play a subtle role in the evaluation and design of duels, the physical nature of their own duets is no less subtle.

Certainly one can observe and record women's "jam sessions," as some linguists have. But if our sample is limited to such conspicuous displays, we will falsely conclude that *all* female interactions are like this, and we will miss any others – perhaps some more important others – that are carried out quietly, even secretly. How should scientists study *these things* that women do in private?

There is room for a different kind of sex bias here, one that inevitably has scientific implications – and complications – for comparative research on duels and duets. These issues include *cultural factors* relating to respect and civility; *technical limitations* including microphones that cannot faithfully record low-volume sounds at a distance; and *ethics principles* that require researchers to tell participants what they plan to do before they do it.

Let's go through these issues one at a time. In civil societies, researchers are expected to show some respect for individuals who are clearly enjoying a moment of intimacy. It might be considered too intrusive to record conversations that focus on personal problems, which, by definition, the discussants would not be inclined to broadcast. Clearly it would be wrong to record such interactions surreptitiously. If, on the other hand, permission is granted, how naturally will women talk with a microphone staring them in the face and the possibility – however remote – that privileged material might fall into the wrong hands?

How women actually *sound* when they are disclosing information about themselves and others – the stuff of intimate relationships – has been largely untouched by science. For example, I am aware of just one published study on the physical nature of *whispering*, and, surprisingly, no papers on who does it, and in what circumstances – save the whispering caused by political repression – and there are only a few odd comments here and there on any uses of subdued speech by children.[2]

There is an analogy in the animal world where, for many years, studies of primate communication focused primarily on *loud vocalizations*. These calls evolved specifically to reach the ears of widely dispersed animals and, for that reason, are fairly easy to record and analyze acoustically. This has made it possible to investigate the "meaning" of primate calls, that is, to classify them as food calls, copulation calls, alarm calls, and so on. To many primatologists, the most important vocalizations were these *signals* that appeared to communicate something.

In baboons, orangutans, and chimpanzees, as we have seen, loud calls are made only by males – usually ones that are physically isolated. But females are far from mute. In fact, they are liberally represented in a class of *quieter* vocalizations that are never hurled across the forest canopy on a "to whom it may concern" basis, but are often exchanged by socially related animals that are huddled together. These animals are familiar with each other. For all we know, they may even "like" and "trust" each other.

For your ears only

Quiet vocalizations are not "signals" in the conventional sense. Their meaning lies on a different level than calls. In 1993, several primatologists wrote that in many species that live in groups, the animals "produce and exchange frequent, quiet vocalizations which are *audible only to group members.*" But these "close" calls, as this class of sounds was labeled, were associated with no particular context. As a consequence, they wrote, "*the functions of this very common social behavior are difficult to divine.*"[3]

Contexts are helpful, of course, perhaps even critical. But there is an additional possibility: to play the sounds over a loudspeaker and watch who does what. That is the strategy of choice for alarm calls, where one has a priori reasons to suspect that monkeys will run up a tree when they hear a leopard call, and this is exactly what monkeys do. But researchers have been less eager to blast monkeys with affiliative sounds, perhaps because they thought that it would be difficult to interpret any responses that amplifications of these soft vocalizations might elicit.

The soft sounds of primates have also been easy to ignore for another reason. They can be hard to record. If a researcher, microphone in hand, approaches animals that are huddled together, grunting and murmuring among themselves, they might scatter or make entirely different kinds of sounds, ones that convey the fear or agitation that the invasion provoked. Fortunately, researchers have found ways around this, and where such calls were recorded and examined in relation to the *social context* in which they occurred, their functions have become evident.

Which brings us into the personal and social world of our closest living relatives. Soft sounds provide reliable information about other animals' emotions and social intentions. To some, this may seem trivial compared to *Leopard!* or *Food!* But calls such as these exist only because animals live in groups and there is someone to warn or advise them in the first place. If internal relations became a serious problem, groups would disband, and each individual would then have to face everything on his own. Close or quiet calls seem to be designed to prevent this.

In our own species, an analogy lurks in "small talk," the speech of amiable individuals who are "passing the time of day." Small talk is fairly common among people who do not know each other. Since they lack mutual acquaintances, they may be unable to gossip. But saying nothing is usually not an acceptable option. Among strangers, silence can be a threat. Comments about the weather or some other public event may seem inane but, like an audible smile, they display friendly intentions, and this reduces the threat. Intellectuals disdain small talk because it has little "content," but this is precisely why it stands out as a friendly gesture.[4]

Quiet vocalizations signal benign intent, and since most primates lack the cognitive or acting ability to deceive, at least vocally, their signals are unavoidably reliable. Other animals can use the information they donate, or give off incidentally, to plan their own actions. Normally, if one female approaches another there is some danger of a fight because she is moving into the other's space. But if she makes soft sounds while approaching, the probability of a fight is reduced. These sounds also put animals in a mood that is conducive to cooperation.[5]

How, then, do we deal with analogous sound-making activities in our own species? If the talking we wish to study is also too faint to record at respectful distances, how do investigators get closer? What if the talkers are conversing too quietly or secretly to be heard? How are the best-intentioned researchers to keep from destroying the very thing that they wish to observe? How do they avoid the injunction, equally embraced by journalists and scientists, to keep themselves out of the story?

These problems might discourage scientists from investigating the physical aspects of duets, but there is still a great deal to be explored when it comes to the social and psychological nature of duets. For as we have seen, duetting women are typically responsive, sympathetic, harmonious, and emotionally intimate; and if some duets are boisterous and others calm or subdued, all are co-authored, coordinated, and personally revealing. By the time we have looked at these things, I think that the essence of women's duets will have come through as clearly as the loud calls of male orangutans.

Evolution of duetting

If duetting is rooted in female biology, then we must embrace biology to understand it, and this includes doing what we can to reconstruct the processes by which duetting evolved. The challenge of doing so might seem to be immense: how do we explore the evolution of duetting without first addressing one of the more challenging problems in intellectual history – the evolution of language?

I think this question has it backwards. Other species did not wait for language to evolve before they began dueling and duetting – in theirs it never did – and in the next chapter I will propose that duetting played a formative role in the evolution of humans, and human language. Here I will look at the emergence of duetting. But evolution is a gradual process, and duetting is a complex behavior, with many "parts," including sociability, vocal sensitivity, social intelligence, intimacy, and empathy. So I will say something about these components, and how they might have emerged.

As with duels, the evolution of duets is a story about the emergence of an adaptive way to deal with competition. But duets involve a *collective approach* to competition. In a collective approach, two or more persons collaborate to reach a common goal, or to help one of them achieve a personal objective. It is important to recognize that cooperation, in this sense, is not the antithesis of aggression, or even an alternative. It is, perhaps surprisingly, an indirect form of it.

We saw earlier that female primates are less overtly aggressive than males. In many species, this is partly because females inherit their mother's rank, and thus do not have to fight for it, as males do. For them, the cost–benefit ratio for aggression is almost all cost – the cost of injury to the combatants and, indirectly, to any present or future infants.[6] Just over thirty years ago, Robert Seyfarth found that among female baboons there were twenty approach–retreat interactions for every act of overt aggression. In males, the ratio of approach–retreats to physical acts was less than two to one.[7] When they do quarrel, females are more likely to threaten and withdraw than to bite and scratch,[8] and when they do fight, Sarah Hrdy commented, they "rarely inflict serious damage on one another in their quarrels."[9] One primatologist, Barbara Smuts, referred to female altercations as generally "low key and chronic."[10] They involve what Jeffrey Walters and Robert Seyfarth called "mild bickering."[11]

At some point in primate evolution, females obviously recognized, on some level, that one-on-one battles with large and strong males were not the answer. But many-to-one confrontations were another matter. They would balance the odds, or even tip them in the females' favor. Clearly, coalesced females could handle the problem posed by menacing males, and they could also discourage other females who were attempting to intrude. The thing was to get together, and then find ways to stay together.

Huddling and grooming

In a number of primate species, the females are particularly disposed to huddle together in small groups, building and reinforcing social relationships by grooming.[12] This activity involves sorting through the fur of another animal, and picking out the lice. It is sometimes referred to as manual grooming, but it is more often called "social" grooming because it is a personal service, one that strengthens the relationship of grooming partners. Joan Silk has found that female baboons that trade places, grooming each other *equitably*, have particularly strong bonds. These females are more likely than others to achieve coalition support, which improves both their social standing and, remarkably, the survival rate of their offspring.[13]

Same-sex relationships are closer in females than in males. Silk has also found that female baboons spend far more time socializing than males, and when a close companion dies, females also appear to be more strongly affected than males. The death of a relative elevates gluco-corticoid levels, a sure sign of increased stress. At such times, females literally reach out and touch someone, grooming each other more frequently than before, and add new members to their grooming networks.[14] My point is this: when modern women literally *come together* in a crisis – which they do – and when they sit together, touch, emote, and speak softly, it is not as though there is no precedent for any of these things in their evolutionary history.[15]

Grooming takes time, of course, and primates have other things to do.[16] They must look for food, reproduce, take care of their infants, and build nests. Only so much time is available for social activities. But when food is scarce and animals need to spend more time foraging, females do not allow grooming to suffer.[17] They take the time from something else, or groom more efficiently. Macaque females occasionally participate in *grooming chains* in which as many as three or four animals groom each other simultaneously.[18]

You scratch my back, I'll scratch yours

Primates may not know that they have lice, or that parasite reduction improves health, but they almost certainly like the sensation of fingers sorting through their fur. Physiological studies suggest that grooming relaxes animals.[19] In one study, it was found that a female monkey experienced a slightly greater cardiac deceleration to stroking than to pincer-like picking movements.[20]

But there is also a higher social or psychological effect, for animals know when another has chosen – or accepted their invitation – to "service" them in this particular way. Indeed, primates maintain a grooming ledger, a mental diary containing the "identities" of animals that have recently groomed them, and a record of their own grooming services.[21] It might escape the eye of casual visitors, but primates have a very busy service-based economy. When animals of a similar rank groom each other, they usually do so reciprocally.[22] When lower-ranking animals groom higher-ranking ones, their efforts may later be compensated with an offer of food or protection.[23] In this sense, a social mind must also include a computational component, one that keeps track of debts.

Humans also groom each other, and there is a female bias here, too. According to Ladurie's book *Montaillou*, the thirteenth-century church records of this tiny village in the French Pyrenees indicate that residents groomed their relatives and friends by sorting through their scalp hair and removing the lice, much as the other primates do. This practice undoubtedly promoted the health of the recipient, but it was pursued in accordance with strict social rules. One rule was that *only* women should groom. Another is that grooming should work upwardly. Like the grooming of apes and monkeys, working-class women groomed women of higher status more than the reverse pattern.

Human grooming is still done. Malinowski observed and photographed it in the Trobriand Islands of New Guinea in the early twentieth century, and it continues today in parts of Africa.[24] Anthropologist Kazuyoshi Sugawara carefully documented it among Kung tribesmen living in the Central Kalahari area of Botswana. There, grooming consists of one person manually removing lice from the scalp or, less commonly, the area under the loincloth. Sugawara's analysis revealed that in about 80 percent of the adult grooming episodes the groomer was a female. Males participated in fewer than 15 percent of the episodes and they never groomed females, although females occasionally groomed their husbands or unrelated adolescent males.[25]

Incidentally, grooming seemed to induce a hedonic state in the Kung. Sugawara noted "the joyful enthusiasm" shown by the groomer and "the intoxicate facial expression of the groomed." The latter, he wrote, while displaying "closed eyes and a rapt expression, emit[s] sharp fricative sounds made by the tongue and teeth, similar to the dental click, just as the groomer flattens lice."[26] Likewise, when rhesus monkeys groom each other, wrote a primate researcher, the recipient "often assumes a very relaxed posture: the limbs go limp and the groomer can manipulate them without resistance."[27]

Physiological evidence indicates that grooming reduces tension. Barry Keverne and his colleagues found that when monkeys groom, it increases levels of endorphins (opiates) in the cerebrospinal fluid of the recipients. Administration of opioid agonists, which presumably reduce the pleasurable feelings produced by opiates, caused increases in grooming and grooming invitations.[28] But these agonists do nothing to alter the frequency of *self*-grooming. The effect of opiate receptor blockades was specific to *social* grooming. In other work it has been found in several different monkey species, and also in humans, that stroking by another individual significantly lowers heart rate. Self-stroking has no such effect.[29]

~

All-female coalitions offer a solution to the problem of external threat, but how are females able to spend so much of their time huddled together in small groups without getting on each other's nerves? It is understood that grooming eases tensions, but how long can animals go on grooming each other?

Social vocalization

Dunbar has argued that in the evolution of language, vocalizations came to take over the affiliative functions of manual grooming, and individuals began what he called "vocal grooming."[30] The vocalizations he had in mind were contact calls, loud sounds that carry across distances. But if one looks at quiet vocalizations, one can see nascent signs of this sonic take-over now, in living primates.

How do monkeys sound when they are being friendly? The quietly social vocalizations of primates include *grunts* – short, harsh sounds made behind closed lips; *girneys* – soft and low-pitched chewing noises that may be accompanied by rapid lip movement; and *coos* – sounds that are made with the lips open and the jaw lowered.[31] Though males make all of the loud calls, females take the lead when it comes to these softer sounds that, significantly, are called "social vocalizations." In one study of rhesus macaques, females issued more than *ten* times the number of social vocalizations than males, and vocalized socially to other adult females more than *thirty* times more often than they vocalized to adult males.[32]

How similar these social vocalizations are to the sounds of speech is a subjective matter, but one team of primatologists compared the vocal pulses of gorillas to syllables, and one investigator has referred to the consonants and vowels produced by gelada monkeys.[33]

Why do females take the lead in this class of vocalizations? In most primate species, as stated, females groom more than males, and animals frequently make girneys or lip-smacking sounds *while grooming*.[34] This means that we can expect females to produce more girneys for that reason alone, but it opens up a new possibility: using the girneys or lip-smacks by themselves. Significantly, lip-smacks seem to stand in for grooming, working as a gesture of friendliness.[35] It is not surprising that in a study of Japanese macaques, females produced 90 percent of all the girneys.[36]

Since girneys and other social vocalizations are known to have an appeasing effect on their recipients, it is interesting that in our own species there is evidence that females smile more often than males, beginning around adolescence.[37] Clearly this is a friendly but silent gesture that is made with the mouth. But what, specifically, are we to make of primates' use of grunts, coos, and girneys and our human uses of quietly social vocalization? Surely it is significant that species that are evolutionarily and genetically related to our own produce somewhat "speechy" sounds when attempting to signal friendly intentions. Considering the psychological benefits of an intimate talk with a close friend, it is interesting that in female baboons, grunting (like grooming) does good things to primate physiology. For grunts also lower the gluco-corticoid levels that rise during periods of stress.[38]

≈

If our evolutionary ancestors were to cooperate, they would have to know how to form and maintain friendships. If they wished to rely on the assistance of friends, they would have to exercise some social skills. They would need the ability to "read" others well enough to manipulate them.

Social intelligence

Group living helps to solve some *external* problems because there are more individuals to look for food and keep an eye out for predators, but all of these individuals have the same needs. This ramps up the competition. Females compete for access to new-born infants. Males fight for mating opportunities. In other words, group living creates *internal* problems. Studies indicate that as groups increase in size, the savings in time devoted to vigilance is largely absorbed by a new perceptual need – eavesdropping – as constituents spend more and more time *watching each other.*[39] This jacks up the need to watch intelligently, for primates, aware that they are being watched, may attempt to outsmart each other by, for example, feigning an unawareness of food when others are watching.

Eavesdropping is a good solution, but it is not enough. Animals need to know who to watch and how to interpret their behaviors. They have to infer the intentions of individuals – especially the sneaky or sinister ones that do not want their intentions inferred – and thus to anticipate their future actions. Members of groups need to know something about the personal and social history of others, especially their rank and relationships – their friendships, alliances, and families. These things require a major commitment of cognitive resources, of "brain power," to problems that are essentially social in nature. But primates can meet the challenge, because they are appropriately wired up to do so. Every ape has a social brain.

Beginning in the early 1990s, Robin Dunbar began to report correlations between the sociality of animals, based on the size of social groups, and the size of their brains, with special reference to the evolutionarily newer cortical areas. Animals that live in large groups, Dunbar and his colleagues discovered, have far more cerebral cortex than solitary or small-group animals. The implication was that the thinking parts of the brain evolved as adaptations to social complexity.[40]

A decade passed before Patrik Lindenfors pointed out that increasing group size only explains changes in *female* brains. First, he demonstrated that changes in the number of males in groups lags behind changes in the number of females. He argued, accordingly, that females were "the driving sex in primate social evolution, with female group size changing first and male group size subsequently adjusting to female number."[41] Then, Lindenfors demonstrated that brain size was determined by the number of females in groups, not the number of males. The increase in male brains, he concluded, was due to genetic correlation or the fact that males must also respond to social challenges of one sort or another.[42]

But Lindenfors and his colleagues did not leave it there. They offered a further claim – that the size of groups is correlated with different brain regions; in females the correlation is with the telencephalon (which includes the cerebral cortex), in males with the diencephalon (the deeper levels of the brain that contain the thalamus, hypothalamus, and other autonomic functions). "This suggests," Dunbar wrote in a response to Lindenfors' work, "that male and female brains have responded to different kinds of social pressures: females to social integration, males to male-male competition and fighting."[43]

In the evolution of our species, the size of social groups expanded well beyond the upper limits of other primate groups. This would have contributed to additional increases in social complexity and competition (and to additional differences in male and female brains). Coalitions would have helped meet the need, but as their value increased, so did competition to get into particularly effective coalitions. Over evolutionary time, adult females found ways to deal with these more complex social problems. The solution, broadly, is what we now call "social intelligence."

Although scientists have not given much attention to social intelligence until recently, the first mention of it occurred nearly a century ago when Edward Thorndike used that term in reference to "the ability to understand and manage men and women," and "to act wisely in human relations."[44] Today, it is sometimes used interchangeably with – and has largely been overtaken by – "emotional intelligence," considered by some to be "a type of social intelligence that involves the ability to monitor one's own and others' emotions, to discriminate among them, and to use the information to guide one's thinking and actions."[45]

If there are arguments about whether men have more aptitude than women in the area of math or physics, there are fewer disputes about which sex has more social intelligence. Studies have consistently shown that women are more sensitive to subtle social cues than men, an advantage that is fully present in infants – and does not increase or decrease in the later developmental stages or adulthood – and they have more advanced social skills.[46]

What explains women's superior facial and vocal sensitivities? The most fertile ground to explore such a thing would be human biology, of course, and there is evidence of face and voice cells in primate brains, and a genetic basis for facial memory in our species.[47] Moreover, within biology a good place to look for the origins of these differences is one we visited earlier: human reproduction. A great deal of what makes women different from men can be traced to differential responsibilities with regard to infant care. I will suggest below that increases in infants' need of care enhanced the ability of mothers to interpret emotional states, and that this sensitivity underpins the capacity for intimate relationships, especially with other women.

The evolution of intimacy: a "skeletal" proposal

If duets are intimate, how did intimacy evolve? To speculate on such a thing might seem adventurous, but archeologists fearlessly discuss the evolution of *cognition* based on stone tools and cave drawings; and scientists now publish articles and whole monographs on the biology of love. So in discussing the evolution of intimacy I at least belong to a select group of theoretical risk-takers.

Clearly, intimacy has a great deal to do with feelings. These feelings are presumably the connective tissue that keeps people together in *sexual relationships.* Cindy Hazan and Phillip Shaver refer to romantic love as "a biological process designed by evolution to *facilitate attachment* between adult sexual partners who, at the time love evolved, were likely to become parents of an infant who would need their reliable care."[48]

Several years ago, in a public presentation I offered a "skeletal" proposal on the evolution of intimacy, and I meant this literally as well as figuratively.[49] It was a "bare bones" outline, but it also made a specific appeal to skeletal remains. I was thinking about this in Chapter 5, when I mentioned the problem of fetal head size in relation to the size of the maternal birth canal. In this ratio, we find a clue to the evolution of human intimacy.

In apes, birth is not a particularly difficult process, mainly because the head of the infant is smaller than the mother's birth canal and the infant is able to pass through it fairly easily. But skeletal evidence suggests that when our ancestors began to stand erect and to walk, this began to change. First, pressures on the hip and pelvis were altered.[50] This eventually shortened the distance between sacroiliac and hip joints.[51] While this made walking and running more efficient, it narrowed and re-morphed the birth canal.

This would have posed no problems had there been parallel reductions in the size of the fetal skull, but this was not the case. In fact, the skulls of adults, and their offspring, were getting larger. Together these things produced an "obstetrical dilemma" of epic proportions.[52] If modern women and their babies are to survive, other women need to pitch in.[53] Merely because they could become pregnant, women have always had to keep their social fences in good repair. In most societies, friends assisted in the birth, and this solidified social relationships among young women, as we saw in the lying-in chambers of seventeenth-century France and England.

If the delivery of human infants seems difficult – in modern societies it's a medical issue – it would be far worse were it not for an adjustment that was made several million years ago. Infants with small heads at parturition were more likely to survive than infants with large heads. This had the effect, over evolutionary time, of shifting the final stages of fetal brain development into the post-natal period when, safely on the outside, increasing head size would no longer pose a threat. This eased the passage of the fetus through the birth canal, but it meant that the new, smaller-headed infants would be less developed at birth, and therefore more helpless than ever. They would require unprecedented levels of care.

If these infants were to survive, a stronger care mechanism would be needed, one that ensured close and continuing contact between mothers and their offspring. Mother–infant attachment has been a concern of psychologists because it fills this need for sustained care, but also – and this is more important here – because it critically affects the future ability of the young to relate to others in an emotionally trusting way. In a rare longitudinal study, Everett Waters and his colleagues compared the attachment scores of subjects when they were 12 months old to their scores *twenty years later.* They found that nearly three-fourths of the subjects fell into the same attachment category in infancy and adulthood. The meaning is clear: the ability to form intimate relationships in adulthood reflects the quality of attachment in infancy.[54]

This, of course, is an intensely female story – there have been few studies of *father*–infant attachment – and we find sprinkled through this saga reasons why modern women, more than men, would enjoy intimate relationships with others.[55] But I have not discussed what women and infants actually do in their intimate relationships, nor have I mentioned the role of the mother's voice.

Mother–infant duets

No less than the other primates, humans have to budget their time, and this applies especially to women. Unlike chimpanzees, where there is a generous birth spacing, women can have several children in need of care at the same time. If ancestral mothers were to apportion their efforts efficiently, giving no more care than was strictly needed, they would have to "read" their infants' vocalizations. This meant, for one thing, learning to discriminate false from genuine cries of distress. Since mothers have always done more parenting than fathers, they would have had a greater need for *vocal sensitivity.*[56]

Evidence of such sensitivity has surfaced in several different kinds of studies. Some years ago, Lynn Murray and Colwyn Trevarthen asked mothers to interact with their infant over closed-circuit television. The mothers assumed that their infant's behavior was live, and in one condition it was, but in another condition what the mother saw was a recording of an interaction that had taken place earlier in the session. In this latter case, the infant *as seen on the screen* could not have been responding to anything that the mother was doing *at the time.* Several of the mothers interpreted their infant's behavior as unresponsive. One said, "You're not interested in mummy, eh?" Another said, "You're ignoring me again then, aren't you?"[57]

Mothers need to control the behavior of infants, and this requires the sort of influence that comes with an emotional relationship. Mothers encourage such a relationship by closely monitoring ongoing streams of infant behavior, waiting for opportunities to jump in. This space-seeking tendency of mothers is present in the first few days of life, when mothers notice that breast or bottle sucking occurs in bursts. When babies pause, mothers naturally assume that something must be done to restart it. Typically, they jiggle the baby or the bottle.[58] This gives the appearance of a perfectly alternating sequence, thanks to the regularity of the sucking infant and the responsiveness of the jiggling mother:

INFANT: suck.... suck.... suck....
MOTHER: ... jiggle.... jiggle.... jiggle.

When it comes to vocal behavior, mothers are no less adept at inserting themselves into the spaces provided by their infant. In studies of vocal "turn taking," it was initially thought that infants were active participants in the back-and-forth "conversations" that occur in the first several months of life. But then it was discovered that young infants' vocalizations were all back and no forth. That is, infants did not wait for the mother to finish speaking before they started in. It was the mothers who did this, creating the illusion that the baby was a fully fledged participant. They also matched their infants' syllables, confusing students of language development who were seeking to study the infant's imitation of its mother.[59]

Overlap

Although vocal turn taking has attracted the attention of numerous researchers, alternation is not the only pattern displayed by mothers and infants. Years ago, Daniel Stern and his colleagues observed that mothers tend to use an alternating pattern when "teaching" their infant, but that the mother and her infant usually *vocalize in unison* with they are just having fun with each other. This is evident in the first three days after birth, when mothers tend to place their vocalizations "on top of," or to overlap with, their infant's vocalizations, a manner of vocalizing called "coactional."[60] Stern and his colleagues found that mothers vocalized in unison with their infants almost twice as often as they vocalized in alternation.

There is a reason why overlapping was the dominant pattern, one that is linked to emotional states that arise naturally in the context of maternal–infant interactions. For it was found that mothers overlapped their infants' clucks and coos mainly during the highest levels of arousal. The alternating pattern was more evident at lower levels. Since the overlapped vocalizations were due to the mother and not the infant, Stern and his colleagues reasoned that the mothers overlapped because they "sought and achieved highly arousing interactions with their infants."[61]

One is reminded of the duets that we saw in Chapter 6, where women were so emotionally aroused, and so eager to co-tell the same stories, that their voices – and their words – overlapped. Stern and his colleagues were evidently aware of such parallels, for they noted that overlapping occurs *throughout life*. "As the interpersonal situation moves toward intense anger, sadness, joy, or expressions of love," they wrote, "the alternating dialogic pattern 'breaks down' and coactional vocalizing again becomes a crucial communicative mode. Mutual declarations of love and vocalizations during love-making are an obvious example. In fact, an operatic love duet can be viewed as an excellent cultural representation of this phenomenon."

Stern's team speculated that choral singing, among other collective behaviors, plays a role "in defining group membership for a given purpose, or to state or establish group bonds." They suggested that *vocalizing in unison was central to the enjoyment of relating* since it uniquely expressed the "mutual experience of joy or excited delight in being with someone."[62]

If the human female's sensitivity to social and emotional cues evolved in the context of infant care, it now facilitates emotional responding in other contexts, providing the psychological framework for duetting. For, as we saw in the previous chapter, women tend to speak in unison with *each other* during periods of high emotional arousal. This is not just a mother–infant phenomenon. Women's duets reflect the capacity to coordinate affective displays that evolved in the context of mother–infant interaction.

Evolution of empathy

Thirty years ago, Eric Trinkaus and Michael Zimmerman, the archaeologists who did the autopsy on the stabbing victim mentioned earlier, analyzed the skeletal remains of Shanidar I, the first of several adult Neandertals named after the area of Iraq where they were found. The analysis revealed that some years before his death, about forty-eight thousand years ago, Shanidar I took a great fall, one that left him brain damaged, semi-paralyzed, and partially blind. His degree of incapacitation suggests that other cave dwellers shared their food and water with him. Given what is known about the time needed for bones to knit, it was surmised that Shanidar I's fellow Neandertals continued their care for some years, even though they knew that he would never be able to return their kindness or pull his own weight. Although the archaeologists started out looking at the bones of a species, they found themselves drawn to the psychological nature and moral values of particular individuals.[63] It was concluded that the friends of Shanidar I were *empathic*, and that all Neandertals may have had some capacity to sense, experience, and respond to the feelings of others.

One assumes that Shanidar I attracted the sympathy of his fellow Neandertals because they "felt his pain." If so, they possessed emotional empathy, which enables people to share in the feelings of others.[64] Emotional empathy also motivates people to behave in an altruistic way toward their family, sexual partners, and allies.

Since duets involve an exchange of feeling, we are surely concerned here with the evolution of this capacity to perceive what others feel. Studies focusing on the affective component clearly reveal that females are more empathic than males across the lifespan.[65] Perhaps, you say, they learn to be empathic, that caring for others is something that our culture expects of women. We encourage this by giving dolls to little girls, and not to boys. But chimpanzee parents do not give dolls to their female off-spring, and yet it has been found, in that species, that medium- and low-ranking females are significantly more likely than males to console victims of aggression.[66]

Of course, in suggesting that the cave-dwelling Neandertals felt the pain experienced by one of their number I neglected some higher-order possibilities. Shanidar I's fellow cave dwellers may have *reasoned* that he needed help. Perhaps, from their assessment of his injuries, they *concluded* that he did, or kept him going because they *surmised* that someday he would recover. My point is that empathy also has a cognitive component, one that involves the ability to get into the minds of others. It is likely that group living promoted the evolution of cognitive empathy because mind reading underlies the ability to understand and predict the behavior of others, to manipulate or deceive people to one's own advantage, and to know when others are lying.

It is less obvious why one sex would be more cognitively empathic than the other, and research confirms that neither is superior in this area. Both types of empathy offer reproductive advantages, a matter to which we will return shortly, but there is a pressing question before us. Having looked at some evolutionary events that prepared women to duet, what do modern women gain from this way of talking today?

Functions of duetting

If duets help to build intimate relationships, as we have seen, they should get some of the credit for women's mental and physical health. It has long been known that people who enjoy close relationships experience better health than others.[67] Women with close friends are less likely than other women to break down following a crisis, and people of both sexes with close relationships are likely to live longer than people who enjoy fewer connections.[68] There is evidence, moreover, that women who have an intimate confidant experience fewer symptoms of depressive illness, such as tiredness and palpitations, than women who have no one with whom they can discuss personal problems.[69] The benefit may stem from the kind of relationship that enables discussion of personal problems, but also from the discussions themselves. For as we saw earlier, self-disclosure – a key ingredient in duets – lowers physiological measures of stress.[70]

The stress-reduction benefits of duets also extend to women in their role as mothers. Thirty years ago, researchers began reporting that when a female companion (called a "doula") merely sits with the mother in the delivery room, there is a shorter period of labor, improved breast-feeding outcomes, greater maternal expression of affection toward the neonate, and reduced incidence of perinatal problems than there is when the mother is alone or accompanied only by a midwife or medical personnel.[71] This casts a different light on the God-sibs, who are now seen as performing an important service just by duetting with, or in the presence of, a woman about to give birth. By duetting, they were "douling."[72]

Indirect aggression

In *The duality of human existence,* David Bakan used the terms "agency" and "communion" to characterize "two fundamental modalities in the existence of living forms." For Bakan, agency involved the person "as an individual." Communion, on the other hand, sees the individual as part of some larger arrangement.

Bakan also noted a number of other contrasts between these basic modalities. "Agency manifests itself in self-protection, self-assertion, and self-expansion," he wrote, while "communion manifests itself in the sense of being at one with other organisms. Agency manifests itself in the formation of separations; communion in the lack of separations. Agency manifests itself in isolation, alienation, and aloneness; communion in contact, openness, and union. Agency manifests itself in the urge to master; communion in noncontractual cooperation."[73]

Psychological research has confirmed Bakan's concepts of agency and communion, finding, additionally, that men rely more on agency, and women more on communion, in their approach to various problems.[74] This illustrates the consistency of human sex differences across a range of life circumstances, including the agentive and communal ways that men and women deal with competition.[75]

It is true, of course, that some women still confront their foes directly, in the manner of their historical ancestors, and they can do so today without fear of bridling or dunking. But it is hard to avoid social reprisal, and for every woman who goes public there are hundreds that deal with their rivals privately.

Privately means indirectly, and when people aggress indirectly they work through third parties. The medium is gossip, which means spreading rumors about the rival or suggesting that she be shunned or ostracized. Gossip "enables one to wrest power, manipulate, and strike out at another without the other's being able to strike back," wrote Samuel Heilman, "since he can never be sure exactly who has generated the offensive against him. While one may at times, with considerable difficulty, learn the substance of gossip focused on oneself, learning the identity of the gossiper is next to impossible."[76]

Are people with good social skills more likely than others to regard "the group" as the strategy of choice? It makes sense that they would, and there is evidence to support this. In a relevant study, Finnish juveniles and adolescents were asked to rate their peers' social intelligence and their tendency to aggress directly and indirectly. No relationship was found between *direct* forms of aggression and social intelligence, but the more individuals habitually used *indirect* aggression, the higher was their level of social intelligence.[77]

Moral gate keeping

When women speak intimately with their friends, they talk about mutual acquaintances and relationships, including family matters. In *The second sex*, Simone de Beauvoir wrote that women, in their talk, "exchange confidences and recipes … They compare experiences: pregnancies, birth, their own and their children's illnesses, and household cares become the essential events of the human story."[78]

What women are doing here is *talking business*, just as surely as cowboys and athletes and bankers do when they gossip. The difference, as we discussed earlier, is that domestic life, including familial and other social relationships, has historically been *women's business*. This particular business accomplishes many things, as we have seen, but there is an additional function that bears mention: the maintenance of local standards regarding behaviors that vitally concern their sex.

Polly Wiessner recorded over three hundred conversations among the Kung Bushmen, a largely egalitarian group of hunter-gatherers. She found that over half of the conversations involved attempts to enforce norms through criticism, but the two sexes criticized different things. In nearly every case where the topic concerned politics or land, and two-thirds of the cases where it involved troublemaking and antisocial behavior, the gossips were men. Where the topic concerned involved jealousy over possessions or failure to share meat, the gossips were women, as they were in over two-thirds of the cases of stinginess, greediness, inappropriate sexual behavior, and failure to meet kinship obligations.[79]

In a southeastern Mexican village that was studied in the 1970s, the most common gossip themes revolved around abuses of alcohol; divorce and child support; illicit sexual relations, incest, fornication; kin disputes; courtship, adultery, and promiscuity.

Adultery was by far the most frequent topic of gossip about married couples.[80] In recent work with American college students, it has been reported that the most interesting stories to women concern the promiscuity or sexual infidelity of other women.[81]

This sort of moral vigilance may be seen as a community service. It certainly broadcasts the things that women can get into trouble for, and may even imply the punishment. Morality is connected to empathy, so we might expect that for this reason, too, women would take the lead in this area. But when women attempt, through other-disclosure, to influence what is acceptable in the local culture, there is a personal benefit. If they're successful, *their own behaviors* will be less likely to be disapproved.

Mechanisms of duetting

We humans live in groups, having discovered long ago that there is safety in numbers. But there is limited value in assembly unless there is a feeling of connection among the constituents. Predictably, there are physiological mechanisms that ensure this connection, and cognitive mechanisms that can handle the flow of socially complex information. When we love or feel compelled to take care of someone, something is happening inside that represents or even causes these feelings. These internal events automatically go to work, ensuring – as much as anything can – that control systems that evolved to do certain things are actually doing them.

I have suggested that characteristics of human reproduction, including the extreme helplessness of the infant, are linked to the quality of mother–infant relationships, which are associated, in turn, with the quality of romantic and other relationships in adulthood. Clearly, a complex system is responsible for these things, and an important element here is oxytocin, a hormone that is synthesized by the hypothalamus and secreted by the posterior pituitary gland. Oxytocin connects up a host of reproductive and social processes. It is stimulated by sexual intercourse (and orgasm) and it controls contractions of the uterus during labor. Oxytocin also regulates the flow of milk, and is stimulated by the activity at the breast that occurs during feeding. After birth, oxytocin levels are correlated with a number of different maternal bonding behaviors, including gaze, speech, positive emotion, and touch.[82] It also occurs during romantic caressing and other acts of affection.[83] Some have called it "the love drug."

Recently, an association between oxytocin and trust – apparently a causal one – was reported. When oxytocin was experimentally administered to men and low-trust women, their level of trust increased.[84] In other work it was found that levels of oxytocin increased following exposure to female vocalization. When children were stressed, *the sound of their mother talking to them* lowered their levels of cortisol, a stress hormone, and boosted their levels of oxytocin.[85] Together these studies expose links between the female voice and hormones associated with connection and stress, and between those hormones and trust. Though more research needs to be done, some of the mechanisms that support duetting seem to be coming into view.

Mini-duets

Since very little in human development appears all at once – in full flower – the emergence of duetting, like its evolution, is marked by the gradual assembly of components. Chief among these are empathy and social intelligence.

In the first chapter we saw that day-old females looked longer at the face of a live female than at an animated mechanical object, male newborns displaying the opposite bias. This orientation to personal attributes continues throughout the lives of females. So does empathy. Early in the second year of life, infants express concern when their mother is sad or distressed – more for her than a stranger – and females take the lead here too. In fact, the greater experience of empathy that is displayed by females in their infancy never stops at any later point in life.[86]

While 2- and 3-year-old infants are still exploring ways to put words together to form sentences, girls already display a preference for *affiliative* speech, which is used to establish or maintain connections with others, over the *self-assertive* commands, criticisms, and disagreements that are favored by boys.[87] This suggests that it cannot be the case that one first acquires language, and then learns how to use it.

There are sex differences in children's nonverbal games, too – not only their riddles and jokes – and these also begin early. It has been noted that girls' games frequently involve turn taking in ordered sequences, and coordinated choral activity with heavy use of rhymes and songs. The groups are often intimate, with just two or three girls playing, and these tend to break up when disputes arise.[88]

In the mid-1970s, Margaret Brady carried out a study of the handclapping, singing, and dancing games played by 7- to 10-year-old girls of varying ethnicity. The girls clapped in rhythm as they sang. This, wrote Brady, created "a rhythmic bond, the fusion of the group into a single cooperative unit." She was impressed that at age 8 the girls were "learning, through play, the significance of group solidarity."[89]

Eight years may seem early, but it is just in the nick of time. By adolescence, which begins about two years later in girls, solidarity is valued as never before. In research carried out on 10- to 14-year-old girls, Donna Eder found that some girls in her sample told stories in such perfect mutuality that they, like the Inuit and Ainu women in their throat singing, had become too collaborative for a single narrator to be discerned.[90] This collaborative style of talk, Eder concluded, reflects female adolescents' "general concern with building solidarity among friends and group members."[91]

In studies of over two thousand adolescents in Finland, Israel, Italy, Poland, and Spain, girls have been found to aggress indirectly, largely through gossip, whereas the boys tended to aggress directly, largely through physical means.[92] Graphs indicate that this verbal difference between the sexes begins to emerge at 8 years of age, is first exhibited reliably at 11, and continues through adolescence into adulthood.[93] The benefits are clear. Indirectness works – girls really can be socially and psychologic- ally injured by gossip – and the perpetrator frequently gets off scot-free. A few years ago, a study of 13-year-old girls reported that victims were aware of aggressors' actions only about 10 percent of the time.[94]

Even when adolescent girls face their rivals directly, they are far more likely than boys to aggress *silently.* This they do by glancing, staring, ignoring, and making faces, as well as through vocal and verbal acts, such as using a snide tone of voice and sarcastic comments.[95]

I'm me and you're not: why men do not duet

There is nothing in the topic of conversations that is special, according to our continuing authority on the subject, Robert Louis Stevenson. In fact, he said there are only a few subjects that are "truly talkable." More than half, he suggested, could be "reduced to three: that I am I, that you are you, and that there are other people dimly understood to be not quite the same as either." He could only have been thinking of men, for they require that their own contributions – and their identity – be kept strictly separate from those of everyone else. How can a man be heroic if he shares the credit with others? How can he be in control if others insist on merging with him?[96]

As we have seen, men cherish their autonomy. They must maintain some distance from others if they are to remain free to act as they wish. But there is no way that they will create this distance and then, in their conversations – the prime place for establishment of personal identity – turn around and jointly negotiate shared meaning with others, or disclose their most closely held secrets. In Chapter 5, we saw that, historically, men have had a morbid fear that intimate confessions and sexual inadequacies would be broadcast by gossipy wives and lovers. By their own admission, the reason that men avoid self-disclosure, according to Lawrence Rosenfeld, is: "If I disclose to you I might project an image I do not want to, which could make me look bad and cause me to lose control over you. This might go so far as to affect relationships I have with people other than you." The reason that men resist self-disclosure, according to Rosenfeld, is that this enables them to maintain control.[97]

Men's reactions to issues surrounding personal privacy tend to confirm this attitude. In *Eavesdropping*, I have written about men's near-paranoid fear that some unauthorized person might see them watching television or taking out the garbage. In their landmark article on "The right to privacy" published in 1890, Richard Warren and Louis Brandeis wrote about the right of a private individual "to prevent his public portraiture."[98] Not all men fancy themselves "painters of life," to use Baudelaire's phrase, but they certainly take themselves to be the best, if not the sole, painter of their own life, and they are not about to hand the brush to someone else.

Testosterone: an anti-duetting hormone?

Duets, by definition, involve an honest exchange of emotion and intimate experience. If a duetting relationship turns sour, this "material" can be used to threaten or weaken the person that supplied it. This, as we have discussed, is not something that would naturally appeal to men. But reasons why men do not duet need not be framed in strictly social and psychological terms. Recently it was found that experimental administration of testosterone decreases trust in women who are normally inclined to give trust easily. The authors suggested that this effect occurred because testosterone normally increases competition, boosting the value of social vigilance. This shows up as a reduction in trust. From other work (cited by the authors), it appears that the relevant mechanism involves two inter-connected areas of the brain, the amygdala and the orbitofrontal cortex.[99] Although more research is needed, it is beginning to appear that the reason why men don't duet has a physiological as well as a psychological answer.

~

When women got in trouble for scolding and other forms of public aggression, they took steps to avoid the risk of direct confrontation. There was no real sacrifice here, since their conflict talk had never really qualified as a display. When social attacks became less threatening, and victims' levels of arousal and provocation fell, an alternative that had long been in the queue took a step forward.

Unlike men, who needed to continually hone their bluffing and posturing skills, ever on the look out for new ways of engaging without enraging, women went more deeply social. The "choice," if we can call it that, was an easy one. For women had long been predisposed by evolutionary events to operate socially, through the services of others. But indirect action posed its own challenges. Women could not devise a strategy without a social map of sorts, one that identified their rival's friends and enemies. They also needed to know the limits on what their own friends could be expected to do to help. If the "plaintiff" wished to recruit allies from her own ranks, these women would have to be brought on board. It would help if she had good social and verbal skills, and knew how to use them to convert acquaintances to friends, and persuade friends to become allies.

In evolution, the heavy lifting ended long ago. Important bequests – empathy, emotional sensitivity, and social intelligence – are now envisaged by the human genome. Given a typically supportive environment, they will develop along with other cognitive mechanisms, facilitating effective inter-action and cooperation in modern adult women. In the next chapter, I will propose that these communal ways of meeting life's challenges, when blended with men's natural preference for individualism and agency, provide the human sexes with significant opportunities to collaborate.

8   Collaboration in language and in life

A great deal has been written about the tendency of men and women to clash in their conversations due to fundamentally different ways of talking. Easily the most important of these writings are Deborah Tannen's *That's not what I meant!* and *You just don't understand.* These books offer insight and, potentially, relief to couples who are failing in their efforts to understand each other.

I do wonder, however, if such books leave us with an impression that the world – certainly the marital world – would be better off if men and women had the *same* speaking style. This impression would seem to follow from the central premise. If members of the sexes have different ways of speaking, and this gets them into trouble, why not work out a single way of speaking – one that puts everyone on the same wavelength? Perhaps it would be best if men and women inhabited the same planet, one that lies halfway between Venus and Mars.

Not for external use

In our own species, many of men's most cherished behaviors appear pre-set to produce adaptive reactions *in other men.* Women are also naturally disposed to act in ways that are easily and appropriately interpreted *by other women.* Men joke with friends, taunt opponents, denigrate competitors, and tell boastful stories about their heroic and masterful adventures. Women commune with friends, divulging secrets about their thoughts, feelings, and relationships while spreading the word about rivals. The stage is thus set for a problem. For when men and women converse, neither sex has a readily available verbal strategy – one that evolved particularly for this purpose. Little wonder that complaints arise. Little wonder that partners say they *just don't understand* each other.

Adopting a uni-sex style might seem like a good idea, but it could pose problems in other areas of life. For one thing, it might reduce the *benefits* of existing differences, which, after all, are not the result of some evolutionary accident. The human sexes dealt with problems differently a million years ago, and they still do. It would be odd if their distinct strategies did not suit them, and work for them. How would some compromise way of talking *serve them better*, as the men and women that they are, in achieving their individual objectives? And when they come together, and turn outwardly to face the world, would they not, as a "bi-dialectal" unit, have greater flexibility in dealing with life's challenges?

One can also question the implications of uni-sex speech for higher levels of social organization. Human societies range from individualistic, in which every individual is considered unique, to collectivist, in which all individuals are regarded as the same.[1] These social and political extremes are associated with psychological traits – individualism with autonomy, collectivism with interdependency – which are characteristic of men and women, respectively. What if men in strongly individualistic societies were forced to quit dueling, and women in highly collectivist societies stopped duetting? Would their cultures begin to gravitate toward the center of the continuum?

From a biological perspective, it would also be anomalous – and certainly maladaptive – if men and women were to adopt some neutral way of talking. Dueling provides information about the ability of men to compete with other men, to mate with women, and to support their families. Members of both sexes make important life decisions based on this information. Duetting regulates social and moral behavior, and helps women to secure the things they need without overt aggression. It is not just convenient that dueling and duetting fulfill these functions. They evolved to do so and no human group has ever existed without them.

I believe there is a more appropriate and natural way of looking at evolved differences in speaking styles. The strategies that ancestral men and women used to address environmental problems antedated the evolution of language. Before words were available, they relied on vocal noises, bodily postures, gestures, and touches to regulate each other's behavior, and to convey personal information – and, as we have seen, the two sexes used these behaviors differently. But these sights and sounds did not merely form a *collage* into which spoken language – when it became available through some independent evolutionary process – was then inserted from the outside. Rather, the ongoing activities of our ancestors were the social ecology – the *crucible* – within which spoken language originated. If the ancestral sexes were already relating and communicating differently before language – for different reasons, in different circumstances – the die was cast. They would also express themselves differently in whatever new communication systems they invented.

Sex and dominance redux

What is the nature of this crucible within which speaking styles, and human language, evolved? In the other primates, as we have seen, males compete with each other for rank and access to females. They are inclined to intimidate other males by bluffing – thumping their chests or roaring – and by fighting. Females are more likely to huddle together, and to groom each other. *But neither sex has a clear-cut strategy for dealing with members of the opposite sex.*

We see this in "consortships," in which a male chimpanzee induces a female to run away with him in order to copulate without arousing sexual competitors. How does the male communicate his wishes? Perhaps the female is willing to be wooed? After all, females do like males who groom or share food with them. But what the male does is gaze at the female, shake branches, and rock back and forth – sometimes all of these. If unsuccessful, he does a very male thing. He beats her up.

Elements of the original crucible can still be witnessed in our own species today. In a study carried out in the Netherlands a few years ago, men and women were asked to interact with a confederate who assumed the role of a subordinate. As expected, the women displayed affiliative tendencies and the men behaved dominantly. The interesting thing is *how* they did so. Both classes of social response were conveyed in the content and style of their speech – no great surprise there – but affiliation and dominance were also expressed in a number of *nonverbal* behaviors, including facial activity, bodily postures, and movements of the hands.[2] As we know from other research, these things occur in humans even when they are not speaking, and they are important elements in the displays of species that cannot speak, including ones that resemble early humans.[3]

My point? If our prelinguistic ancestors were already responding to social challenges by strutting, posturing, and gesturing dominantly, or by cowering in submission, it would have been difficult for them, when they acquired some rudimentary level of language, to adopt an emotionally neutral way of talking in the same situations, and there would have been no reason to do so. That is, the interaction frames of our early human ancestors – replete with physical and vocal acts of threat, appeasement, deference, aggression, and reconciliation – would necessarily have influenced the verbal styles that arose within the same frames. Since dominance and submission are the stock and trade of our competitive species, it is not surprising that some decidedly agonistic and conciliatory ways of talking evolved.

If human language is built the way *it is* because the designers, the ancient human architects, were built the way that *they were* – with the goals and strategies that they had – then the shape of language would have been formed around these innately scripted preferences and priorities. But how did this happen? How did the human sexes' ways of relating and interacting affect the design of spoken language? In previous sections we looked at things that language, as a communicative tool, has done for men and women. Here I will ask what men and women did for language.

Separate paths

Historically, women devoted a great deal of their resources to the gestation and birth of each child, and to its subsequent care, and were limited to a few offspring in their reproductive lifetime. Men, on the other hand, invested little or nothing in the production and care of offspring, and enjoyed an extended period of fecundity. With such a glaring disparity, the sexes did exactly what one would expect. The men competed for mating opportunities – some got hundreds, others none – and the women carefully evaluated their suitors in order to weed out substandard quality fathers and mates.

Traits that gave males a competitive advantage were selected and thereby found their way into the genes of succeeding generations. One such trait was size. In evolution, a significant size and strength disparity gave males an advantage over females, just as larger males were able to dominate smaller ones. Large males also enjoyed preferential access to females. With sex and dominance playing such a powerful role in human evolution, and continuing to do so today, some of the lexical tendencies noted by Robin Lakoff in the first chapter begin to look rather trivial. What can it possibly signify that men use fewer intensifiers like "*so* wonderful" and unusual color terms like "magenta"?

This is not to suggest that there is *no* biology at work in these cases. Even these seemingly trivial things may reflect basic sex differences in emotional experience and sensitivity to color.[4] Less trivially, women's tendency to hedge assertions and end statements with a rising pitch imply a submissive stance, as evolutionary theory would predict. But even while linguists were documenting these "gendered" differences in words and pitches, there were larger fish waiting to be fried. Below the surface were critical concerns with mating and status – things that really *mattered* to individuals, and to the species – and these things had a way of bubbling up when men and women spoke.

This, of course, is what we have pursued here as we worked our way from the existence of rituals, which reveal the purity and depth of our dispositions to duel and duet, to the evolution and development of these different ways of addressing life problems. But where is all this leading us? What are the implications for the ways that men and women talk to each other today?

Monogamous speech?

If evolution shaped men's speech to men, and women's speech to women, there is little indication that evolution also hammered out an *additional* strategy that inter-sexual partners would use when talking *with each other*. This "oversight" makes sense. Once men and women entered into a stable relationship, and produced offspring, what would have been the *reproductive* need for communication in the future? What was the strategic need for "monogamous speech"?

Outside of romantic and marital relationships, it is not even clear that modern men and women seek out members of the opposite sex for friendships.[5] When men are asked to name their best friends, they come up with a list of men, and women list women.[6] In fact, many books have been written on whether men and women are even *able to be friends* outside of marriage.

In same-sex friendships, participants are free to use the verbal style with which they feel most comfortable. No vocal, lexical, or topical accommodations are necessary. Insults and jokes need not be edited or suppressed. Indirect statements need not be issued more bluntly or assertively. Neither sex must feign interest in topics of far greater concern to the other.

Many of men's most cherished speech habits appear pre-set to produce adaptive reactions *in other men*. Women are also naturally disposed to act in ways that are easily and appropriately interpreted *by other women*. Men joke with friends, challenge opponents, denigrate competitors, and tell boastful stories about their heroic and masterful adventures. Women commune with friends, divulging secrets about their thoughts, feelings, and relationships while spreading the word about rivals and out-group intruders. Each of us automatically uses the vocal and verbal style that is most readily available by virtue of our genetic constitution as men and women. Duels and duets are the "default" mode of speaking for men and women. Our natural tendency is to "revert to" these ways of speaking.

Two psychologists described a workshop that they conducted for men and women in relationships. The workshop began with an introductory session in which all members were present. Then the group broke up into male and female subgroups in order to complete a questionnaire. "Once the men and women split up," the authors commented, "the whole atmosphere changed. What a relief, for each gender to be away from the other! They loved it! The men immediately shook hands and each started writing down his own individual answers; the women started talking noisily in small groups, with a lot of laugher and waving of hands."[7]

Neither sex talks in the default mode exclusively, of course, for reasons that should be obvious. Men are not always intent on fortifying their status or facing down rivals, nor do women constantly seek to connect with others, or to rally support from their friends. When released from these needs, men and women are obviously able to drift into other ways of relating and speaking, and they often do.

The verbal clashes that have been documented so persuasively begin to make sense in this context. The men are not merely boorish and the women hypersensitive. Each sex is *treating* – interacting with, reacting to, *and* talking to – members of the opposite sex as though they belonged to the same sex. The men are talking to women *as though they were men*, and the women are talking to men *as though they were women*. In their conversations, they undoubtedly modulate their same-sex speaking strategies to some degree, but they have no third way of talking that is equally available to them in the social contexts in which verbal clashes occur.

When a man speaks to a woman in a dominant way, leaving her little room to get in a word edgewise, she wonders if the man cares at all about her feelings, or values her opinions. When a woman, speaking to a man, uses tentative and indirect phrasing, and oblique suggestions, the man wonders why, if she has something to say, she doesn't just say it. When conversations fail, the surprise – and the disappointment – can be greater in those who are unaware that each sex evolved to talk differently.

How, then, are we to view Deborah Tannen's wonderful books? That males and females do not acquire a satisfactory way of talking to each other by the time they reach adulthood merely makes my point. A third verbal style does not exist, because evolution failed to provide it. So self-help books are needed to close the gap created when cultures – or at least a few of the thousands of cultures in the world – have conditioned people to expect behaviors that evolution had not adequately provisioned.

One might think that even without monogamous speech, the sexes could still adopt some "gender-appropriate" way of talking when they encounter a member of the opposite sex. This might seem to be a simple thing to do. When adults interact with a young child, they typically use simpler vocabulary, and may speak more slowly than usual, or in a higher pitch. Research journals carry countless articles about this deeply entrenched tendency. Most of us also talk differently when addressing foreigners with a heavy accent, and elderly people whom we suppose may be hard of hearing or muddled. No one ever taught us to do these things. Indeed, many people are surprised to learn that they make these adjustments. But when a man sees a woman, he does not immediately begin to whisper intimate confessions, nor does she put up her verbal dukes.

When couples do "learn" to talk to each other, *learning* is indeed the process involved. But let's not go overboard here. There is nothing *cultural* about this learning, at least in the sense that there is something "out there" that can be imported from the environment. If they're lucky, men and women in long-term relationships learn what they must do to communicate with one another in a satisfying way. But this is no different in principle from learning about any other special sensitivities or requirements that either party might bring into the partnership, including personal things like an inability to trust or being afraid of the dark. There is no reason to believe that if Couple A learns to converse with each other in a satisfying manner, it will spread to others automatically, like truly cultural phenomena, facilitating similar adjustments in Couples B and C.

Clashing and meshing

Much has been written about the verbal styles that cause men and women to *clash* in their conversations. In stable relationships, men and women can come to communicate more smoothly – that is, do less clashing – merely by recognizing that their own natural tendency is likely to be rather different from the natural tendency of their partner. One can say to the other: "You are dueling, which is often okay, but right now I need to duet." Or: "I know you would like to discuss this in greater detail, but right now I just need a yes or a no." But the differences that can lead to clashing also enable *meshing*.

The human sexes come equipped with differing sets of abilities, and there is plenty of room – and need – for both. Partnerships are collaborations. They work best when each party has something different to contribute. In a climate of mutual understanding and respect, two people are potentially stronger for their differences, not weaker. Evolution contributed to our verbal clashes but it also gave us important opportunities to mesh.

I believe that innately supported sex differences in verbal behavior facilitate effective collaboration in modernity, and may even have contributed, in evolutionary history, to the complex system of communication that ultimately became human language. To get a sense of how men and women might have collaborated, imagine a world in which everyone behaved identically. Life would be boring, to be sure, but it would also be inefficient. We humans thrive on group action. This requires cooperation, which presupposes some level of familiarity and trust, but we also need to collaborate. More is required, here, than congeniality and a chance to work together. Collaboration cannot take place unless each of the participants *brings something to the collaboration* – some unique knowledge or ability or skill, something different.

Some years ago, corporations began to set up teams. The assumption was that these teams would outperform the same individuals working independently *if* the team members had different kinds of knowledge and talent *and* they pooled it. The team principle makes sense. In *Cognition in the wild*, Edwin Hutchins pointed out that sailing a naval vessel is only possible because the crew has different abilities and the disposition to share them in a timely fashion.[8]

Historically, collaboration was made easier, not harder, when design differences were built into the sexes. There are no indications that men and women fought over who "got to" go hunting and who was "relegated" to gathering. Men, being physically larger and stronger than women, did the hunting because this activity required size and strength. It was also dangerous, and men who enjoyed risky activities undoubtedly were drawn to that aspect of hunting, too. Through the meat they brought back to camp, everyone obtained large amounts of iron, protein, and other nutrients – and calories – that were required by their bodies and massive human brains.[9]

Hunting also gave groups an important social opportunity. Men could use hunting to display their fitness. The hunter who acquired the most meat was clearly an exceptional individual – strong, swift, and intelligent – and if he brought it back to camp for distribution, he would also be considered generous or even altruistic. What male hunting party could afford to go off without him? What woman could ignore the potential benefits that would accrue to her and any children if she chose to mate with him?[10]

A balanced diet requires fruit and vegetables, too. Except in extreme conditions, some sort of plant life could usually be found near the camp, without extensive and risky excursions, and women collected it. Meat, on the other hand, has a mind of its own. It fights back, and roams, and is not always available.

One could say, well, that was then, this is now; surely we have made some progress since our ancestors turned from hunting and gathering to agriculture. But evolution is conservative. As research regularly demonstrates, *then is now too*. Over evolutionary time, the tasks that our ancestors divided up on sexual grounds produced different cognitive abilities in modern males and females. For example, on visual performance tasks administered in a number of different cultures, men out-perform women on tests that are sensitive to aiming and tracking ability, as needed for hunting, and women surpass men on tests of spatial memory, as needed for gathering.[11]

Even in modernity, men and women's gathering patterns are predictable on evolutionary grounds, and they too may be complementary. According to a recent study, male and female residents of Tlaxcala, in central Mexico, forage for mushrooms in a complementary way. In the study, men and women were taken to a location and asked, basically, to go get mushrooms. In hunter-like fashion, the men explored more distant areas, and ascended higher terrain – expending more energy in order to do so – but came back with the same amount of mushroom (by weight) as the women, who chose to explore more local territory. The sexes went about gathering in rather different ways, but their nutritional harvest was the same.[12]

It is not hard to find examples of complementarity in everyday life, of one person zigging when another is zagging. Efficiency is an important benefit but it is not the only one. Complementarity also has social and psychological benefits, and it makes sense that it would. If, in evolution, certain behaviors were selected because they improved reproductive success, the enabling mechanisms are likely to be available to us today, too, prompting us to undertake similar actions without *knowing* that, or why, we should do so. I suggest that complementarity, as a disposition, is the psychological mechanism that supports collaboration and the felt need to mesh.

Several years ago, a study was done that supports this. It began with an observation, one that is already familiar to us here:

people who expand their physical presence are considered dominant. Individuals who physically constrict tend to be perceived as subordinate or submissive. The authors reasoned that others, viewing such displays, have two choices. The first is that they might mimic the acts. There are indications that mimicry is likely when affiliation is the primary goal of the participants. The alternative is that the participants would behave in a complementary way, puffing themselves up when around constricted individuals, and shrinking when others expand their physical presence – in chimpanzees evidently the latter maneuver seems to avert aggression.[13] In the experiment, young adults were asked to interact with an experiment assistant who had been instructed to assume an expanded or dominant posture, or a constricted or submissive posture. It was found that the subjects responded in a complementary way, assuming a posture that was the opposite of the assistant's posture. In the less frequent cases where there was a postural match, the subjects experienced some discomfort, and reported that the assistant seemed less "likeable."[14] In later work, participants were told that they would be expected to work with the assistant, and the complementarity effect was even larger.[15]

Others have found that when work groups are made up of people with different personalities – not just different abilities – they operate more efficiently, and offer more enjoyment to the participants, than groups in which the members are similar in personality. This provides some evidence for the idea that "opposites attract," at least in the context of a working relationship.[16]

Collaborating on language

There is something highly natural about complementarity. It goes back millions of years, and it is obviously very useful to species that live in groups. Complementarity would seem to facilitate collaborative action. Our evolutionary ancestors split up hunting and infant care on sexual grounds, as the other primates do. What about the construction of language? Did men and women (unconsciously) divide this up too?

I think it is likely that ancestral men and women unwittingly brought their disparate abilities into the construction of this new and complex form of human communication. The idea is so intuitively appealing that one wonders how our evolutionary ancestors could have avoided doing so. For our male and female ancestors were already engaged in chest-thumping duels and mutual-grooming duets when more complex forms of social communication arose. The question is: *how* did the sex-specific interaction patterns of our evolutionary ancestors influence language and speech? My speculation is that men and women made different contributions to two broadly different areas of linguistic evolution. One area is the complexity of utterances at all levels, from sounds to words and sentences. The other area is the propagation of new linguistic material.

Vocal and verbal ornamentation

How much grammar does it take to build a boat, or to sail one? It is an odd question, to be sure, but it has been raised by serious scholars, ones who see few reasons why modern languages should be so *ornate* or grammatically complex.[17] Linguists have claimed that before fully fledged language evolved, our ancestors worked out the ability to use words, ordered in simple ways, to express their basic needs, and this obviously worked for them.[18] It may even have been enough to design and build a boat.

So why did our ancestors push past this level of complexity? The skeptics would seem to have a point, at least if the only reason for complexity is transmission of thought that is equally complex. But there are two reasons to believe that the skeptics are wrong. For one thing, even before language became available survival pressures would have ramped up pre-existing levels of social complexity, as larger and larger groups of individuals were forced to compete in increasingly fierce contests for the same finite supply of precious resources. If our ancestors began to compete vocally, either by adding new elements to their repertoire, or by uttering familiar elements in novel sequences, communication systems would have diversified. Natural selection for vocal control would have laid the groundwork for complexity at other levels, too, expanding a host of attention, perception, and storage systems, thus preparing the human brain to deal with utterances that would eventually approach the rate, duration, and intricacy of sentences in modern languages.

The other reason relates to sexual selection. In the first chapter we saw that female birds prefer males that sing complex songs, and that male impresarios are usually more healthy and virile than males who lack "a way with songs." In early stages of linguistic evolution, it is reasonable to speculate that human males who vocalized extravagantly were able to command attention, an important step on the ladder to social and sexual success. My claim here is that selection for vocal extravagance expanded the capacity to control longer sequences of phonetic material and to process material of this length and complexity.

Duels would have done something to hike up the level of complexity, for these contests force men to top each other in all things "speechy," from wit to originality. Effective dueling requires the ability to walk a verbal tightrope, to say something that is almost, but not quite, true; to deliver an insult in a way that scratches but stops short of puncturing.

Women played an evaluative role, so they deserve some of the credit for men's contributions to complexity. But what about women's own expressive contributions? As we have seen, female primates take the lead when it comes to the production of social vocalizations, which are rather more differentiated, from an articulatory standpoint, than the grunts and barks that are more nearly the province of males.

Females almost certainly made contributions at higher levels too. We know that their biological roles have required them to develop and to operate within social relationships. The utterances needed to manage entangling alliances can be no less complex than the relationships they are meant to manage. Recall that if a woman is to operate indirectly, she must rally friends to her cause or point of view without accidentally turning them against her. This, too, is tricky. It also requires a judicious use of language.

I realize that our ancestors, in the popular conception, sat around campfires and said things no more engaging than "Where food?" and "Fire hot." But in actuality the Kung hunter-gatherers spend most of their time talking about each other. They use speech to police their food-sharing networks, which are based on mutual reciprocity.[19] Much of the time that they are not actually looking for food is devoted to discussions of "who had what and did or did not give it to whom."[20] One anthropologist said that Kung talk centers on "accusations of improper meat distribution, improper gift exchange ... laziness, and stinginess."[21]

Precision is required here. Picking up on the food-sharing topic, Steven Pinker and Paul Bloom wrote, "It makes a difference whether you understand me as saying that if you give me some of your fruit I will share meat that I will get, or that you should give me some fruit because I shared meat that I got, or that if you don't give me some fruit I will take back that meat that I got."[22] In order to communicate, people have to manipulate utterances that are as complex as their mental representations of those relationships.

How, then, do we add up the contributions of the sexes to linguistic complexity? Men, in their dueling, get some of the credit for lexical ingenuity. Women, in their discussions of complex social relationships, get some of the credit for contributions at the level of narratives and meaningful discourse.

Spreading the word

There is a second broad area where the sexes would have played differing roles in the construction of language. When men were busily advertising *themselves* – their verbal plumage – across their broad social networks, they were also showing off their knowledge of *language*. That means, in effect, that they were unintentionally hawking this new medium, strictly for self-serving purposes. Men's need to display their verbal skills, and deeper biological wares, would surely have played a key role in the evolution of a system that would only work if everyone knew it.

Let's look at social factors. Even when they remain in place, men prefer larger to smaller groups, public to private places, and louder to softer vocalizations. Women, being less likely to show off, clown around, hurl insults, order people around, tell stories, or pontificate, would have done less to advertise speech and language.

When it comes to spreading the word, the advantage goes to those who wield the most power and influence, and these individuals are usually the men. They are the more strongly inclined to broadcast their behaviors, as we have seen, and they have more acquaintanceships and superficial friendships than women.[23] Historically, men also enjoyed greater mobility than women, and ranged farther from home. They would have seen and interacted with more people in the course of a day.

Andrew Fyfe's account of the mobility of men and women in New Guinea is typical. He found that men tended to disperse across greater ranges than women. "At maturity," he wrote, "men were expected to demonstrate some facility for securing ties in other communities and a man's social worth was sometimes measured according to the number and value of these allegiances." This mobility had predictable effects on the spread of culture through space. The important men, Fyfe reported, "conveyed ideas and knowledge across social boundaries that most other members of their communities rarely if ever crossed."[24] Others working in the same area found that the women, by contrast, led a far less expansive existence. In one group, the majority of women "never travelled further than a day's walk from their local ... valley [while] the majority of men have travelled many times to areas at least four or five days' walk away." Women's social networks were made up mainly of relatives.[25]

From a generational perspective, the role of men in broadcasting language would have been a horizontal one for the most part, words, phrases, and other material passing from adults to adults; but this is not the only type of diffusion that is needed to propagate and change languages. In fact, when it comes to the establishment of a native language, women – indisputably – have the first crack at the young. We know this because the learning of prosody, the rhythm of language, occurs prenatally, when the fetus is able to hear the mother's voice but not the father's.[26] Once, Anthony De Casper, a pioneer in this research, suggested that the term "mother tongue" was well chosen for that reason. But preferential modeling rights continue after birth. Everything we can reconstruct about life in the Pleistocene, and know about the infant stage of development in ancient and modern humans, suggests that mothers, sisters, and grandmothers would have tended to the young round-the-clock for the first several years of life, when the foundations of language were being laid. These women would have spent far more time talking to infants than men did.[27]

Of course, women do not merely display their knowledge of language when they talk to children. They also tell them stories. In many traditional societies there is a designated storyteller – almost invariably a man – but women tell stories to other women too – ancient paintings and photographs depict them doing so – and they are typically the tellers of children's stories, providing morality and wisdom along with language.

Tongue and groove

I have suggested that through their disparate ways of communicating the sexes unconsciously divided up the evolutionary linguistic labor, with social and genetic sharing processes blending their individual contributions into a broadly based faculty of language.[28]

In describing actions that are socially complementary, I have described ones that are physically *opposite*. But the unconscious tendency to shrink when another expands, and vice versa, is socially and functionally *harmonious*. Complementarity lays the groundwork for an effective working relationship.

This reminds me of tongue and groove joints that hold two pieces of wood together. In these joints, the pieces that form the tongue and the groove are *exactly* the opposite. In every place where one piece goes in, the other goes out. But it is in this oppositeness that their strength resides. Tongue and groove joints require no glue, and they do not weaken in time.

I think, in significant ways, the sexes work like tongue and groove joints. It is in our design. The ways we men and women present our selves, treat others, and talk, are all reflections of this basic design. So, why not celebrate it, and do what we can to benefit from it? In an article titled "Feminist biologies," Celeste Condit suggested that individuals should select "people with masculine styles when they perceive that a dominance-seeking individual is desirable, and they should select people with feminine styles when they perceive the need to maintain relations and distribute resources among mutually interested parties."[29]

In *The evolution of sex*, published over a century ago, Scottish naturalists Patrick Geddes and John Arthur Thompson sensed the mutualism – possibly even the magnificence – of men and women. "The two sexes are complementary and mutually dependent," they wrote. "Each is higher in its own way..."[30]

Notes to chapters

Chapter 1

1 Gray 1992; McElvaine 2001
2 Mulac *et al.* 1986
3 Maccoby 1990; Maltz and Borker 1983
4 Tannen 1990, p. 77
5 See a review of such "mini-pragmatic" developments in Locke 1993
6 Eckel *et al.* 2008
7 Philips 1980
8 Daly and Wilson 1988, p. 153
9 Locke 2009, 2010a, in press; Locke and Bogin 2006
10 Jespersen 1922, p. 237
11 Frazer 1959, p. 190
12 Eckel *et al.* 2008
13 Darwin, quoted in Piggott 1972, p. 949
14 Coates 1996; 2003, p. 147
15 Tannen 1990, p. 140
16 Tannen 1990, p. 140
17 Anderson *et al.* 1992; Furnham and Baguma 1994
18 Sobal and Stunkard 1989
19 Nelson and Morrison 2005, p. 172
20 Gould and Marler 1987
21 Berenbaum *et al.* 2008; Terman and Miles 1936
22 Hines *et al.* 2002, cited by Berenbaum *et al.* 2008; Berenbaum and Hines 1992
23 Alexander 2006
24 Draper and Harpending 1982
25 Connellan *et al.* 2000; if such early differences were to increase with development, this would not necessarily represent non-genetic factors (e.g. Byrd-Craven and Geary 2007).
26 If sex differences do increase with age, however, this is not necessarily attributable to cultural learning, as Byrd-Craven and Geary (2007) and others have pointed out.

27 Lytton and Romney 1991
28 Hayes 1962 (also see Bouchard and Loehlin 2001; Johnson 2009)
29 Rudman and Glick 2008
30 Alexander and Hines 2002
31 Alexander 2003
32 Larry Summers, Remarks given at the Conference on Diversifying the Science and Engineering Workforce, January 14, 2005
33 Troemel-Ploetz 1991
34 Buss and Reeve 2003; DeBruine 2009
35 Dunbar 1993; Dunbar 2007a; Dunbar and Shultz 2007
36 Tomaszycki *et al.* 2001
37 Brockelman and Schilling 1984; Geissmann 1984
38 Brockelman and Schilling 1984, p. 634
39 Owren *et al.* 1993

Chapter 2

1 Clover 1980, p. 451
2 Parks 1990, p. 6
3 Clover 1980
4 Clover 1980
5 Harris 1979; also see Clover 1980
6 Russom 1978, p. 11
7 Clover 1980, p. 445
8 Harris 1979
9 Russom 1978, quotations of Eystein and Sigurd from p. 11
10 Lönnroth 1979; Harris 1979
11 Parks 1990, p. 24
12 Parks 1990, p. 24
13 Huxley 1966a, p. 250
14 Issa and Edwards 2006; also see Huxley 1966b; Moynihan 1998
15 Cox and Le Boeuf 1977; Semple 1998
16 Frevert 1995; Spierenburg 1998; Nye 1993
17 Wilson 1988
18 Andrew 1980, p. 411
19 Shoemaker 2004, p. 195

20 Alcohol contributed to many militant duels (e.g. Hopton 2007; Johnson and Lipsett-Rivera 1998).
21 Gallant 2000
22 Gallant 2000; Pitt-Rivers 1966; Wyatt-Brown 1982
23 Reproduced in Peltonen 2003, p. 121; also see Andrew 1980; Baldick 1965
24 Miller 1993, p. 116
25 Miller 1993
26 Shoemaker 2004
27 Gallant 2000; in some societies, the same has been true of verbal dueling. In his description of poetic duels in Lebanon, Adnan Haydar wrote that if famed poets turned down a request to duel, they would "suffer loss of prestige among their critical public" (1989, p. 192).
28 Parks 1990, p. 13
29 Nisbett and Cohen 1996
30 Fischer 1989, p. 690
31 Nisbett and Cohen 1996
32 Andrew 1980, p. 419
33 Endler and Bassolo 1998; Ryan 1990
34 Nye 1993, p. 186 (also see pp. 200–10)
35 Baldick 1965, p. 32
36 Spierenburg 1998, p. 117; also see Hopton 2007
37 Parks 1990
38 von Oettingen, quoted in McAleer 1994, p. 171; also see Baldick 1965; McAleer 1994; Nye 1993
39 Shoemaker 2004, p. 188
40 Shoemaker 2004
41 Andrew 1980
42 Gowing 1996
43 Ziv 1981; also see Mio and Graesser 1991; O'Connell 1960
44 Hill and Öttchen 1995
45 Progovac and Locke 2009
46 Samarin 1969
47 Radcliffe-Brown 1965, p. 90
48 Radcliffe-Brown 1965, p. 91
49 Dollard 1939, p. 4
50 Jones and Yarbrough 1985, p. 41
51 Pagliai 2009

52 Sung duels: Bowen 1989; sung poetic duels: Caraveli 1985; Herndon and McLeod 1980; Mathias 1976

53 Mathias 1976, p. 491

54 Elliott 1960; Mirsky 1937

55 Brenneis and Padarath 1975; Herndon and McLeod 1980; Hoebel 1964; McLean 1965; Mirsky 1937; Solomon 1994; Travassos 2000; Weyer 1932

56 Hoebel 1964, p. 93

57 Doukanari 1997

58 Haydar 1989

59 Foley 2007

60 Sowayan 1989, pp. 153–54

61 Ray 2004

62 Eliasoph, 1998, pp. 11–12, quoted in Ray 2004, p. 6

63 Ray 2004, pp. 12–13

64 Mickle 1977, p. 339

65 Mickel 1977, p. 342

66 Ryon 1995, p. 218

67 Dandy 1991, p. 87

68 Brown 1990, p. 354

69 Ayoub and Barnett 1965; Bronner 1978

70 Ayoub and Barnett 1965, p. 338

71 Bronner 1978

72 Tetreault 2010

73 Brown 1990, p. 354

74 Abrahams 1989; Labov 1972; Labov 1973

75 Anderson 1990, p. 115

76 Also see Edwards and Sienkowitz 1990; Peek 1981

77 For examples, see Abrahams 1970a, b; Haydar 1989; Sowayan 1989

78 Manning, 1973, p. 63

79 LeMasters 1975, p. 140

80 Decapua and Boxer 1999, p. 19

81 Laughter, according to a recent analysis, is capable of "dampening friction and violent competition between individuals" (Gervais and Wilson 2005, p. 403).

82 Speer 1985, p. 30, italics mine

83 Kulick 1993, p. 513

84 William Sheppard (or Shepherd) (1675). *A Grand Abridgment of the Common and Statute Law of England*. London.
85 Capp 2003, pp. 199, 257
86 Fairly precise statistics over a period of several centuries may be found in McIntosh (1998).
87 Gowing 1996; Leneman 2000
88 Gowing 1996, p. 2
89 Thomas 1959
90 Schuster 1983, p. 324
91 Buss *et al.* 1992; Sagarin *et al.* 2003
92 Burbank 1987
93 Winstanley 1678, p. 1
94 Friedley and Manchester 1985
95 Manchester and Friedley 2003, p. 25
96 Stepp and Gardner 2001
97 Manchester and Friedley 2003
98 Manchester and Friedley 2003, p. 32
99 Bruschke and Johnson 1994; Friedley and Manchester 1987
100 Bruschke and Johnson 1994, p. 7
101 Stepp 1997, p. 182
102 Meade 1973
103 Burgoon 1975, p. 4
104 Stein *et al.* 1996
105 Women among humorists. *New York Times Saturday Review*, January 20, 1900, p. 40.
106 Sheppard 1986
107 Apte 1985
108 Apte 1985
109 Zillmann and Stocking 1976

Chapter 3

1 Abrahams 1970b, pp. 145–46
2 Abrahams 1970b, p. 146
3 Bauman 1986
4 Reay 1959, p. 118
5 Malinowski 1922, p. 432
6 Read 1954, p. 6

7 Holmes 1969, p. 344

8 Salmond 1975, p. 50

9 Santos-Granero 1991, p. 301

10 Seeger 1981, pp. 85, 186

11 Dabbs and Ruback 1984; Kendon and Cook 1969; Mulac 1989

12 Bass 1949; Hayes and Meltzer 1972; Mullen *et al.* 1989; Sorrentino and Boutillier 1975

13 Questions continue as to whether other species, lacking language as they do, have or even can have a culture (Laland and Galen 2009).

14 Hale 1994

15 Hale 1994

16 Wilbert 1977

17 Faris 1966, 1972

18 Bauman 1972, pp. 333, 334

19 Bauman 1972, p. 337

20 Andersson 1994

21 Kruger *et al.* 2003

22 Wachtmeister and Enquist 1999

23 Abrahams and Gay 1975; Anderson 1990; Dandy 1991; Smitherman 1977

24 Anderson 1990, pp. 114, 115

25 Dandy 1991, pp. 76–77

26 Hannerz 1969, p. 84

27 Folb 1980, pp. 91, 101

28 Janus *et al.* 1978; Sheppard 1985

29 Ziv and Gadish 1989

30 Sheppard 1985, p. 190

31 Mio and Graesser 1991, p. 90

32 Turnbull 1965, p. 182

33 Apte 1985, p. 72

34 Emler 1992, p. 24

35 Coates 2003; Johnstone 1993

36 Georgakopoulou 1995, p. 463, italics mine

37 Fentress and Wickham 1992

38 Bauman 1972

39 Manguel 2006

Chapter 4

1 Tinbergen 1963
2 Bax 1981; Bax and Padmos 1983
3 Foster 1996
4 Oliveira *et al.* 2001
5 Oliveira *et al.* 1998
6 Naguib and Todt 1997; Otter *et al.* 1999; Peake *et al.* 2001
7 Leboucher and Pallot 2004; Vallet and Kreutzer 1995; I discuss eavesdropping in Locke (2010b).
8 Leboucher and Pallot 2004
9 Leboucher and Pallot 2004; Vallet and Kreutzer 1995
10 Doutrelant and McGregor 2000; Kunc *et al.* 2006; Leboucher and Pallot 2004
11 Kunc *et al.* 2006
12 Mennill *et al.* 2003
13 Cowlishaw and Dunbar 1991
14 Silk 2007
15 Based on data reported in Smith and Jungers 1997
16 Moynihan 1955, p. 248
17 Jablonski and Chaplin 1993; Livingstone 1962
18 Hauser 1993
19 Fitch and Hauser 2002
20 Kingsley 1982, 1988
21 Delgado 2006; Harris *et al.* 2006; Hewitt *et al.* 2002
22 Lewis and van Schaik 2007; Setia and van Schaik 2007; though see Mitani 1985
23 Irschick and Lailvaux 2006
24 Utami *et al.* 2002
25 Fischer *et al.* 2004; Kitchen *et al.* 2003
26 Nieuwenhuijsen and de Waal 1982
27 Hewitt *et al.* 2002
28 de Boer 2008
29 Trinkaus and Zimmerman 1982
30 Burbank 1994
31 Daly and Wilson 1988, p. 146
32 Buss and Shackleford 1997
33 Betzig 1992

34 Salzano *et al.* 1967; by contrast, women had about six children, averaging one birth every five years between the ages of 15 and 40 years.

35 Anderson 2010

36 When some men "gain more than their 'fair share' of copulations... other males are shut out entirely," wrote evolutionary psychologists David Buss and Todd Shackleford. "Such a system leads to more ferocious competition" among men (Buss and Shackleford 1997, p. 613).

37 Daly and Wilson 1988, p. 146, italics mine

38 Daly and Wilson 1988, p. 176

39 Smith and Jungers 1997

40 See Bribiescas 2008, p. 56, for relevant speculation. It is also possible, of course, that females increased in size for unrelated reasons.

41 Marsh 1978, pp. 11, 17, 28

42 Marsh *et al.* 2009; Renninger *et al.* 2004

43 Bereczkei *et al.* 1997; Davis 1990; Fisman *et al.* 2006

44 Radway 1984

45 Salmon and Symons 2001

46 Buss 1989

47 Bruckert *et al.* 2006; Dabbs and Mallinger 1999; Pedersen *et al.* 1986

48 Puts *et al.* 2006

49 Apicella *et al.* 2007

50 Wilson 1984

51 Collins 2000; Collins and Missing 2003; Feinberg *et al.* 2006; Oguchi and Kikuchi 1997; Puts *et al.* 2006

52 Feinberg *et al.* 2006; Puts 2005

53 Hughes *et al.* 2009

54 See Miller (2000) for a sexual selection-based account of verbal intelligence (and humor).

55 See Locke and Bogin 2006 for supporting evidence.

56 Deary and Der 2005; Whalley and Deary 2001

57 Arden *et al.* 2009

58 Binet 1911

59 Bale *et al.* 2006

60 Vetterli and Furedy 1997

61 Franks and Rigby 2005

62 Rosenberg and Tunney 2008

63 Marley 2002, p. 83

64 Provine 2000a, b

65 Howrigan and MacDonald 2008

66 Bressler and Balshine 2006; quote due to Bressler *et al.* 2006, p. 122

67 See, for example, Lundy *et al.* 1998

68 Ziv and Gadish 1989

69 Zillmann and Stocking 1976

70 Prokosch *et al.* 2009

71 Sell *et al.* 2010; since the men's speech consisted of phrases and sentences that were supplied by the experimenters, and read aloud, measures of language could not have influenced the women's preferences, nor could vocal pitch, which did not differ in the stronger and weaker men.

72 Wrangham and Peterson 1997; Daly and Wilson 1988

73 Mazur and Booth 1998

74 Dabbs *et al.* 2001

75 Dabbs and Ruback 1988, p. 246

76 Dabbs *et al.* 1990

77 Walter 1988, pp. 31–32

78 Dabbs *et al.* 1998, p. 91

79 Gwilliam 2009, p. 1

80 I am indebted to Barry Krengel for this anecdote.

81 Dabbs *et al.* 1998

82 Walter 1988

83 According to information provided by the American Trial Lawyers Association, membership is "limited to the Top 100 Trial Lawyers from each state ... based on superior qualifications, leadership, reputation, influence, stature, and profile in the Trial Lawyer community."

84 Almli *et al.* 2001; Eaton and Ennis 1986

85 Tremblay 2002; Tremblay 2003; Tremblay *et al.* 2004

86 Tremblay *et al.* 1999; Baillargeon *et al.* 2005; Fagot and Hagan 1985

87 Whiting and Edwards 1973

88 Björkqvist *et al.* 1994; Tremblay 2004

89 Gossen 1976
90 Wyatt 1995
91 Wyatt 1995, pp. 14–15
92 McGhee 1976, p. 180
93 Haring 1985, p. 178
94 Haring 1985, p. 178
95 Mio and Graesser 1991, pp. 96–97
96 McCloskey and Coleman 1992
97 Eder 1991; McGhee 1976
98 Apte 1985, p. 99
99 Dundes *et al.* 1970, p. 340
100 Dundes *et al.* 1970, p. 136
101 Dundes *et al.* 1970, p. 135; Glazer 1976
102 Dundes *et al.* 1970, p. 131
103 Dabbs *et al.* 2002

Chapter 5

1 Wilson 1985
2 Cressy 1997, p. 84
3 Cressy 1997, p. 85
4 Fabre-Nys *et al.* 1982; Martel *et al.* 1993, 1995; Martensz *et al.* 1986
5 Kraft and Vraa 1975
6 Krebs and Dawkins 1984
7 Coates 1996, p. 117
8 Coates 1996, p. 151
9 Coates 1991, p. 298
10 Rucas *et al.* 2006
11 Warner 1993, p. 22
12 Emler 1992, pp. 23, 24
13 Gambetta 1994, p. 1
14 Gearing 1663; Hooton 1709
15 Harper 1638
16 Capp 2003, p. 376
17 The residents of small towns tend to experience anxiety when they discover or suspect that personal information about them is in circulation (Blumenthal 1932).

18 Capp 2003, p. 64
19 Capp 2003, p. 63
20 Cressy 1997, p. 84; Capp 2003, p. 376
21 Sommerville 1997, p. 10
22 Oldenburg 1989
23 Cressy 1997
24 Cressy 1997
25 Manguel 2006
26 Berlin 1969, p. 131
27 Bos *et al.* 2010
28 Bischoping 1993; also see Locke 2005
29 Wiessner 2005
30 Ellickson 1991, p. 214
31 Kniffin and Wilson 2005
32 Smoreda and Licoppe 2000
33 Bell 1981, p. 83
34 Harding 1975, pp. 286–87

Chapter 6

1 Beaudry 1988; Nattiez 1999, p. 403, italics mine
2 I am indebted to Steven Brown for bringing these games to my attention.
3 Description based on accounts by Beaudry 1978, 1988; Cavanagh 1976; Charron 1978; Nattiez 1983, 1999
4 Charron 1978, p. 246
5 Charron 1978; Nattiez 1999
6 Beaudry 1988
7 Charron 1978, p. 258
8 Falk 1979, 1980
9 Falk 1979, p. 52
10 Coates 1991, pp. 299, 301
11 Coates 1996, p. 198
12 Coates 1996, p. 112
13 LaFrance *et al.* 2003
14 Makri-Tsilipakou 1994
15 Makri-Tsilipakou 1994, pp. 416, 417
16 Maccoby 1990, p. 518

17 Watson and Potter 1962, pp. 255–56
18 Morton 1978
19 Locke 2010b
20 Aiello 1977a, b; Argyle and Dean 1965
21 Slotko and Langmeyer 1977
22 Jones and Yarbrough 1985
23 Derlega *et al.* 1993
24 Laurenceau *et al.* 1998, p. 1239
25 Reis and Shaver 1988
26 Laurenceau *et al.* 1998, p. 1246
27 Morton 1978
28 Aries and Johnson 1983; Booth (1972) found that women confided in 52 percent of their female friendships, men in just 38 percent of theirs.
29 Aukett *et al.* 1988
30 Derlega *et al.* 1993; also see Bell 1981
31 Coates 2003
32 Bell 1981, p. 63
33 Bell 1981, pp. 81–82
34 Rosenfeld 1979
35 Kelvin 1977, quoted in Derlega *et al.* 1993, p. 67
36 Goodman and O'Brien 2000, p. 42

Chapter 7

1 Woolley 1910, p. 340
2 Figes (2007) describes an entire society that was reduced to whispering.
3 Harcourt *et al.* 1993, p. 89, italics mine
4 Interested readers might wish to inspect *Small talk* (Coupland 2000).
5 Greeno and Semple 2009; Harcourt *et al.* 1993; Silk 2001
6 Campbell 1999
7 Seyfarth 1976
8 Campbell 1999, p. 207
9 Hrdy 1981, p. 106
10 Smuts 1987, p. 402
11 Walters and Seyfarth 1987, p. 308

12 Walters 1987
13 Silk 2007
14 Silk 2007
15 Taylor *et al.* 2000; Taylor 2002
16 Dunbar 1996
17 Silk 2001
18 Cooper and Bernstein 2000
19 Aurelli *et al.* 1999
20 Boccia *et al.* 1989
21 Silk 2007, p. 1348
22 Gomes *et al.* 2009
23 de Waal 1982
24 Malinowski 1922
25 Sugawara 1984
26 Sugawara 1984, pp. 36–37
27 Sade 1965, p. 6
28 Fabre-Nys *et al.* 1982; Martel *et al.* 1993, 1995
29 Aurelli *et al.* 1999; Boccia *et al.* 1989; Drescher *et al.* 1980, 1982
30 Dunbar 1996
31 Hauser *et al.* 1993
32 Greeno and Semple 2009
33 Harcourt *et al.* 1993; Richman 1976; Richman 1987
34 Walters 1987
35 Marler and Tenaza 1977; Redican 1975
36 Blount 1985
37 Dodd *et al.* 1999; La France *et al.* 2003
38 Crockford *et al.* 2008
39 Locke 2005, 2010b
40 Dunbar 1993, 2007a, b; Dunbar and Shultz 2007
41 Lindenfors *et al.* 2004, p. S102
42 Lindenfors 2005
43 Dunbar 2007b, p. 2; Lindenfors *et al.* 2007a, b
44 Thorndike 1920, p. 228
45 Mayer and Salovey 1993, p. 433
46 Blanck *et al.* 1981; Hall 1978; Petrides and Furnham 2000; Rosenthal and DePaulo 1979
47 Wilmer *et al.* 2010
48 Hazan and Shaver 1987, p. 523

49 Locke 2003
50 LeBarre 1954; McHenry 1975
51 Leutenegger 1974, 1980
52 Washburn 1960
53 Trevathan 1999
54 Waters *et al.* 2000; also Feeney and Noller 1991
55 Fox *et al.* 1991; van IJzendoorn and De Wolff 1997
56 Locke 2006
57 Murray and Trevarthen 1986
58 Kaye 1977, 1982; Kaye and Wells 1980; mothers discover that as long as they are jiggling, the infant will not resume sucking, so they learn to keep their jiggles short.
59 Locke 1993, 2004
60 Anderson *et al.* 1977; Beebe *et al.* 1988; Rosenthal 1982
61 Stern *et al.* 1975, p. 46
62 Stern *et al.* 1975, pp. 46, 47, 48. This is a maternal-female story. Are fathers as likely to vocalize in unison with their infants? There is little evidence on this, but it has been reported that fathers in two countries, Greece and Scotland, are less imitative of their infants' vocalizations than the mothers (Kokkinaki and Vassdekis 2003).
63 Trinkaus and Zimmerman 1982
64 Hoffman 1977; Smith 2006
65 Eisenberg and Lennon 1983; de Wied *et al.* 2007; Lennon and Eisenberg 1987; Staats *et al.* 2006
66 Romero *et al.* 2010
67 Sarason *et al.* 1990
68 Berkman and Syme 1979; Brown and Harris 1978
69 Miller and Ingham 1976
70 Pennebaker *et al.* 1989
71 Campbell *et al.* 2006; Mottl-Santiago *et al.* 2008; Sosa *et al.* 1980
72 Mottl–Santiago *et al.* 2008
73 Bakan 1966, pp. 14–15
74 Diehl *et al.* 2004; Eisenberg and Lennon 1983
75 Hess and Hagen 2006
76 Heilman 1973, p. 156
77 Kaukiainen *et al.* 1999
78 de Beauvoir 1953, p. 542

79 Wiessner 2005
80 Haviland 1977
81 McAndrew and Milenkovic 2002
82 Feldman *et al.* 2007; Uvnas-Moberg 1998
83 Carter 1998; Debuse 1998
84 Bos *et al.* 2010; De Dreu *et al.* 2010
85 Seltzer *et al.* 2010
86 Hoffman 1977; van der Mark *et al.* 2002; Zahn-Waxler and Radke-Yarrow 1982
87 Leaper and Smith 2004
88 Hughes 1988
89 Brady 1975, pp. 8, 10
90 Eder 1988
91 Eder 1988, p. 233
92 Österman *et al.* 1988; Toldos 2005
93 Burbank 1994; Björkqvist *et al.* 1992a; Björkqvist *et al.* 1992b; Björkqvist *et al.* 1994; also see Crick and Bigbee 1998; Galen and Underwood 1997
94 Xie *et al.* 2002
95 Galen and Underwood 1997
96 Stevenson 1897, pp. 138–39
97 Rosenfeld 1979, p. 72
98 Warren and Brandeis 1890, p. 213
99 Bos *et al.* 2010

Chapter 8

1   Triandis 2001; Triandis *et al.* 1998
2   Luxen 2005
3   Marsh 1978; Morris 1967
4   Barrett *et al.* 1998; Janeson *et al.* 2001
5   McPherson and Smith-Lovin 1986; McPherson *et al.* 2001
6   Bell 1981; Wright 1995
7   Shem and Surrey 1999
8   Hutchins 1995
9   Aiello and Wheeler 1995; Stanford 1999
10 Smith 2004
11 Ecuyer-Dab and Robert 2007; Silverman *et al.* 2007

12 Pacheco-Cobos *et al.* 2010

13 de Waal 1982

14 Tiedens and Fragale 2003

15 Tiedens *et al.* 2007

16 Kristof-Brown *et al.* 2005

17 Gil 2008

18 Bickerton 1995

19 Wiessner 1982

20 Wiessner 1982, p. 68

21 Lee 1979, p. 372; also see Wiessner 2005

22 Pinker and Bloom 1990, p. 725

23 Aukett *et al.* 1988; also see Milardo 1987

24 Fyfe 2009, p. 136

25 Bercovitch 1989, quoted in Fyfe 2009, p. 137

26 DeCasper and Fifer 1980

27 I am aware that in some modern cultures fathers are responsible for much of the linguistic input to infants (e.g. Rowe and Pan 2004), but this effect is undoubtedly limited to societies that bear little resemblance to ancestral groups.

28 Amundsen 2000; Lande 1980; Plavcan 2001; West-Eberhard 2003

29 Condit 2008, p. 501

30 Geddes and Thompson 1889, p. 289

References

Abrahams, R. D. (1970a). *Deep down in the jungle*. Chicago, IL: Aldine.

(1970b). Rapping and capping: Black talk as art. In J. F. Szwed (ed.), *Black America*. New York: Basic Books.

(1989). Black talking on the streets. In R. Bauman and J. Sherzer (eds.), *Explorations in the ethnography of speaking*. Cambridge: Cambridge University Press.

Abrahams, R. D. and Gay, G. (1975). Talking black in the classroom. In P. Stoller (ed.), *Black English: its use in the classroom and in the literature*. New York: Dell Publishing.

Aiello, J. R. (1977a). A further look at equilibrium theory: visual interaction as a function of interpersonal distance. *Environmental Psychology and Nonverbal Behavior*, **1**: 122–40.

(1977b). Visual interaction at extended distances. *Personality and Social Psychology Bulletin*, **3**: 83–86.

Aiello, L. C. and Wheeler, P. (1995). The Expensive Tissue Hypothesis: the brain and the digestive system in human evolution. *Current Anthropology*, **36**: 199–221.

Alexander, G. M. (2003). An evolutionary perspective of sex-typed toy preferences: pink, blue, and the brain. *Archives of Sexual Behavior*, **32**: 7–14.

(2006). Associations among gender-linked toy preferences, spatial ability, and digit ratio: evidence from eye-tracking analysis. *Archives of Sexual Behavior*, **35**: 699–709.

Alexander, G. M. and Hines, M. (2002). Sex differences in response to children's toys in nonhuman primates (*Cercopithecus aethiops sabaeus*). *Evolution and Human Behavior*, **23**: 467–79.

Almli, C. R., Ball, R. H., and Wheeler, M. E. (2001). Human fetal and neonatal movement patterns: gender differences and fetal-to-neonatal continuity. *Developmental Psychobiology*, **38**: 252–73.

Amundsen, T. (2000). Female ornaments: genetically correlated or sexually selected? In Y. Espmark, T. Amundsen, and G. Rosenqvist (eds.), *Animal signals*. Trondheim: Tapir Academic Press.

Anderson, B. J., Vietze, P., and Dokecki, P. R. (1977). Reciprocity in vocal interactions of mothers and infants. *Child Development,* **48**: 1676–81.

Anderson, E. (1990). *Streetwise: race, class, and change in an urban community.* Chicago, IL: University of Chicago Press.

Anderson, J. L., Crawford, C. B., Nadeau, J., and Lindberg, T. (1992). Was the Duchess of Windsor right? A cross-cultural review of the socioecology of ideals of female body shape. *Ethology & Sociobiology,* **13**: 197–227.

Anderson, S. (2010). The polyganists. *National Geographic,* February, pp. 34–61.

Andersson, M. (1994). *Sexual selection.* Princeton, NJ: Princeton University Press.

Andrew, D. T. (1980). The code of honour and its critics: the opposition to duelling in England, 1700–1850. *Social History,* **5**: 409–34.

Apicella, C. L., Feinberg, D. R., and Marlowe, F. W. (2007). Voice pitch predicts reproductive success in male hunter-gatherers. *Biology Letters,* **3**: 682–84.

Apte, M. L. (1985). *Humor and laughter: an anthropological approach.* Ithaca, NY: Cornell University Press.

Arden, R., Gottfredson, L. S., Miller, G., and Pierce, A. (2009). Intelligence and semen quality are positively correlated. *Intelligence,* **37**: 277–82.

Argyle, M. and Dean, J. (1965). Eye-contact, distance and affiliation. *Sociometry,* **28**: 289–304.

Aries, E. and Johnson, F. (1983). Close friendship in adulthood: conversational content between same-sex friends. *Sex Roles,* **9**: 1183–96.

Aukett, R., Ritchie, J., and Mill, K. (1988). Gender differences in friendship patterns. *Sex Roles,* **19**: 57–66.

Aurelli, F., Preston, S. D., and de Waal, F. B. M. (1999). Heart rate responses to social interactions in free-moving rhesus macaques (*Macaca mulatta*): a pilot study. *Journal of Comparative Psychology,* **113**: 59–65.

Ayoub, M. R. and Barnett, S. A. (1965). Ritualized verbal insult in white high school culture. *Journal of American Folklore,* **78**: 337–44.

Baillargeon, R. H., Tremblay, R. E., and Willms, J. D. (2005). Gender differences in the prevalence of physically aggressive behaviors in the Canadian population of 2- and 3-year-old children. In D. J. Pepler, K. C. Madsen, C. Webster, and K. S. Levene (eds.), *The development and treatment of girlhood aggression.* Mahwah, NJ: Erlbaum.

Bakan, D. (1966). *The duality of human existence: isolation and communion in Western man.* Boston, MA: Beacon Press.

Baldick, R. (1965). *The duel: a history of dueling.* New York: Charles Potter.

Bale, C., Morrison, R., and Caryl, P. G. (2006). Chat-up lines as male sexual displays. *Personality and Individual Differences*, **40**: 655–64.

Barrett, L. F., Robin, L., Pietromonaco, P. R., and Eyssell, K. M. (1998). Are women the "more emotional" sex? Evidence from emotional experiences in social context. *Cognition and Emotion*, **12**: 555–78.

Bass, B. M. (1949). An analysis of the leaderless group discussion. *Journal of Applied Psychology*, **33**: 527–33.

Bauman, R. (1972). The La Have Island general store: sociability and verbal art in a Nova Scotia community. *Journal of American Folklore*, **85**: 330–43.

   (1986). *Story, performance, and event: contextual studies of oral narrative.* Cambridge: Cambridge University Press.

Bax, M. (1981). Rules for ritual challenges: a speech convention among medieval knights. *Journal of Pragmatics*, **5**: 423–44.

Bax, M. and Padmos, T. (1983). Two types of verbal dueling in Old Icelandic: the interactional structure of the *senna* and the *mannjafnaðr* in Harbardsljod. *Scandinavian Studies*, **55**: 149–74.

Beaudry, N. (1978). Toward transcription and analysis of Inuit throat-games: macro-structure. *Ethnomusicology*, **22**: 261–73.

   (1988). Singing, laughing and playing: three examples from the Inuit, Dene and Yupik traditions. *Canadian Journal of Native Studies*, **8**: 275–90.

Beebe, B., Alson, D., Jaffe, J., Feldstein, S., and Crown, C. (1988). Vocal congruence in mother–infant play. *Journal of Psycholinguistic Research*, **17**: 245–59.

Bell, R. R. (1981). *Worlds of friendship.* Newbury Park, CA: Sage Publications.

Bercovitch, E. (1989). Disclosure and concealment: a study of secrecy among the Nalumin people of Papua New Guinea. PhD thesis, Stanford University.

Berenbaum, S. A. and Hines, M. (1992). Early androgens are related to childhood sex-typed toy preferences. *Psychological Science*, **3**: 203–6.

Berenbaum, S. A., Martin, C. L., Hanish, L. D., Briggs, P. T., and Fabes, R. A. (2008). Sex differences in children's play. In J. B. Becker,

K. J. Berkley, N. Geary, E. Hampson, J. Herman, and E. Young (eds.), *Sex differences in the brain: from genes to behavior*. New York: Oxford University Press.

Bereczkei, T., Voros, S., Gal, A., and Bernath, L. (1997). Resources, attractiveness, family commitment: reproductive decisions in human mate choice. *Ethology*, **103**: 681–99.

Berkman, L. F. and Syme, L. (1979). Social networks, host resistance, and mortality: a nine-year follow-up study of Alameda County residents. *American Journal of Epidemiology*, **109**: 186–204.

Berlin, I. (1969). *Four essays on liberty*. Oxford: Oxford University Press.

Betzig, L. (1992). Roman polygyny. *Ethology and Sociobiology*, **13**: 309–49.

Bickerton, D. (1995). *Language and human behaviour*. London: UCL Press.

Binet, A. (1911). New investigation on the measure of the intellectual level among school children. *L'Année psychologique*, **17**: 145–201. Reproduced in A. Binet, and T. Simon (1916/1980). *The development of intelligence in children*. Translated by E. S. Kite. Nashville, TN: Williams Printing Company.

Bischoping, K. (1993). Gender differences in conversation topics, 1922–1990. *Sex Roles*, **28**: 1–18.

Björkqvist, K., Lagerspetz, K. M. J., and Kaukiainen, A. (1992a). Do girls manipulate and boys fight? Developmental trends regarding direct and indirect aggression. *Aggressive Behavior*, **18**: 117–27.

Björkqvist, K., Österman, K., and Kaukiainen, A. (1992b). The development of direct and indirect aggressive strategies in males and females. In K. Björkqvist and P. Niemelä (eds.), *Of mice and women: aspects of female aggression*. San Diego, CA: Academic Press.

Björkqvist, K., Österman, K., and Lagerspetz, K. M. J. (1994). Sex differences in covert aggression among adults. *Aggressive Behavior*, **20**: 27–33.

Blanck, P. D., Rosenthal, R., Snodgrass, S. E., DePaulo, B. M., and Zuckerman, M. (1981). Sex differences in eavesdropping on nonverbal cues: developmental changes. *Journal of Personality and Social Psychology*, **41**(2): 391–96.

Blount, B. G. (1985). "Girney" vocalizations among Japanese macaque females: context and function. *Primates*, **26**: 424–35.

Blumenthal, A. (1932). *Small town stuff*. Chicago, IL: University of Chicago Press.

Boccia, M. L., Reite, M., and Laudenslager, M. (1989). On the physiology of grooming in a pigtail macaque. *Physiology & Behavior*, **45**: 667–70.

Boose, L. E. (1991). Scolding brides and bridling scolds: taning the woman's unruly member. *Shakespeare Quarterly*, **42**: 179–213.

Booth, A. (1972). Sex and social participation. *American Sociological Review*, **37**: 183–92.

Bos, P. A., Terburg, D., and van Honk, J. (2010). Testosterone decreases trust in socially naïve humans. *Proceedings of the National Academy of Sciences*, **107**: 9991–9995.

Bouchard, T. J. and Loehlin, J. C. (2001). Genes, evolution, and personality. *Behavior Genetics*, **31**: 243–73.

Bowen, J. R. (1989). Poetic duels and political change in the Gayo Highlands of Sumatra. *American Anthropologist*, **91**: 25–40.

Brady, M. K. (1975). "This little lady's gonna boogaloo": elements of socialization in the play of black girls. In *Black girls at play: folkloric perspectives on child development*. Early Elementary Program, Southwest Educational Development Laboratory, Austin, Texas.

Brenneis, D. and Padarath, R. (1975). "About those scoundrels I'll let everyone know": challenge singing in a Fiji Indian community. *Journal of American Folklore*, **88**: 283–91.

Bressler, E. R. and Balshine, S. (2006). The influence of humor on desirability. *Evolution and Human Behavior*, **27**: 29–39.

Bressler, E. R., Martin, R. A., and Balshine, S. (2006). Production and appreciation of humor as sexually selected traits. *Evolution and Human Behavior*, **27**: 121–30.

Bribiescas, R. (2008). *Men: evolutionary and life history.* Cambridge, MA: Harvard University Press.

Brockelman, W. Y. and Schilling, D. (1984). Inheritance of stereotyped gibbon calls. *Nature*, **312**: 634–36.

Bronner, S. J. (1978). A re-examination of dozens among white American adolescents. *Western Folklore*, **37**: 118–28.

Brooks, C. W. (1998). *Lawyers, litigation and English society since 1450.* London: The Hambledon Press.

Brown, G. W. and Harris, T. (1978). *Social origins of depression: a study of psychiatric disorder in women.* New York: Free Press.

Brown, H. R. (1990). Street smarts. In A. Dundes (ed.), *Mother wit from the laughing barrel: readings in the interpretation of Afro-American folklore.* Jackson, MS: University Press of Mississippi.

Bruckert, L., Lienard, J.-S., Lacroix, A., Kreutzer, M., and Leboucher, G. (2006). Women use voice parameters to assess men's characteristics. *Proceedings of the Royal Society of London B*, **273**: 83–89.

Bruschke, J. and Johnson, A. (1994). An analysis of differences in success rates of male and female debaters. *Argumentation & Advocacy*, **30**: 105–14.

Burbank, V. K. (1987). Female aggression in cross-cultural perspective. *Behavior Science Research*, **21**: 70–100.

(1994). *Fighting women: anger and aggression in Aboriginal Australia.* Berkeley, CA: University of California Press.

Burgoon, J. K. (1975). Evaluation criteria as predictors of debate success. *Journal of the American Forensic Association*, **12**: 1–4.

Buss, D. M. (1989). Sex differences in human mate preferences: evolutionary hypothesis testing in 37 cultures. *Behavioral and Brain Sciences*, **12**: 1–49.

Buss, D. M., Larsen, R. L., Westen, D., and Semmelroth, J. (1992). Sex differences in jealousy, evolution, physiology, and psychology. *Psychological Sciences*, **3**: 251–55.

Buss, D. M. and Reeve, H. K. (2003). Evolutionary psychology and developmental dynamics: comment on Lickliter and Honeycutt (2003). *Psychological Bulletin*, **129**: 848–53.

Buss, D. M. and Shackleford, T. K. (1997). Human aggression in evolutionary psychological perspective. *Clinical Psychology Review*, **17**: 605–19.

Byrd-Craven, J. and Geary, D. C. (2007). Biological and evolutionary contributions to developmental sex differences. *Reproductive BioMedicine*, **15**: 12–22.

Campbell, A. (1999). Staying alive: evolution, culture and women's intra-sexual aggression. *Behavioral and Brain Sciences*, **22**: 203–52.

Campbell, D. A., Lake, M. F., Falk, M., and Backstrand, J. R. (2006). A randomized control trial of continuous support in labor by a lay doula. *Journal of Obstetrical, Gynecologic, and Neonatal Nursing*, **35**: 456–64.

Capp, B. (2003). *When gossips meet: women, family, and neighbourhood in early modern England.* Oxford: Oxford University Press.

Caraveli, A. (1985). The symbolic village: community born in performance. *Journal of American Folklore*, **98**: 259–86.

Carter, C. S. (1998). Neuroendocrine perspectives on social attachment and love. *Psychoneuroendocrinology*, **23**: 779–818.

Cavanagh, B. (1976). Some throat-games of Netsilik Eskimo women. *Canadian Folk Music Journal*, **4**: 43–47.

Charron, C. (1978). Toward transcription and analysis of Inuit throat-games: micro-structure. *Ethnomusicology*, **22**: 245–59.

Clover, C. J. (1980). The Germanic context of the Unferth episode. *Speculum*, **55**: 444–68.

Coates, J. (1991). Women's cooperative talk: a new kind of conversational duet. In C. Uhlig and R. Zimmermann (eds.), *Proceedings of the Anglistentag 1990, Marburg*. Tübingen: Max Niemeyer Verlag.

(1996). *Women talk: conversation between women friends*. Oxford: Blackwell.

(2003). *Men talk: stories in the making of masculinity*. Oxford: Blackwell.

Collins, S. A. (2000). Men's voices and women's choices. *Animal Behaviour*, **60**: 773–80.

Collins, S. A. and Missing, C. (2003). Vocal and visual attractiveness are related in women. *Animal Behaviour*, **65**: 997–1004.

Condit, C. M. (2008). Feminist biologies: revising feminist strategies and biological science. *Sex Roles*, **59**: 492–503.

Connellan, J., Baron-Cohen, S., Wheelwright, S., Batki, A., and Ahluwalia, J. (2000). Sex differences in human neonatal social perception. *Infant Behavior & Development*, **23**: 113–18.

Cooper, M. A. and Bernstein, I. S. (2000). Social grooming in Assamese macaques (*Macaca assamensis*). *American Journal of Primatology*, **50**: 77–85.

Coupland, J. (ed.) (2002). *Small talk*. Harlow: Pearson Education.

Cowlishaw, G. and Dunbar, R. I. M. (1991). Dominance rank and mating success in male primates. *Animal Behaviour*, **41**: 1045–56.

Cox, C. R. and Le Boeuf, B. J. (1977). Female incitation of male competition: a mechanism in sexual selection. *American Naturalist*, **111**: 317–35.

Cressy, D. (1997). *Birth, marriage and death: ritual, religion, and the life-cycle in Tudor and Stuart England*. Oxford: Oxford University Press.

Crick, N. R. and Bigbee, M. A. (1998). Relational and overt forms of peer victimization: a multiinformant approach. *Journal of Consulting and Clinical Psychology*, **66**: 337–47.

Crockford, C., Wittig, R. M., Whitten, P. L., Seyfarth, R. M., and Cheney, D. L. (2008). Social stressors and coping mechanisms in wild female baboons (*Papio hamadryas ursinus*). *Hormones and Behavior*, **53**: 254–65.

Dabbs, J. M., Alford, E. C., and Fielden, J. A. (1998). Trial lawyers and testosterone: blue-collar talent in a white-collar world. *Journal of Applied Social Psychology*, **28**: 84–94.

Dabbs, J. M., Bernieri, F. J., Strong, R. K., Campo, R., and Milun, R. (2001). Going on stage: testosterone in greetings and meetings. *Journal of Research in Personality*, **35**: 27–40.

Dabbs, J. M., Karpas, A. E., Dyomina, N., *et al.* (2002). Experimental raising or lowering of testosterone level affects mood in normal men and women. *Social Behavior and Personality*, **30**: 795–806.

Dabbs, J. M., La Rue, D., and Williams, P. M. (1990). Testosterone and occupational choice: actors, ministers, and other men. *Journal of Personality and Social Psychology*, **59**: 1261–65.

Dabbs, J. M. and Mallinger, A. (1999). Higher testosterone levels predict lower voice pitch among men. *Personality and Individual Differences*, **27**: 801–4.

Dabbs, J. M. and Ruback, R. B. (1984). Vocal patterns in male and female groups. *Personality and Social Psychology Bulletin*, **10**: 518–25.

(1988). Saliva testosterone and personality of male college students. *Bulletin of the Psychonomic Society*, **26**: 244–247.

Daly, M. and Wilson, M. (1988). *Homicide.* New York: Aldine de Gruyter.

Dandy, E. B. (1991). *Black communications: breaking down the barriers.* Chicago, IL: African-American Images.

Davis, S. (1990). Men as success objects and women as sex objects: a study of personal advertisements. *Sex Roles*, **23**: 43–50.

Deary, I. J. and Der, G. (2005). Reaction time explains IQ's association with death. *Psychological Science*, **16**: 64–69.

de Beauvoir, Simone (1953). *The second sex.* New York: Knopf. (Quotation from p. 542.)

de Boer, B. (2008). The joy of sacs. In A. D. M. Smith, K. Smith, and R. Ferrer I Cancho (eds.), *The evolution of language.* Singapore: World Scientific.

DeBruine, L. M. (2009). Beyond "just-so stories": how evolutionary theories led to predictions that non-evolution-minded researchers would never dream of. *The Psychologist*, **22**: 930–31.

Debuse, M. (1998). *Endocrine and reproductive sytems.* St. Louis, MO: Mosby.

Decapua, A. and Boxer, D. (1999). Bragging, boasting and bravado: male banter in a brokerage house. *Women and Language*, **22**: 5–22.

DeCasper, A. and Fifer, W. P. (1980). On human bonding: newborns prefer their mothers' voices. *Science*, **208**: 1174–76.

De Dreu, C. K. W., Greer, L. L., Handgraaf, M. J. J., *et al.* (2010). The neuropeptide oxytocin regulates parochial altruism in intergroup conflict among humans. *Science*, **328**: 1408–11.

de Waal, F. B. M. (1982). *Chimpanzee politics: sex and power among apes.* Baltimore, MD: Johns Hopkins University Press.

de Wied, M., Branje, J. T., and Meeus, W. H. J. (2007). Empathy and conflict resolution in friendship relations among adolescents. *Aggressive Behavior*, **33**: 48–55.

Delgado, R. A. (2006). Sexual selection in the loud calls of male primates: signal content and function. *International Journal of Primatology*, **27**: 5–25.

Derlega, V. J., Metts, S., Petronio, S., and Margulis, S. T. (1993). *Self-disclosure.* Newbury Park, CA: Sage.

Diehl, M., Owen, S. K., and Youngblade, L. M. (2004). Agency and communication attributes in adults' spontaneous self-representations. *International Journal of Behavioral Development*, **28**: 1–15.

Dodd, D. K., Russell, B. L., and Jenkins, C. (1999). Smiling in school yearbook photos: gender differences from kindergarten to adulthood. *Psychological Record*, **49**: 543–54.

Dollard, J. (1939). The dozens: dialectic of insult. *The American Imago*, **1**: 3–25.

Doukanari, E. (1997). The presentation of gendered self in Cyprus rhyming improvisations: a sociolinguistic investigation of Kipriaka chattista in performance. PhD dissertation, Georgetown University.

Doutrelant, C. and McGregor, P. K. (2000). Eavesdropping and mate choice in female fighting fish. *Behaviour*, **137**: 1655–69.

Draper, P. and Harpending, H. (1982). Father absence and reproductive strategy: an evolutionary perspective. *Journal of Anthropological Research*, **38**: 255–73.

Drescher, V. M., Gantt, W. H., and Whitehead, W. E. (1980). Heart rate response to touch. *Psychosomatic Medicine*, **42**: 559–65.

Drescher, V. M., Hayhurst, V., Whitehead, W. E., and Joseph, J. A. (1982). The effects of tactile stimulation on pulse rate and blood pressure. *Biological Psychiatry*, **17**: 1347–52.

Dunbar, R. I. M. (1993). Coevolution of neocortical size, group size and language in humans. *Behavioral and Brain Sciences*, **16**: 681–94.

(1996). *Grooming, gossip and the evolution of language*. London: Faber and Faber.

(2007a). Evolution of the social brain. In S. W. Gangestad and J. A. Simpson (eds.), *The evolution of mind: fundamental questions and controversies*. New York: Guilford Press.

(2007b). Male and female brain evolution is subject to contrasting selection pressures in primates. *BMC Biology*, **5**: 1–3.

Dunbar, R. I. M. and Shultz, S. (2007). Evolution in the social brain. *Science*, **317**: 1344–47.

Dundes, A., Leach, J. W., and Özkök, B. (1970). The strategy of Turkish boys' verbal dueling rhymes. In J. J. Gumperz and D. Hymes (eds.), *Directions in sociolinguistics: the ethnography of communication*. New York: Holt, Rinehart and Winston.

Eaton, W. O. and Ennis, L. R. (1986). Sex differences in human motor activity level. *Psychological Bulletin*, **100**: 19–28.

Eckel, L. A., Arnold, A. P., Hampson, E., Becker, J. B., Blaustein, J. D., and Herman, J. P. (2008). Research and methodological issues in the study of sex differences and hormone-behavior relations. In J. B. Becker, K. J. Berkley, N. Geary, E. Hampson, J. P. Herman, and E. A. Young (eds.), *Sex differences in the brain: from genes to behavior*. Oxford: Oxford University Press.

Ecuyer-Dab, I. and Robert, M. (2007). The female advantage in object location memory according to the foraging hypothesis: a critical analysis. *Human Nature*, **18**: 365–85.

Eder, D. (1988). Building cohesion through collaborative narration. *Social Psychology Quarterly*, **51**: 225–35.

(1991). The role of teasing in adolescent peer culture. In S. Cahill (ed.), *Sociological studies of child development*, Vol. **4**. Greenwich, CT: JAI Press.

Edwards, V. and Sienkowitz, T. J. (1990). *Oral cultures past and present: rappin' and Homer*. Oxford: Blackwell.

Eisenberg, N. and Lennon, R. (1983). Sex differences in empathy and related capacities. *Psychological Bulletin*, **94**: 100–31.

Eliasoph, N. (1998). *Avoiding politics: how Americans produce apathy in everyday life.* Cambridge: Cambridge University Press.

Ellickson, R. C. (1991). *Order without law: how neighbors settle disputes.* Cambridge, MA: Harvard University Press.

Elliott, R. C. (1960). *The power of satire: magic, ritual, art.* Princeton, NJ: Princeton University Press.

Emler, N. (1992). The truth about gossip. *Social Psychology Newsletter*, **27**: 23–37.

Endler, J. A. and Basolo, A. L. (1998). Sensory ecology, receiver biases and sexual selection. *Trends in Ecology and Evolution*, **13**: 415–20.

Fabre-Nys, C., Meller, R. E., and Keverne, E. B. (1982). Opiate antagonists stimulate affiliative behaviour in monkeys. *Pharmacology, Biochemistry & Behaviour*, **16**: 653–59.

Fagot, B. I. and Hagan, R. (1985). Aggression in toddlers: responses to the assertive acts of boys and girls. *Sex Roles*, **12**: 341–51.

Falk, J. (1979). The duet as a conversational process. PhD dissertation, Princeton University.

(1980). The conversational duet. *Proceedings of the 6th Annual Meeting of the Berkeley Linguistics Society*, 507–14.

Faris, J. C. (1966). The dynamics of verbal exchange: a Newfoundland example. *Anthropologica*, **8**: 235–48.

(1972). *Cat Harbour: a Newfoundland fishing settlement.* Toronto: University of Toronto Press.

Feeney, J. A. and Noller, P. (1991). Attachment style as a predictor of adult romantic relationships. *Journal of Personality and Social Psychology*, **58**: 281–91.

Feinberg, D. R., Jones, B. C., Law Smith, M. J., Moor, F. R., DeBruine, L. M., Cornwell, R. E., Hillier, S. G., and Perrett, D. I. (2006). Menstrual cycle, trait estrogen level, and masculinity preferences in the human voice. *Hormones and Behavior*, **49**: 215–22.

Feldman, R., Weller, A., Zagoory-Sharon, O., and Levine, A. (2007). Evidence for a neuroendocrinological foundation of human affiliation. *Psychological Science*, **18**: 965–70.

Fentress, J. and Wickham, C. (1992). *Social memory.* Oxford: Blackwell.

Figes, O. (2007). *The whisperers: private life in Stalin's Russia.* New York: Henry Holt.

Fischer, D. H. (1989). *Albion's seed: four British folkways in America.* Oxford: Oxford University Press.

Fischer, J., Kitchen, D. M., Seyfarth, R. M., and Cheney, D. L. (2004). Baboon loud calls advertise male quality: acoustic features and their relation to rank, age, and exhaustion. *Behavioral Ecology and Sociobiology*, **56**: 140–48.

Fisman, R., Iyengar, S. S., Kamenica, E., and Simionson, I. (2006). Gender differences in mate selection: evidence from a speed dating experiment. *Quarterly Journal of Economics*, **121**: 673–97.

Fitch, W. T. and Hauser, M. D. (2002). Unpacking "honesty": the vocal production and the evolution of acoustic signals. In A. M. Simmons, R. R. Fay, and A. N. Popper (eds.), *Acoustic communication*. New York: Springer.

Folb, E. (1980). *Runnin' down some lines: the language and culture of black teenagers*. Cambridge, MA: Harvard University Press.

Foley, J. M. (2007). Basque oral poetry championship. *Oral Tradition*, **22**: 3–11.

Foster, W. A. (1996). Duelling aphids: intraspecific fighting in *Astegopteryx minuta* (Homoptera: Hormaphididae). *Animal Behaviour*, **51**: 645–55.

Fox, N. A., Kimmerly, N. L., and Schafer, W. D. (1991). Attachment to mother/attachment to father: a meta-analysis. *Child Development*, **62**: 210–25.

Franks, B. K. and Rigby, K. (2005). Deception and mate selection: some implications for relevance and the evolution of language. In M. Tallerman (ed.), *Language origins: perspectives on evolution*. Oxford: Oxford University Press.

Frazer, J. G. (1900/1959). *The new golden bough*. New York: Criterion Books.

Frevert, U. (1995). *Men of honour: a social and cultural history of the duel*. Translated by Anthony Williams. Cambridge: Polity Press.

Friedley, S. A. and Manchester, B. B. (1985). An analysis of male/female participation at select national championships. *National Forensic Journal*, **3**: 1–12.

  (1987). An examination of male/female judging decisions in individual events. *National Forensic Journal*, **5**: 11–20.

Furnham, A. and Baguma, P. (1994). Cross-cultural differences in the evaluation of male and female body shapes. *International Journal of Eating Disorders*, **15**: 81–89.

Fyfe, A. (2009). Exploring spatial relationships between material culture and language in the Upper Sepik and Central New Guinea. *Oceania*, **79**: 121–61.

Galen, B. R. and Underwood, M. K. (1997). A developmental investigation of social aggression among children. *Developmental Psychology*, **33**: 589–600.

Gallant, T. W. (2000). Honor, masculinity, and ritual knife fighting in nineteenth-century Greece. *American Historical Review*, **105**: 359–82.

Gambetta, D. (1994). Godfather's gossip. *Archives Européennes de Sociologie*, **35**: 199–223.

Gearing, W. (1663). *A Bridle for the Tongue; or, a treatise for ten sins of the tongue*. London: Thomas Parkhurst.

Geddes, P. and Thompson, J. A. (1889). *The evolution of sex*. Chicago, IL: University of Chicago Press.

Geissmann, T. (1984). Inheritance of song parameters in the gibbon song, analysed in 2 hybrid gibbons (*Hylobates pileatus* x *H. lar*). *Folia Primatologica*, **42**: 216–35.

Georgakopoulou, A. (1995). Women, men, and conversational narrative performances: aspects of gender in Greek storytelling. *Anthropological Linguistics*, **37**: 460–86.

Gervais, M. and Wilson, D. S. (2005). The evolution and functions of laughter and humor: a synthetic approach. *Quarterly Review of Biology*, **80**: 395–430.

Gil, D. (2008). How much grammar does it take to sail a boat? (Or, what can material artefacts tell us about the evolution of language?). In A. D. M. Smith, K. Smith, and R. Ferrer I Cancho (eds.), *The evolution of language*. Singapore: World Scientific.

Glazer, M. (1976). On verbal dueling among Turkish boys. *Journal of American Folklore*, **89**: 87–89.

Gomes, C. M., Mundry, R., and Boesch, C. (2009). Long-term reciprocation of grooming in wild West African chimpanzees. *Proceedings of the Royal Society B*, **276**: 699–706.

Goodman, E. and O'Brien, P. (2000). *I know just what you mean: the power of friendship in women's lives*. New York: Simon & Schuster.

Gossen, G. H. (1976). Verbal dueling in Chamula. In B. Kirshenblatt (ed.), *Speech play: research and resources for the study of linguistic creativity*. Philadelphia: University of Pennsylvania Press.

Gould, J. L. and Marler, P. (1987). Learning by instinct. *American Scientist*, **255**: 74–85.

Gowing, L. (1996). *Domestic dangers: women, words, and sex in early modern London*. Oxford: Clarendon Press.

Gray, J. (1992). *Men are from Mars, women are from Venus*. New York: HarperCollins.

Greeno, N. C. and Semple, S. (2009). Sex differences in vocal communication among adult rhesus macaques. *Evolution and Human Behavior*, **30**: 141–45.

Gwilliam, J. G. (2009). Trial lawyers: actors or boxers? *Plaintiff Magazine*, December: 1.

Hale, T. A. (1994). Griottes: female voices from West Africa. *Research in African Literatures*, **25**: 71–91.

Hall, J. A. (1978). Gender effects in decoding nonverbal cues. *Psychological Bulletin*, **85**: 845–57.

Hall, M. L. (2004). A review of hypotheses for the functions of avian duetting. *Behavioral Ecology and Sociobiology*, **55**: 415–30.

Hannerz, U. (1969). *Soulside*. New York: Columbia University Press.

Harcourt, A. H., Stewart, K., and Hauser, M. D. (1993). The social use of vocalizations by gorillas: I. Social behaviour and vocal repertoire. *Behaviour*, **124**: 89–122.

Harding, S. (1975). Women and words in a Spanish village. In R. Reiter (ed.), *Towards an anthropology of women*. New York: Monthly Review Press.

Haring, L. (1985). Magagasy riddling. *Journal of American Folklore*, **98**: 163–90.

Harper, R. (1638). *The Anatomy of a Woman's Tongue*. London. In Harleian Miscellany II (1744), 167–78.

Harris, J. (1979). The *senna*: from description to literary theory. *Michigan Germanic Studies*, **5**: 65–73.

Harris, T. R., Fitch, W. T., Goldstein, L. M., and Fashing, P. J. (2006). Black and white colobus monkey (*Colobus guereza*) roars as a source of both honest and exaggerated information about body mass. *Ethology*, **112**: 911–20.

Hauser, M. D. (1993). The evolution of nonhuman primate vocalizations: effects of phylogeny, body weight, and social context. *American Naturalist*, **142**: 528–42.

Hauser, M. D., Evans, C. S., and Marler, P. (1993). The role of articulation in the production of rhesus monkey, *Macaca mulatta*, vocalizations. *Animal Behaviour*, **45**: 423–33.

Haviland, J. B. (1977). *Gossip, reputation, and knowledge in Zinacantan*. Chicago: University of Chicago Press.

Haydar, A. (1989). The development of Lebanese *zajal*: genre, meter, and verbal duel. *Oral Tradition*, **4**: 189–212.

Hayes, D. P. and Meltzer, L. (1972). Interpersonal judgments based on talkativeness: fact or artifact? *Sociometry*, **35**: 538–61.

Hayes, K. J. (1962). Genes, drives and intellect. *Psychological Reports*, **10**: 299–342.

Hazan, C. and Shaver, P. (1987). Romantic love conceptualized as an attachment process. *Journal of Personality and Social Psychology*, **52**: 511–24.

Heilman, S. C. (1973). *Synagogue life: a study in symbolic interaction*. Chicago, IL: University of Chicago Press.

Herndon, M. and McLeod, N. (1980). The interrelationship of style and occasion in the Maltese *spirtu pront*. In N. McLeod and M. Herndon (eds.), *The ethnography of musical performance*. Norwood, PA: Norwood Editions.

Hess, N. H. and Hagen, E. H. (2006). Sex differences in indirect aggression: psychological evidence from young adults. *Evolution and Hormone Behavior*, **27**: 231–45.

Hewitt, G., MacLarnon, A., and Jones, K. E. (2002). The functions of laryngeal air sacs in primates: a new hypothesis. *Folia Primatologica*, **73**: 70–94.

Hill, W. F. and Öttchen, C. J. (1995). *Shakespeare's insults: educating your wit*. New York: Crown Trade Paperbacks.

Hines, M., Golombok, S., Rust, J., Johnston, K. J., and Golding, J. (2002). Testosterone during pregnancy and gender role behavior of preschool children: a longitudinal, population study. *Child Development*, **73**: 1678–87.

Hoebel, E. A. (1964). *The law of primitive man: a study in comparative legal dynamics*. Cambridge, MA: Harvard University Press.

Hoffman, M. L. (1977). Sex differences in empathy and related behaviors. *Psychological Bulletin*, **84**: 712–22.

Holmes, L. D. (1969). Samoan oratory. *Journal of American Folklore*, **82**: 342–52.

Hooton, H. (1709). *A bridle for the tongue*. London: W. Taylor.

Hopton, R. (2007). *Pistols at dawn: a history of dueling*. London: Piatkus Books.

Howrigan, D. P. and MacDonald, K. B. (2008). Humor as a mental fitness indicator. *Evolutionary Psychology*, **6**: 652–66.

Hrdy, S. B. (1981). *The woman that never evolved*. Cambridge, MA: Harvard University Press.

Hughes, L. A. (1988). "But that's not *really* mean": competing in a cooperative mode. *Sex Roles*, **19**: 669–87.

Hughes, S., Harrison, M. A., and Gallup, G. G. (2009). Sex specific body configurations can be estimated from voice samples. *Journal of Social, Evolutionary, and Cultural Psychology*, **3**: 343–55.

Hutchins, E. (1995). *Cognition in the wild*. Cambridge, MA: MIT Press.

Huxley, J. (1966a). Introduction. In J. Huxley (ed.) (1966b).

Huxley, J. (ed.) (1966b). A discussion on ritualization of behaviour in animals and man. *Philosophical Transactions of the Royal Society of Britain*, **251**: 249–71.

Irschick, D. J. and Lailvaux, S. P. (2006). Age-specific forced polymorphism: implications of ontogenetic changes in morphology for male mating tactics. *Physiological and Biochemical Zoology*, **79**: 73–82.

Issa, F. A. and Edwards, D. H. (2006). Ritualized submission and the reduction of aggression in an invertebrate. *Current Biology*, **16**: 2217–21.

Jablonski, N. G. and Chaplin, G. (1993). Origin of habitual terrestrial bipedalism in the ancestor of the Hominidae. *Journal of Evolution*, **24**: 259–80.

Janus, S. S., Bess, B. E., and Janus, B. R. (1978). The great comediennes: personality and other factors. *American Journal of Psychoanalysis*, **38**: 367–72.

Janeson, K. A., Highnote, S. M., and Wasserman, L. M. (2001). Richer color experience in observers with multiple photopigment opsin genes. *Psychonomic Bulletin & Review*, **8**: 244–61.

Jespersen, O. (1922). *Language: its nature, development and origin*. London: Allen & Unwin.

Johnson, L. J. and Lipsett-Rivera, S. (1998). *The faces of honor: sex, shame, and violence in colonial Latin America*. Albuquerque, NM: University of New Mexico Press.

Johnson, W. (2009). Extending and testing Tom Bouchard's experience producing drive theory. *Personality and Individual Differences*, **49**, 296–301.

Johnstone, B. (1993). Community and contest: Midwestern men and women creating their worlds in conversational storytelling.

In D. Tannen (ed.), *Gender and conversational interaction.* Oxford: Oxford University Press.

Jones, S. E. and Yarbrough, A. E. (1985). A naturalistic study of the meanings of touch. *Communication Monographs,* **52**: 19–56.

Kaukiainen, A., Bjorkqvist, K., Lagerspetz, K., Osterman, K., Salmivalli, C., Rothberg, S., and Ahlbom, A. (1999). The relationships between social intelligence, empathy, and three types of aggression. *Aggressive Behavior,* **25**: 81–89.

Kaye, K. (1977). Toward the origin of dialogue. In H. R. Schaffer (ed.), *Studies in mother–infant interaction.* New York: Academic Press.

(1982). *The mental and social life of babies: how parents create persons.* Chicago, IL: University of Chicago Press.

Kaye, K. and Wells, A. (1980). Mothers' jiggling and the burst-pause pattern in neonatal sucking. *Infant Behavior and Development,* **3**: 29–46.

Kelvin, P. (1977). Predictability, power and vulnerability in interpersonal attraction. In S. Duck (ed.), *Theory and practice in interpersonal attraction.* New York: Academic Press.

Kendon, A. and Cook, M. (1969). The consistency of gaze patterns in social interaction. *British Journal of Psychology,* **60**: 481–94.

Kingsley, S. K. (1982). Causes of non-breeding and the development of the secondary sexual characteristics in the male orang-utan: a hormonal study. In L. E. M. de Boer (ed.), *The orang-utan: its biology and conservation.* The Hague: Dr W. Junk.

Kingsley, S. (1988). Physiological development of male orangutans and gorillas. In J. Schwartz (ed.), *Orangutan biology.* Oxford: Oxford University Press.

Kitchen, D. M., Seyfarth, R. M., Fischer, J., and Cheney, D. L. (2003). Loud calls as indicators of dominance in male baboons (*Papio cynocephalus ursinus*). *Behavioral Ecology and Sociobiology,* **53**: 374–84.

Kniffin, K. M. and Wilson, D. S. (2005). Utilities of gossip across organizational levels: multilevel selection, free-riders, and teams. *Human Nature,* **16**: 278–92.

Kokkinaki, T. and Vasdekis, V. G. S. (2003). A cross-cultural study on early vocal imitative phenomena in different relationships. *Journal of Reproductive and Infant Psychology,* **21**: 85–101.

Kraft, L. W. and Vraa, C. W. (1975). Sex composition of groups and pattern of self-disclosure by high school females. *Psychological Reports*, **37**: 733–34.

Krebs, J. R. and Dawkins, R. (1984). Animal signals: mind-reading and manipulation. In R. Krebs and N. B. Davies (eds.), *Behavioural ecology: an evolutionary approach*. Second edition. Oxford: Blackwell Scientific.

Kristof-Brown, A., Barrick, M. R., and Stevens, C. K. (2005). When opposites attract: a multi-sample demonstration of complementary person–team fit on extraversion. *Journal of Personality*, **73**: 935–57.

Kruger, D. J., Fisher, M., and Jobling, I. (2003). Proper and dark heroes as dads and cads: alternative mating strategies in British romantic literature. *Human Nature*, **14**: 305–17.

Kuiper, K. (1996). *Smooth talkers: the linguistic performance of auctioneers and sportscasters*. Mahwah, NJ: Lawrence Erlbaum.

Kulick, D. (1993). Speaking as a woman: structure and gender in domestic arguments in a New Guinea village. *Cultural Anthropology*, **8**: 510–41.

Kunc, H. P., Amrhein, V., and Naguib, M. (2006). Vocal interactions in nightingales, *Luscinia megarhynchos*: more aggressive males have higher pairing success. *Animal Behaviour*, **72**: 25–30.

Labov, W. (1972). Rules for ritual insults. In T. Kochman (ed.), *Rappin' and stylin' out*. Urbana, IL: University of Illinois Press.

(1973). The linguistic consequences of being a lame. *Language and Society*, **2**: 81–115.

LaFrance, M., Hecht, M. A., and Paluck, E. L. (2003). The contingent smile: a meta-analysis of sex differences in smiling. *Psychological Bulletin*, **129**: 305–34.

Lakoff, R. (1975). *Language and woman's place*. New York: Harper & Row.

Laland, K. N. and Galen, B. G. (2009). *The question of animal culture*. Cambridge, MA: Harvard University Press.

Lande, R. (1980). Sexual dimorphism, sexual selection, and adaptation in polygenic characters. *Evolution*, **33**: 292–305.

Laurenceau, J.-P., Barrett, L. F., and Pietromonaco, P. R. (1998). Intimacy as an interpersonal process: the importance of self-disclosure, partner disclosure, and perceived partner responsiveness in interpersonal exchanges. *Journal of Personality and Social Psychology*, **74**: 1238–51.

Leaper, C. and Smith, T. E. (2004). A meta-analytic review of gender variations in children's language use: talkativeness, affiliative speech, and assertive speech. *Developmental Psychology*, **40**: 993–1027.

LeBarre, W. (1954). *The human animal*. Chicago, IL: University of Chicago Press.

Leboucher, G. and Pallot, K. (2004). Is he all he says he is? Intersexual eavesdropping in the domestic canary, *Serinus canaria*. *Animal Behaviour*, **68**: 957–63.

Lee, R. B. (1979). *The !Kung San: men, women, and work in a foraging society*. Cambridge: Cambridge University Press.

LeMasters, E. E. (1975). *Blue-collar aristocrats: life-styles at a working-class tavern*. Madison, WI: University of Wisconsin Press.

Leneman, L. (2000). Defamation in Scotland, 1750–1800. *Continuity and Change*, **15**: 209–34.

Lennon, R. and Eisenberg, N. (1987). Gender and age differences in empathy and sympathy. In N. Eisenberg and J. Strayer (eds.), *Empathy and its development*. Cambridge: Cambridge University Press.

Le Roy Ladurie, E. (1978). *Montaillou: Cathars and Catholics in a French village 1294–1324*. Translated by Barbara Bray. London: Scolar Press.

Lessing, D. (1964). *A proper marriage*. New York: Harper Perennial.

Leutenegger, W. (1974). Functional aspects of pelvic morphology in Simian primates. *Journal of Human Evolution*, **3**: 207–22.

(1980). Encephalization and obstetrics in primates with particular reference to human evolution. In E. Armstrong and D. Falk (eds.), *Primate brain evolution: methods and concepts*. New York: Plenum.

Lewis, R. J. and van Schaik, C. P. (2007). Bimorphism in male verreaux's sifaka in the Kirindy Forest of Madagascar. *International Journal of Primatology*, **28**: 159–82.

Lindenfors, P. (2005). Neocortex evolution in primates: the "social brain" is for females. *Biology Letters*, **1**: 407–10.

Lindenfors, P., Fröberg, L., and Nunn, C. L. (2004). Females drive primate social evolution. *Proceedings of the Royal Society of London B (Suppl.)*, **271**: S101–3.

Lindenfors, P., Gittleman, J. L., and Jones, K. E. (2007a). Sexual size dimorphism in mammals. In D. J. Fairbairn, W. U. Blanckenhorn, and T. Szekely (eds.), *Sex, size and gender roles: evolutionary studies of sexual size dimorphism*. Oxford: Oxford University Press.

Lindenfors, P., Nunn, C. L., and Barton, R. A. (2007b). Primate brain architecture and selection in relation to sex. *BMC Biology*, **5**. Online.

Livingstone, F. B. (1962). Reconstructing man's Pliocene pongid ancestor. *American Anthropologist*, **64**: 301–5.

Locke, J. L. (1993). *The child's path to spoken language*. Cambridge, MA: Harvard University Press.

(2003). The evolution of human intimacy: a "skeletal" proposal. Invited address, Department of Anthropology, University of Vienna, Austria.

(2004). Trickle up phonetics: a vocal role for the infant. *Behavioral and Brain Sciences*, **27**: 516.

(2005). Looking for, looking at: social control, honest signals, and intimate experience in human evolution and history. In P. K. McGregor (ed.), *Animal communication networks*. Cambridge: Cambridge University Press.

(2006). Parental selection of vocal behavior: crying, cooing, babbling and the evolution of spoken language. *Human Nature*, **17**: 155–68.

(2009). Evolutionary developmental linguistics: naturalization of the faculty of language. *Language Sciences*, **31**: 33–59.

(2010a). The development of linguistic systems: insights from evolution. In J. Guendouzi, F. Loncke, and M. J. Williams (eds.), *Handbook of psycholinguistic and cognitive processes: perspectives in communication disorders*. London: Taylor & Francis.

(2010b). *Eavesdropping: an intimate history*. Oxford: Oxford University Press.

(in press). Vocal and verbal complexity: a fitness account of language, situated in development. In M. Tallerman and K. Gibson (eds.), *Oxford handbook on language evolution*. Oxford: Oxford University Press.

Locke, J. L. and Bogin, B. (2006). Language and life history: a new perspective on the evolution and development of linguistic communication. *Behavioral and Brain Science*, **29**: 259–325.

Lönnroth, L. (1979). The double scene of Arrow-Odd's drinking contest. In H. Bekker-Nielsen, P. Foot, A. Haarder, and P. M. Sorensen (eds.), *Medieval narrative: a symposium*. Odense: Odense University Press.

Lundy, D. E., Tan, J., and Cunningham, M. R. (1998). Heterosexual romantic preferences: The importance of humour and physical attractiveness for different types of relationships. *Personal Relationships*, **5**: 311–25.

Luxen, M. F. (2005). Gender differences in dominance and affiliation during a demanding interaction. *Journal of Psychology,* **139**: 331–47.

Lytton, H. and Romney, D. M. (1991). Parents' differential socialization of boys and girls: a meta-analysis. *Psychological Bulletin,* **109**: 267–96.

Maccoby, E. (1990). Gender and relationships: a developmental account. *American Psychologist,* **45**: 513–20.

Mainardi, P. (2003). *Husbands, wives, and lovers: marriage and its discontents in nineteenth-century France.* New Haven, CT: Yale University Press.

Makri-Tsilipakou, M. (1994). Interruption revisited: affiliative vs. dis-affiliative intervention. *Journal of Pragmatics,* **21**: 401–26.

Malinowski, B. (1922). *Argonauts of the Western Pacific: an account of native enterprise and adventure in the Archipelagoes of Melanesian New Guinea.* Prospect Heights, IL: Waveland Press (reprinted in 1984).

Malm, W. P. (1963). *Traditional Japanese music and musical instruments.* Tokyo: Kodansha International.

Maltz, D. N. and Borker, R. A. (1983). A cultural approach to male–female miscommunication. In J. Gumperz (ed.), *Language and Social identity.* New York: Cambridge University Press.

Manchester, B. B. and Friedley, S. A. (2003). Revisiting male/female participation and success in forensics: has time changed the playing field? *National Forensic Journal,* **21**: 20–35.

Manguel, A. (2006). Review of Stephen Miller's *Conversation: a history of a declining art. Times Literary Supplement* (Social Studies). *Times Online,* July 12, 2006.

Manning, F. E. (1973). *Black clubs in Bermuda: ethnography of a play world.* Ithaca, NY: Cornell University Press.

Marler, P. and Tenaza, R. (1977). Signaling behavior of apes with special reference to vocalization. In T. A. Sebeok (ed.), *How animals communicate.* Bloomington, IN: Indiana University Press.

Marley, C. (2002). Popping the question: questions and modality in written dating advertisements. *Discourse Studies,* **4**: 75–98.

Marsh, A. A., Yu, H. H., Schechter, J. C., and Blair, R. J. R. (2009). Larger than life: humans' nonverbal status cues alter perceived size. *PLOS One,* **4**: 1–8.

Marsh, P. (1978). *Aggro: the illusion of violence.* London: Dent.

Martel, F. L., Nevison, C. M., Rayment, F. D., Simpson, M. J. A., and Keverne, E. B. (1993). Opioid receptor blockade reduces maternal affect and social grooming in rhesus monkeys. *Psychoneuroendocrinology,* **18**: 307–21.

Martel, F. L., Nevison, C. M., Simpson, M. J. A., and Keverne, E. B. (1995). Effects of opioid receptor blockade on the social behavior of rhesus monkeys living in large family groups. *Developmental Psychobiology,* **28**: 71–84.

Martensz, N. D., Vellucci, S. V., Keverne, E. B., and Herbert, J. (1986). B-endorphin levels in the cerebrospinal fluid of male talapoin monkeys in social groups related to dominance status and the luteinizing hormone response to naloxone. *Neuroscience,* **18**: 651–58.

Mathias, E. (1976). *La Gara Poetica*: Sardinian shepherds' verbal dueling and the expression of male values in an agro-pastoral society. *Ethos,* **4**: 483–507.

Mayer, J. D. and Salovey, P. (1993). The intelligence of emotional intelligence. *Intelligence,* **17**: 433–42.

Mazur, A. and Booth, A. (1998). Testosterone and dominance in men. *Behavioral and Brain Sciences,* **21**: 353–63.

McAleer, K. (1994). *Dueling: the cult of honor in fin-de-siècle Germany.* Princeton, NJ: Princeton University Press.

McAndrew, F. T. and Milenkovic, M. A. (2002). Of tabloids and family secrets: the evolutionary psychology of gossip. *Journal of Applied Social Psychology,* **32**: 1064–82.

McCloskey, L. A. and Coleman, L. M. (1992). Difference without dominance: children's talk in mixed- and same-sex dyads. *Sex Roles,* **27**: 241–57.

McElvaine, R. S. (2001). *Eve's seed: biology, the sexes, and the course of history.* New York: McGraw-Hill.

McGhee, P. E. (1976). Sex differences in children's humor. *Journal of Communication,* **26**: 176–89.

McHenry, H. M. (1975). Biomechanical interpretation of the early hominid hip. *Journal of Human Evolution,* **4**: 343–55.

McIntosh, M. K. (1998). *Controlling misbehavior in England, 1370–1600.* Cambridge: Cambridge University Press.

McLean, M. (1965). Song loss and social context among New Zealand Maori. *Ethnomusicology,* **9**: 296–304.

McPherson, M. and Smith-Lovin, L. (1986). Sex segregation in voluntary associations. *American Sociological Review*, **51**: 61–79.

McPherson, M., Smith-Lovin, L., and Cook, J. M. (2001). Birds of a feather: homophily in social networks. *Annual Review of Sociology*, **27**: 415–44.

Meade, M. (1973). *Bitching*. Englewood Cliffs, NJ: Prentice Hall.

Mennill, D. J., Boag, P. T., and Ratcliffe, L. M. (2003). The reproductive choice of eavesdropping female black-capped chickadees, *Poecile atricapillus*. *Naturwissenschaften*, **90**: 577–82.

Mickle, I. (1977). *A gentleman of much promise: the diary of Isaac Mickle, 1837–1845*. Vol. 2. Edited by Philip E. Mackey. Philadelphia: University of Pennsylvania Press.

Milardo, R. M. (1987). Changes in social networks of women and men following a divorce: a review. *Journal of Family Issues*, **8**: 78–96.

Miller, G. (2000). *The mating mind: how sexual choice shaped the evolution of human nature*. London: William Heinemann.

Miller, P. M. and Ingham, J. G. (1976). Friends, confidants, and symptoms. *Social Psychiatry*, **11**: 51–58.

Miller, W. I. (1993). *Humiliation: and other essays on honor, social discomfort, and violence*. Ithaca, NY: Cornell University Press.

Mio, J. S. and Graesser, A. C. (1991). Humor, language and metaphor. *Metaphor and Symbolic Activity*, **6**: 87–102.

Mirsky, J. (1937). The Eskimo of Greenland. In M. Mead (ed.), *Cooperation and competition among primitive peoples*. Boston: Beacon Press.

Mitani, J. C. (1985). Sexual selection and adult male orangutan long calls. *Animal Behaviour*, **33**: 272–83.

Morris, D. (1967). *The naked ape: a zoologist's study of the human animal*. New York: Crown.

Morton, T. L. (1978). Intimacy and reciprocity of exchange: a comparison of spouses and strangers. *Journal of Personality and Social Psychology*, **36**: 72–81.

Mottl–Santiago, J., Walker, C., Ewan, J., Vragovic, O., Winder, S., and Stubblefield, P. (2008). A hospital-based doula program and childbirth outcomes in an urban, multicultural setting. *Maternal and Child Health Journal*, **12**: 372–77.

Moynihan, M. H. (1955). Types of hostile display. *Auk*, **72**: 247–59.

(1998). *The social regulation of competition and aggression in animals*. Washington, DC: Smithsonian Institution Press.

Mulac, A. (1989). Men's and women's talk in same-sex and mixed-sex dyads: power or polemic? *Journal of Language and Social Psychology*, **8**: 249–70.

Mulac, A., Lundell, T. L., and Bradac, J. J. (1986). Male/female language differences and attributional consequences in a public speaking situation: toward an explanation of the gender-linked language effect. *Communication Monographs*, **53**: 115–29.

Mullen, B., Salas, E., and Driskell, J. E. (1989). Salience, motivation, and artifact as contributions to the relation between participation rate and leadership. *Journal of Experimental Social Psychology*, **25**: 545–59.

Murray, L. and Trevarthen, C. (1986). The infant's role in mother–infant communications. *Journal of Child Language*, **13**: 15–29.

Naguib, M. and Todt, D. (1997). Effects of dyadic vocal interactions on other conspecific receivers in nightingales. *Animal Behaviour*, **54**: 1535–43.

Nattiez, J.-J. (1983). Some aspects of Inuit vocal games. *Ethnomusicology*, **27**: 457–75.

(1999). Inuit throat-games and Siberian throat singing: a comparative, historical, and semiological approach. *Ethnomusicology*, **43**: 399–418.

Nelson, L. D. and Morrison, E. L. (2005). The symptoms of resource scarcity: judgements of food and finances influence preferences for potential partners. *Psychological Science*, **16**: 167–73.

Nieuwenhuijsen, K. and de Waal, B. M. (1982). Effects of spatial crowding on social behavior in a chimpanzee colony. *Zoo Biology*, **1**: 5–28.

Nisbett, R. E. and Cohen, D. (1996). *Culture of honor*. Boulder, CO: Westview Press.

Nye, R. A. (1993). *Masculinity and male codes of honour in modern France*. Oxford: Oxford University Press.

O'Connell, W. E. (1960). The adaptive functions of wit and humor. *Journal of Abnormal and Social Psychology*, **61**: 263–70.

Oguchi, T. and Kikuchi, H. (1997). Voice and interpersonal attraction. *Japanese Psychological Research*, **39**: 56–61.

Oldenburg, R. (1989). *The great good place: cafés, coffee shops, community centers, beauty parlors, general stores, bars, hangouts, and how they get you through the day*. New York: Paragon House.

Oliveira, R. F., Lopes, M., Carneiro, L. A., and Canário, A. V. M. (2001). Watching fights raises fish hormone levels. *Nature*, **409**: 475.

Oliveira, R. F., McGregor, P. K., and Latruffe, C. (1998). Know thine enemy: fighting fish gather information from observing conspecific interactions. *Proceedings of the Royal Society of London B*, **265**: 1045–49.

Österman, K., Björkqvist, K., Lagerspetz, K. M. J., Kaukiainen, A., Landau, S., Fraczek, A., and Caprara, G. V. (1988). Cross-cultural evidence of female indirect aggression. *Aggressive Behavior*, **24**: 1–8.

Otter, K. A., McGregor, P. K., Terry, A. M. R., Burford, F. R. L., Peake, T. M., and Dabelsteen, T. (1999). Do female great tits (Parus major) assess males by eavesdropping? A field study using interactive song playback. *Proceedings of the Royal Society of London B*, **266**: 1305–9.

Owren, M. J., Dieter, J. A., Seyfarth, R. M., and Cheney, D. L. (1993). Vocalizations of rhesus (*Macaca mulatta*) and Japanese (*M. fuscata*) macaques cross-fostered between species show evidence of only limited modification. *Developmental Psychobiology*, **26**: 389–406.

Pacheco-Cobos, L., Rosetti, M., Cuatinquiz, C., and Hudson, R. (2010). Sex differences in mushroom gathering: men expend more energy to obtain equivalent benefits. *Evolution and Human Behavior*, **31**: 289–97.

Pagliai, V. (2009). The art of dueling with words: toward a new understanding of verbal duels across the world. *Oral Tradition*, **24**: 61–88.

Parks, W. (1990). *Verbal dueling in heroic narrative: the Homeric and Old English traditions*. Princeton, NJ: Princeton University Press.

Peake, T. M., Terry, A. M. R., McGregor, P. K., and Dabelsteen, T. (2001). Male great tits eavesdrop on simulated male-to-male vocal interactions. *Proceedings of the Royal Society of London B: Biological Science*, **268**: 1183–87.

Pedersen, M. F., Moller, S., Krabbe, S., and Bennett, P. (1986). Fundamental voice frequency measured by electroglottography during continuous speech: a new exact secondary sex characteristic in boys in puberty. *International Journal of Pediatric Otorhinolaryngology*, **11**: 21–27.

Peek, P. (1981). The power of words in African verbal arts. *The Journal of American Folklore*, **94**: 19–43.

Peltonen, M. (2003). *The duel in early modern England: civility, politeness and honour*. Cambridge: Cambridge University Press.

Pennebaker, J. W., Barger, S. D., and Tiebout, J. (1989). Disclosure of traumas and health among Holocaust survivors. *Psychosomatic Medicine*, **51**: 577–89.

Petrides, K. V. and Furnham, A. (2000). Gender differences in measured and self-estimated trait emotional intelligence. *Sex Roles*, **42**: 449–61.

Philips, S. U. (1980). Sex differences and language. *Annual Review of Anthropology*, **9**: 523–44.

Piggott, S. (1972). Conclusion. In P. J. Ucko, R. Tringham, and G. W. Dimbleby (eds.), *Man, settlement and urbanism*. London: Duckworth.

Pinker, S. and Bloom, P. (1990). Natural language and natural selection. *Behavioral and Brain Sciences*, **13**: 707–84.

Pitt-Rivers, J. (1966). Honour and social status. In J. Peristiany (ed.), *Honour and shame: the values of Mediterranean society*. London: Weidenfeld & Nicolson.

Plavcan, J. M. (2001). Sexual dimorphism in primate evolution. *Yearbook of Physical Anthropology*, **44**: 25–53.

Progovac, L. and Locke, J. L. (2009). Exocentric compounds, ritual insult, and the evolution of syntax. *Biolinguistics*, **3**: 337–54.

Prokosch, M. D., Coss, R. G., Scheib, J. E., and Blozis, S. A. (2009). Intelligence and mate choice: intelligent men are always appealing. *Evolution and Human Behavior*, **30**: 11–20.

Provine, R. R. (2000a). Laughing, tickling, and the evolution of speech and self. *Current Directions in Psychological Science*, **13**: 215–18.

(2000b). *Laughter: a scientific investigation*. New York: Penguin Books.

Puts, D. A. (2005). Mating context and menstrual phase affect women's preferences for male voice pitch. *Evolution and Human Behavior*, **26**: 388–97.

Puts, D. A., Gaulin, S. J. C., and Verdolini, K. (2006). Dominance and the evolution of sexual dimorphism in human voice pitch. *Evolution and Human Behavior* **27**: 283–96.

Radcliffe-Brown, A. R. (1965). On joking relationships. In A. R. Radcliffe-Brown, *Structure and function in primitive society*. New York: The Free Press. Reprinted from *Africa*, **8** (1940): 195–210.

Radway, J. (1984). *Reading the romance: women, patriarchy, and popular literature*. Chapel Hill, NC: University of North Carolina Press.

Ray, A. G. (2004). The permeable public: rituals of citizenship in antebellum men's debating clubs. *Argumentation and Advocacy*, **41**: 1–16.

Read, K. E. (1954). Cultures of the Central Highlands, New Guinea. *Southwestern Journal of Anthropology*, **10**: 1–43.

Reay, M. (1959). *The Kuma: freedom and conformity in the New Guinea Highlands.* Carlton, Victoria: Melbourne University Press.

Redican, W. K. (1975). Facial expressions in non-human primates. In L. A. Rosenblum (ed.), Primate behavior: developments in field and laboratory research. New York: Academic Press.

Reis, H. T. and Shaver, P. (1988). Intimacy as an interpersonal process. In S. Duck (ed.), *Handbook of personal relationships.* Chichester: Wiley.

Renninger, L. A., Wade, T. J., and Grammer, K. (2004). Getting that female glance: patterns and consequences of male nonverbal behavior in courtship contexts. *Evolution and Human Behavior,* **25**: 416–31.

Richman, B. (1987). Rhythm and melody in gelada vocal exchanges. *Primates,* **28**: 199–223.

Richman, N. (1976). Some vocal distinctive features used by gelada monkeys. *Journal of the Acoustical Society of America,* **60**: 687–95.

Romero, T., Castellanos, M. A., and de Waal, F. B. M. (2010). Consolation as possible expression of sympathetic concern among chimpanzees. *Proceedings of the National Academy of Sciences,* **107**: 12110–15.

Rosenberg, J. and Tunney, R. J. (2008). Human vocabulary use as display. *Evolutionary Psychology,* **6**: 538–49.

Rosenfeld, L. B. (1979). Self-disclosure avoidance: why I am afraid to tell you who I am. *Communication Monographs,* **46**: 63–74.

Rosenthal, M. K. (1982). Vocal dialogues in the neonatal period. *Developmental Psychology,* **18**: 17–21.

Rosenthal, R. and DePaulo, B. M. (1979). Sex differences in eavesdropping on nonverbal cues. *Journal of Personality and Social Psychology,* **37**: 273–85.

Rowe, M. L. and Pan, B. A. (2004). A comparison of fathers' and mothers' talk to toddlers in low-income families. *Social Development,* **13**: 278–91.

Rucas, S. L., Gurven, M., Kaplan, H., Winking, J., Gangestad, S., and Crespo, M. (2006). Female intrasexual competition and reputational effects on attractiveness among the Tsimane of Bolivia. *Evolution and Human Behavior,* **27**: 40–52.

Rudman, L. A. and Glick, P. (2008). *The social psychology of gender: how power and intimacy shape gender relations.* New York: Guilford Press.

Russom, G. R. (1978). A Germanic concept of nobility in *The gifts of men* and *Beowulf*. *Speculum*, **53**: 1–15.

Ryan, M. J. (1990). Sexual selection, sensory systems and sensory exploitation. *Oxford Surveys of Evolutionary Biology*, **7**: 157–95.

Ryon, R. N. (1995). Craftsmen's union halls, male bonding, and female industrial labor: the case of Baltimore, 1880–1917. *Labor History*, **36**: 211–31.

Sade, D. S. (1965). Some aspects of parent–offspring and sibling relations in a group of rhesus monkeys, with a discussion of grooming. *American Journal of Physical Anthropology*, **23**: 1–18.

Sagarin, B. J., Becker, D. V., Guadagno, R. E., Nicastle, L. D., and Millevoi, A. (2003). Sex differences (and similarities) in jealousy: the moderating influence of infidelity experience and sexual orientation of the infidelity. *Evolution and Human Behavior*, **24**: 17–23.

Salmon, C. and Symons, D. (2001). *Warrior lovers*. London: Weidenfeld & Nicolson.

Salmond, A. (1975). Mana makes the man: a look at Maori oratory and politics. In M. Bloch (ed.), *Political language and oratory in traditional society*. London: Academic Press.

Salzano, F. M., Neel, J. V., and Maybury-Lewis, D. (1967). Further studies on the Xavante Indians. I. Demographic data on two additional villages: genetic structure of the tribe. *American Journal of Human Genetics*, **19**: 463–89.

Samarin, W. J. (1969). The art of Gbeya insults. *International Journal of American Linguistics*, **35**: 323–29.

Santos-Granero, F. (1991). *The power of love: the moral use of knowledge amongst the Amuesha of Central Peru*. London: Athlone Press.

Sarason, B. R., Pierce, G. R., and Sarason, I. G. (1990). Social support: the sense of acceptance and the role of relationships. In B. R. Sarason, I. G. Sarason, G. R. Pierce (eds.), *Social support: an interactional view*. New York: John Wiley & Sons.

Schuster, I. (1983). Women's aggression: an African case study. *Aggressive Behavior*, **9**: 319–31.

Seeger, A. (1981). *Nature and society in Central Brazil: the Suya Indians of Mato Grosso*. Cambridge, MA: Harvard University Press.

Sell, A., Bryant, G. A., Cosmides, L., *et al.* (2010). Adaptation in humans for assessing physical strength from the voice. *Proceedings of the Royal Society of London B*, **277**: 3509–18.

Seltzer, L. J., Ziegler, T. E., and Pollak, S. D. (2010). Social vocalizations can release oxytocin in humans. *Proceedings of the Royal Society of London B*, **277**: 2661–66.

Semple, S. (1998). The function of Barbary macaque copulation calls. *Proceedings of the Royal Society of London B*, **265**: 287–91.

Setia, T. M. and van Schaik, C. P. (2007). The response of adult orang-utans to flanged male long calls: inferences about their function. *Folia Primatologica*, **78**: 215–26.

Seyfarth, R. M. (1976). Social relationships among adult female baboons. *Animal Behaviour*, **24**: 917–38.

Shem, S. and Surrey, J. (1999). *We have to talk: healing dialogues between women and men.* New York: Basic Books.

Sheppard, A. (1985). Funny women: social change and audience response to female comedians. *Empirical Studies in the Arts*, **3**: 179–95.

(1986). From Kate Sanborn to feminist psychology: the social context of women's humor, 1885–1985. *Psychology of Women Quarterly*, **10**: 155–70.

Shoemaker, R. (2004). *The London mob: violence and disorder in eighteenth-century England.* London: Hambledon and London.

Silk, J. B. (2001). Grunts, girneys, and good intentions: the origins of strategic commitment in nonhuman primates. In R. M. Nesse (ed.), *Evolution and the capacity for commitment.* New York: Russell Sage Press.

(2007). The adaptive value of sociality in mammalian groups. *Philosophical Transactions of the Royal Society*, **362**: 539–59.

Silverman, I., Choi, J., and Peters, M. (2007). The hunter-gatherer theory of sex differences in spatial abilities: data from 40 countries. *Archives of Sexual Behavior*, **36**: 261–68.

Slotko, V. P. and Langmeyer, D. (1977). The effects of interaction distance and gender on self-disclosure in the dyad. *Sociometry*, **40**: 178–82.

Smith, A. (2006). Cognitive empathy and emotional empathy in human behavior and evolution. *Psychological Record*, **56**: 3–21.

Smith, E. A. (2004). Why do good hunters have higher reproductive success? *Human Nature*, **15**: 343–64.

Smith, R. J. and Jungers, W. L. (1997). Body mass in comparative primatology. *Journal of Human Evolution*, **32**: 523–59.

Smitherman, G. (1977). *Talkin and testifyin: the language of black America.* Detroit, MI: Wayne State University.

Smoreda, Z. and Licoppe, C. (2000). Gender-specific use of the domestic telephone. *Social Psychology Quarterly*, **63**: 238–52.

Smuts, B. B. (1987). Gender, aggression, and influence. In B. B. Smuts, D. L. Cheney, R. M. Seyfarth, R. W. Wrangham, and T. T. Struhsaker (eds.), *Primate societies*. Chicago, IL: University of Chicago Press.

Sobal, J. and Stunkard, A. J. (1989). Socioeconomic status and obesity: a review of the literature. *Psychological Bulletin*, **105**: 260–75.

Solomon, S. T. (1994). Coplas de Todos Santos in Cochamba: language, music, and performance in Bolivian Quechua song dueling. *Journal of American Folklore*, **107**: 378–414.

Sommerville, C. J. (1997). Surfing the coffeehouse. *History Today*, **47**: 8–10.

Sorrentino, R. M. and Boutillier, R. G. (1975). The effect of quantity and quality of verbal interaction on ratings of leadership ability. *Journal of Experimental Social Psychology*, **11**: 403–11.

Sosa, R., Kennell, J., Klaus, M., Robertson, S., and Urrutia, J. (1980). The effect of a supportive companion on perinatal problems, length of labor, and mother–infant interaction. *New England Journal of Medicine*, **303**: 7–10.

Sowayan, S. A. (1989). "Tonight my gun is loaded": poetic dueling in Arabia. *Oral Tradition*, **4**: 151–73.

Speer, J. H. (1985). Waulking o' the web: women's folk performance in the Scottish Isles. *Text and Performance Quarterly*, **6**: 24–33.

Spierenburg, P. (1998). Knife fighting and popular codes of honor in early modern Amsterdam. In P. Spierenburg (ed.), *Men and violence: gender, honor, and rituals in Modern Europe and America*. Columbus, OH: Ohio State University Press.

Staats, S., Long, L., Manulik, K., and Kelley, P. (2006). Situated empathy: variations associated with target gender across situations. *Social Behavior and Personality*, **34**: 431–42.

Stanford, C. B. (1999). *The hunting apes: meat eating and the origins of human behavior*. Princeton, NJ: Princeton University Press.

Stein, M. B., Walker, J. R., and Forde, D. R. (1996). Public-speaking fears in a community sample: prevalence, impact on functioning, and diagnostic classification. *Archives of General Psychiatry*, **53**: 169–74.

Stepp, P. L. (1997). Can we make intercollegiate debate more diverse? *Argumentation and Advocacy*, **33**: 176–90.

Stepp, P. L. and Gardner, M. B. (2001). Ten years of demographics: who debates in America. *Argumentation and Advocacy*, **38**: 69–82.

Stern, D. N., Jaffe, J., Beebe, B., and Bennett, S. L. (1975). Vocalizing in unison and in alternation: two modes of communication within the mother–infant dyad. *Annals of the New York Academy of Sciences*, **263**: 89–100.

Stevenson, R. L. (1897). Talk and talkers. In *Memories and portraits*. New York: Charles Scribner's Sons.

Sugawara, K. (1984). Spatial proximity and bodily contact among the Central Kalahari San. *African Study Monographs*, **3**: 1–43.

Tannen, D. (1990). *You just don't understand: women and men in conversation.* New York: Quill.

Taylor, S. E. (2002). *The tending instinct: how nurturing is essential for who we are and how we live.* New York: Henry Holt.

Taylor, S. E., Klein, L. C., Lewis, B. P., Gruenewald, T. L., Gurung, R. A. R., and Updegraff, J. A. (2000). Biobehavioral responses to stress in females: tend-and-befriend, not fight-or-flight. *Psychological Review*, **107**: 411–29.

Terman, L. M. and Miles, C. C. (1936). Sex and personality: studies in masculinity and femininity. New York: McGraw-Hill.

Tetreault, C. (2010). Collaborative conflicts: teens performing aggression and intimacy in a French cité. *Journal of Linguistic Anthropology*, **20**: 72–86.

Thomas, K. (1959). The double standard. *Journal of the History of Ideas*, **20**: 195–216.

Thorndike, E. L. (1920). Intelligence and its use. *Harper's Magazine*, **140**: 227–35.

Tiedens, L. Z. and Fragale, A. R. (2003). Power moves: complementarity in dominant and submissive nonverbal behavior. *Journal of Personality and Social Psychology*, **84**: 558–68.

Tiedens, L. Z., Unzueta, M. M., and Young, M. J. (2007). An unconscious desire for hierarchy? The motivated perception of dominance complementarity in task partners. *Journal of Personality and Social Psychology*, **93**: 402–14.

Tinbergen, N. (1963). On aims and methods of ethology. *Zeitschrift fur Tierpsychologie*, **20**: 410–423. Reprinted (2005) in Animal Biology, **55**: 297–321.

Toldos, M. P. (2005). Sex and age differences in self-estimated physical, verbal and indirect aggression in Spanish adolescents. *Aggressive Behavior*, **31**: 13–23.

Tomaszycki, M. L., Davis, J. E., Gouzoules, H., and Wallen, K. (2001). Sex differences in infant rhesus macaque separation-rejection vocalizations and effects of prenatal androgens. *Hormones and Behavior*, **39**: 267–76.

Travassos, E. (2000). Ethics in the sung duels of northeastern Brazil: collective memory and contemporary practice. *British Journal of Ethnomusicology*, **9**: 61–94.

Tremblay, R. E. (2002). Prevention of injury by early socialization of aggressive behavior. *Injury Prevention*, **8** (Supplement 4): 17–21.

(2003). Why socialization fails? The case of chronic physical aggression. In B. B. Lahey, T. E. Moffitt, and A. Caspi (eds.), *Causes of conduct disorder and juvenile delinquency*. New York: Guilford.

(2004). Development of physical aggression during infancy. *Infant Mental Health Journal*, **25**: 399–407.

Tremblay, R. E., Apel, C., Perusse, D., Boivin, M., Zoccolillo, M., Montplaisir, J., and McDuff, P. (1999). The search for the age of 'onset' of physical aggression. Rousseau and Bandura revisited. *Criminal Behavior and Mental Health*, **9**: 8–23.

Tremblay, R. E., Nagin, D. S., Séguin, J. R., Zoccolillo, M., Zelazo, P., Boivin, M., Pérusse, D., and Japel, C. (2004). Physical aggression during early childhood: trajectories and predictors. *Pediatrics*, **114**: e43–e50.

Trevathan, W. (1999). Evolutionary obstetrics. In W. Trevathan, E. O. Smith, and J. J. McKenna (eds.), *Evolutionary medicine*. Oxford: Oxford University Press.

Triandis, H. C. (2001). Individualism-collectivism and personality. *Journal of Personality*, **69**: 907–924.

Triandis, H. C. and Gelfand, M. J. (1998). Converging measurement of horizontal and vertical individualism and collectivism. *Journal of Personality and Social Psychology*, **74**: 118–28.

Trinkaus, E. and Zimmerman, M. R. (1982). Trauma among the Shanidar Neandertals. *American Journal of Physical Anthropology*, **57**: 61–76.

Troemel-Ploetz, S. (1991). Review essay: selling the apolitical (review of Deborah Tannen's *You just don't understand*). *Discourse Society*, **2**: 489–502.

Turnbull, C. M. (1965). *Wayward servants: the two worlds of the African pygmies*. Garden City, NJ: The Natural History Press.

Utami, S. S., Goossens, B., Bruford, M. W., de Ruiter, J. R., and van Hooff, J. A. R. A. M. (2002). Male bimaturism and reproductive success in Sumatran orang-utans. *Behavioral Ecology*, **13**: 643–52.

Uvnas-Moberg, K. (1998). Oxytocin may mediate the benefits of positive social interaction and emotions. *Psychoneuroendocrinology*, **23**: 819–35.

Vallet, E. and Kreutzer, M. (1995). Female canaries are sexually responsive to special song phrases. *Animal Behaviour*, **49**: 1603–10.

van der Mark, I. L., van IJzendoorn, M. H., and Bakermans-Kranenburg, M. J. (2002). Development of empathy in girls during the second year of life: associations with parenting, attachment, and temperament. *Social Development*, **11**, 451–68.

van IJzendoorn, M. H. and De Wolff, M. S. (1997). In search of the absent father – meta-analyses of infant–father attachment: a rejoinder to our discussants. *Child Development*, **68**: 604–9.

Von Oettingen, A. (1989). *Zur duellfrage*. Dorpat: E. J. Karow.

Vetterli, C. F. and Furedy, J. J. (1997). Correlates of intelligence in computer measured aspects of prose vocabulary: word length, diversity, and rarity. *Personality and Individual Differences*, **22**: 933–35.

Wachtmeister, C. -A. and Enquist, M. (1999). The evolution of female coyness – trading time for information. *Ethology*, **105**: 983–92.

Walter, B. (1988). *The jury summation as speech genre: an ethnographic study of what it means to those who use it*. Philadelphia: John Benjamins.

Walters, J. R. (1987). Transition to adulthood. In B. B. Smuts *et al.* (eds.), *Primate Societies*. Chicago, IL: University of Chicago Press.

Walters, J. R. and Seyfarth, R. M. (1987). Conflict and cooperation. In B. B. Smuts *et al.* (eds.), *Primate societies*. Chicago, IL: University of Chicago Press.

Warner, M. (1993). Provocations: Marina Warner on gossip. *The Independent Magazine*, May 1, 22–23.

Warren, S. D. and Brandeis, L. D. (1890). The right to privacy. *Harvard Law Review*, **4**, 193–220.

Washburn, S. L. (1960). Tools and human evolution. *Scientific American*, **203**: 63–75.

Waters, E., Merrick, S., Treboux, D., Crowell, J., and Albersheim, L. (2000). Attachment security in infancy and early adulthood: a twenty-year longitudinal study. *Child Development*, **71**: 684–89.

Watson, J. and Potter, R. J. (1962). An analytic unit for the study of interaction. *Human Relations*, **15**: 245–63.

West-Eberhard, M. J. (2003). *Developmental plasticity and evolution.* Oxford: Oxford University Press.

Weyer, E. M. (1932). *The Eskimos: their environment and folkways.* New Haven, CT: Yale University Press.

Whalley, L. J. and Deary, I. J. (2001). Longitudinal cohort study of childhood IQ and survival up to age 76. *British Medical Journal*, **322**: 819–22.

Whiting, B. and Edwards, C. P. (1973). A cross-cultural analysis of sex differences in the behavior of children aged three through 11. *Journal of Social Psychology*, **91**: 171–88.

Wiessner, P. (1982). Risk, reciprocity and social influences on !Kung San economics. In E. Leacock and R. Lee (eds.), *Politics and history in band societies.* Cambridge: Cambridge University Press.

(2005). Norm enforcement among the Ju/'hoansi Bushmen: a case of strong reciprocity? *Human Nature*, **16**: 115–45.

Wilbert, J. (1977). *Folk literature of the Yamana Indians.* Berkeley, CA: University of California Press.

Wilmer, J. B., Germine, L., Chabris, C. F., Chatterjee, G., Williams, M., Loken, E., Nakayama, K., and Duchaine, B. (2010). Human face recognition is specific and highly heritable. *Proceedings of the National Academy of Science*, **107**: 5238–41.

Wilson, A. (1985). Participant or patient? Seventeenth-century childbirth from the mother's point of view. In R. Porter (ed.), *Patients and practitioners: lay perceptions of medicine in pre-industrial society.* Cambridge: Cambridge University Press.

Wilson, G. D. (1984). The personality of opera singers. *Personality and Individual Differences*, **5**: 195–201.

Wilson, S. (1988). *Feuding, conflict and banditry in nineteenth-century Corsica.* Cambridge: Cambridge University Press.

Winstanley, W. (1678). *Poor Robin's character of a scold: or, the shrew's looking-glass.* London.

Woolley, H. T. (1910). A review of recent literature on the psychology of sex. *Psychological Bulletin*, **7**: 335–42.

Wrangham, R. and Peterson, D. (1997). *Demonic males: apes and the origins of human violence.* London: Bloomsbury.

Wright, E. R. (1995). Personal networks and anomie: exploring the sources and significance of gender composition. *Sociological Focus*, **28**: 261–82.

Wyatt, T. A. (1995). Language development in African American English child speech. *Linguistics and Education*, **7**: 7–22.

Wyatt-Brown, B. (1982). *Southern honor: ethics and behavior in the Old South*. Oxford: Oxford University Press.

Xie, H., Swift, D. J., Cairns, B. D., and Cairns, R. B. (2002). Aggressive behaviors in social interaction and developmental adaptation: a narrative analysis of interpersonal conflicts during early adolescence. *Social Development*, **11**: 205–24.

Zahn-Waxler, C. and Radke-Yarrow, M. (1982). The development of altruism: alternative research strategies. In N. Eisenberg (ed.), *The development of prosocial behavior*. New York: Academic Press.

Zillmann, D. and Stocking, S. H. (1976). Putdown humor. *Journal of Communication*, Summer: 154–63.

Ziv, A. (1981). The self concept of adolescent humorists. *Journal of Adolescence*, **4**: 187–97.

Ziv, A. and Gadish, O. (1989). Humor and marital satisfaction. *Journal of Social Psychology*, **129**: 759–68.

Index